IN CELEBRATION OF THE 100TH ANNIVERSARY OF THE PROVINCE
OF ALBERTA, ON SEPTEMBER 1, 2005,
CANMEDIA INC. IS HONOURED TO PUBLISH THIS LIMITED
EDITION ALBERTA CENTENNIAL COMMEMORATIVE HISTORY BOOK.

THIS IS NO. _____7745_____ OF 35,000 COPIES PRINTED.

Curtis Stewart
President

Rodney Dietzmann
Publisher

Paul Stanway
Author and Editor

CMI
CanMedia Inc.

ALBERTA IN THE 20TH CENTURY

A JOURNALISTIC HISTORY OF THE PROVINCE

CENTENNIAL LIMITED EDITION

THE ALBERTANS:
FROM SETTLEMENT
TO SUPER PROVINCE
1905 - 2005

CanMedia Inc.
Edmonton
2005

Author and Editor
PAUL STANWAY

Layout and Design
DEAN PICKUP

Proofreading and Research
NICOLE STANWAY

Index
LOUISE HENEIN

Published By
CanMedia Inc.

President
CURTIS STEWART

Publisher
RODNEY DIETZMANN

Suite 202,
10479 - 184 Street,
Edmonton, Alberta.
T5S 2L1
Phone (780) 489-1555
Fax (780) 486-6726
Toll Free: 1-866-404-1555
www.canmediapublishing.com

Printed in Canada
By Friesens Corporation, Altona, Manitoba

THE ALBERTANS:
FROM SETTLEMENT
TO SUPER PROVINCE

Alberta in the 20th Century; Centennial Limited Edition.
Includes bibliographical references and Index.
ISBN 0-9736529

I. Alberta - History - 1905-2005
II. Stanway, Paul, 1950- III. Series.

Alberta in the 20th Century; set.
ISBN 0-9736529-0-X

Alberta in the 20th Century

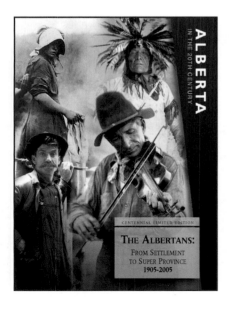

The Cover:

An evocative collage of images from Alberta's age of settlement, created by graphic designer Dean Pickup from photos supplied by the Provincial Archives of Alberta and Calgary's Glenbow Archives. The province's achievements in its first century are the direct result of the talents and determination of such people - from the original native inhabitants to the latest wave of immigrants. The story of Alberta is the story of its people - past, present, and future.

Foreword

There may be some who labour under the mistaken view that Canadian history is devoid of drama, colourful characters and thundering controversy. I can only assume that they are unfamiliar with the story of Alberta's first century, particularly as told in the remarkable series upon which this book is based - *Alberta in the 20th Century*. In addition to being that rarest of birds, a commercially successful provincial history, that 12-volume series is a vivid and unpretentious telling of one of the great sagas of the 20th century - the settlement and development of a rugged and beautiful frontier, and its astonishing growth from a remote outpost of empire to one of the most prosperous and flourishing societies on earth.

The beginning of Alberta's story is full of voices extolling the province's potential and the promise of great things to come. As we stand on the threshold of Alberta's second century, what is perhaps even more remarkable is that the great-grandchildren of those who celebrated the birth of Alberta exhibit the very same confidence in the future. There are surely few places on earth where you could find such an enduring sense of optimism and an ingrained belief that, with hard work and determination, anything is possible. That attitude helps differentiate Albertans from their generally more cautious fellow citizens, and does much to fuel their ongoing frustration with Canada's political and economic status quo. Some might say this is entirely the result of the province's resource wealth, but as anyone who knows the history of the province can attest, the robust independence of Albertans predates the discovery of oil and gas and has endured through the bad times as well as the good.

This book is, therefore, an unabashed and unapologetic celebration of the people of Alberta in their centennial year. It is an attempt to both encapsulate and bring up to date (with condensed narrative and more than 50 new photographs) the story of the province as told in the original dozen volumes. It could not hope to contain the encyclopaedic detail of the original, but I hope it provides the reader with a satisfying glimpse of the varied and rich history of the province and its people - and whets your appetite for more.

The visual impact of the book is due entirely to the prodigious talents of graphic artist Dean Pickup, who designed and created the pages. I am also forever indebted to all those who helped create *Alberta in the 20th Century*, in particular the researchers and 75 writers (most Albertans themselves) who worked on the project over a period of 13 years. I must also offer heartfelt thanks to an old friend, the inimitable Ted Byfield, who envisioned that original history and made it a reality. In a life full of accomplishments, it surely stands as one of the most remarkable. And to another friend and colleague, Paul Bunner, who took over from Byfield as editor for the final three volumes of *Alberta in the 20th Century* and invited me to become a contributor and editor. Without his professionalism and determination the landmark series might never have been completed. Lastly, to Curtis Stewart and Rodney Dietzman of CanMedia Inc., who recognized the potential and importance of a comprehensive Alberta history, and had the courage to keep it in print and available to the people of this province.

Paul Stanway

February 2005.

The Publisher gratefully acknowledges the work of all those who contributed to the original 12-volume history, *Alberta in the 20th Century*, including the following writers: Don Baron. Rick Bell. Kenneth Boessenkool. Robert Bott. Brian Brennan. Ian Brodie. Paul Bunner. Link Byfield. Mike Byfield. Ted Byfield. Virginia Byfield. Chris Champion. Brad Clark. Fred Cleverley. Larry Collins. Robert Collins. Colby Cosh. Frank Dabbs. Michael Dawe. Carol Dean. Phillipa Dean. Calvin Demmon. Hugh A. Dempsey. Ric Dolphin. Mary Frances Doucedame. Faron Ellis. Fil Fraser. Eleanor Gasparik. Lorne Gunter. Nigel Hannaford. Janet Harvey. Joanne Hatton. Greg Heaton. Ralph Hedlin. Don Hill. Brian Hutchinson. D'Arcy Jenish. Terry Johnson. Stephani Keer. George Koch. Les Kozma. Daniel S. Levy. Charles Mandel. Don Martin. Mike Maunder. Victoria Maclean. Tom McFeely. Mike McGarry. Celeste McGovern. Candis McLean. Paul McLoughlin. Kelly Morstad. Andrew Nikiforuk. George Oake. Shafer Parker. Barrett Pashak. J.F.J. Pereira. Davis Sheremata. Greg Shilliday. John Short. Carla Smithson. Paul Stanway. David Staples. Mark Stevenson. Sid Tafler. Courtney Tower. Janice Tyrwhitt. Peter Verburg. Ron Wallace. Stephen Weatherbe. Paul Willcocks. Carmen Wittmeier. Deborah Witwicki. Joe Woodard.

Table of Contents

CHAPTER ONE

Amid uproar and argument Alberta becomes a province

MUCH TO CALGARY'S DISGUST, EDMONTON IS NAMED THE 'PROVISIONAL CAPITAL', BUT CAN THE OLD FUR TRADING POST ASSEMBLE ENOUGH PEOPLE FOR A PARTY?

To its original nomadic inhabitants the territory that would become Alberta was part of a vast jig-saw puzzle of tribal homelands. The great northern boreal forests, drained by the Peace and Slave rivers, were home to the Beaver, Slavey and Chipewyan. In the poplar woodlands of the North Saskatchewan basin lived the Cree, masters of a sprawling empire which stretched all the way to Hudson Bay. The foothills of the Rockies were the territory of the Assiniboine, relatives of the Sioux. And on the wide grasslands south of the Battle River lived the Blackfoot, Blood, Peigan, Sarcee and Gros Ventre, a much-feared warrior confederacy that roamed the Great Plains as far as the Dakota badlands and the Missouri valley. These original Albertans knew as little of the outside world as it knew of them, but for the curious and the land-hungry their enormous territory radiated a powerful and irresistible attraction.

For more than a century increasing numbers of Europeans had found their way to this remote and rugged frontier, drawn by its furs, the promise of a back-door route to the Klondike gold fields, and finally by its potential for settlement. At the end of the 19th century Canada's North-West Territories, a vast sprawl of land the size of Western Europe, still hung in economic and political limbo between the young provinces of Manitoba and British Columbia — but that was changing. The great global depression of the 1880s, which had stifled investment and hampered development of the Canadian West, was by now a fading memory. The railway at last provided access to the population centres of the East and to the potential markets of the Pacific. After 1896 the NWT even elected its own democratic representatives,

who governed from the tiny territorial capital of Regina, population 2,100.

In fact, Regina was indicative of the one resource the territories sorely lacked — people. The 1901 census listed just 165,555 residents on scattered farms and in small communities from the American border to the Arctic Ocean. The largest town, by far, was Dawson City in the Yukon, which courtesy of the Klondike gold rush was home to almost 10,000 people. In the pivotal year of 1896, when Clifford Sifton became minister of the interior in the new Liberal government of Prime Minister Wilfrid Laurier, a mere 1,857 new homesteads had been settled across the territories.

Sifton approached the issue of immigration with typical energy and enthusiasm. He abandoned Ottawa's genteel pursuit of new Canadians in favour of a full-blooded, American-style marketing campaign, which aggressively recruited the sort of immigrant Sifton favoured — rugged, self-sufficient farmers. His agents were suddenly to be found everywhere, from Manchester to Moscow, from St. Louis to Stockholm, and by 1905 the number of new homesteads settled in what was now promoted as the "Last, Best West" had swelled to 30,819. The towns were also growing. Calgary, a divisional point on the Canadian Pacific Railway and a bustling ranching centre, could now boast 4,000 residents - making it the second largest community on the Prairies (after Winnipeg), and double the size of Edmonton, Lethbridge and Medicine Hat.

The result of all this development was a demand for something the politicians and lawyers called "autonomy": the evolution of the territories into one or more provinces, which would take their rightful place in Confederation. The idea of the NWT's District of Alberta becoming a province in its own right was first advanced by the *Calgary Herald* in 1891 — with Calgary as the provincial capital, of course. This did not sit well with residents of Edmonton, the much older, fur-trading outpost which already regarded itself as the capital of the northern frontier. "We notice that the hoglike propensities of Calgary are still to the fore," huffed an editorial in the *Edmonton Bulletin*. But despite such arguments, by the end of the 19th century there was a groundswell of public support and broad agreement across the West that the time had come to create new provinces.

Fort Edmonton in 1871, looking west from the river flats. The York Boat (centre) and the Red River cart (right) were the two main vehicles for western travel before the arrival of the railroad.

The man charged with making it happen was Frederick Haultain, the charming and popular premier of the NWT. As might be expected of a frontier territory, in those days the business of government at Regina was decidedly informal. Haultain, a Conservative, led a cabinet of mostly Liberals, and debates, although lively, were less politically partisan than in later times. And at the end of the day the entire 35-member assembly would retire to the Palmer House for lavish oyster suppers lubricated by large quantities of whiskey. The evenings tended to devolve into a raucous singsong, led by the premier himself, who was a church chorister and possessed of a fine voice.

This non-partisan, collegial approach did not sit well with at least one young member of the legislature. Richard Bedford Bennett, an outspoken Conservative lawyer, was elected from Calgary in 1898. Bennett appointed himself the leader of the opposition, and since Haultain favoured the creation of a single, large Prairie province, Bennett became the chief spokesman for a two-province model — with Calgary the capital of the western jurisdiction, naturally. Since he did not drink, the serious-minded Bennett did not join the post-session revelry at the Palmer House. Such foolishness, to his mind, was simply a waste of time.

In May 1900 Haultain delivered a three-hour speech to the legislature (the best of his career according to some) in which he outlined his proposal for one great Prairie province, called Buffalo, lying between Manitoba and B.C. and stretching from the U.S. border to the 57th parallel. With an eye on Bennett, he dismissed those in favour of dividing the territories into two or more provinces as "Little Westerners." But always the practical politician, Haultain's actual resolution called only for an "inquiry" into provincial status and avoided the sticky question of whether there ought to be one province or more. It passed unanimously on July 20, 1900, and was presented to the cabinet of Prime Minister Wilfrid Laurier a week later.

Haultain's proposal resulted in a cordial meeting in Ottawa with the prime minister and his minister of the interior, Clifford Sifton, but there were some significant political obstacles. One was Manitoba, the "postage stamp province" created out of Winnipeg and the Red River country after the Riel rebellion. Its borders had been extended twice, but denied control over crown land it remained dependent on Ottawa. Its premier, Rodmond Roblin, saw in Manitoba's westward expansion an opportunity for equality and financial stability. He suggested to the federal government that it extend Manitoba's borders to Regina, and then create a single new province between Manitoba and B.C.

A debate between Roblin and Haultain was organized at Indian Head in the District of Assiniboia a week before Christmas, 1901. Both men were noted orators and the issue was such

John Black's store in Fort Macleod, 1898. Black (just left of centre, holding the horse) was one of Alberta's earliest independent entrepreneurs. As the sign over his store suggests, he revelled in his reputation as a rebel merchandiser. He died, aged 43, the year after this photograph was taken.

8

Edmonton fur trader Colin Fraser sorting his purchases in 1900. At the dawn of the 20th century the fur trade was still big business in northern Alberta, with the Hudson's Bay Company's long domination of the trade facing new competition from the likes of freelancer Fraser and the French fur company, Revillon. Fraser alone is said to have bought 30,000 muskrat skins from the lower Athabasca and Slave rivers.

Territorial Lieutenant-Governor Edgar Dewdney turning the first sod in Calgary for construction of the Calgary and Edmonton Railway in 1890. Built in 13 months, the C & E finally provided Edmonton with a rail link - but it terminated on the south side of the North Saskatchewan valley, spurring development of New Edmonton (later to become Strathcona). Edmontonians were not well pleased.

that the community hall was packed with farmers, many of whom had travelled long distances to be there. Roblin made a strong case for extending Manitoba's borders, bringing the advantages of an established government and immediate help in building roads and establishing schools and hospitals. Who knew how long it would take for the NWT to achieve provincial status? Haultain pointed out that joining Manitoba would mean shouldering at least a portion of that province's not inconsiderable debt. He also argued, convincingly, that a brand new province could chart its own destiny, rather than being subservient to established interests in Winnipeg. After the debate, Roblin's plan found little support in the territories.

For Haultain the greater political problem became one the territorial legislators had not even considered. Their quest for provincehood threatened to upset the political balance in Ottawa, and within the Laurier government, between French and English, and between Quebec and Ontario. The issue was education. The provision of French-language, Catholic schools had been authorized by the North-West Territories Act of 1875, but they existed in effect as part of a single public system. Would any new western province, or provinces, be required to provide a separate school system?

It was far from a minor question. Laurier had won the 1896 election, ending the Conservatives' long grip on federal power, at least in part by promising a compromise on the explosive issue of francophone education in Manitoba. The province's founding legislation had guaranteed such schooling, but the Manitoba government had abolished separate schools. Laurier had found a compromise, and his government now included both powerful French Catholics and staunch English Protestants (among them Sifton, who as Manitoba's attorney-general had been a leading proponent of unified public schooling and provincial rights). But it was an uneasy coalition, and the last thing Laurier wanted was another divisive debate over education.

10

So in January 1902 the federal cabinet flatly rejected Haultain's proposal. The timing, said Laurier, was not yet right. Sifton said the problem was that the people of the territories were not agreed on how many new provinces there ought to be. That, said Haultain, was plainly nonsense. "Could you ever get a people to be unanimous on any question? By far the greater number are in favour of one province and I am simply acting on their behalf."

The stalemate continued for two years, but with a federal election looming, and Haultain continuing to rouse public support in the NWT for "autonomy," Laurier eventually softened and promised that the appropriate legislation would be introduced the following year — as long as the Liberals were returned to power. They were, and early in 1905 serious negotiations began between the Laurier government and territorial representatives. Various delegations arrived in Ottawa from the West to lobby for their particular cause. Manitoba wanted to make sure it got whatever rights or powers might be conferred on any new provinces. Fort Saskatchewan wanted a bridge over the North Saskatchewan River. Father Albert Lacombe and Bishop Emile Legal wanted to safeguard Catholic education. And Calgary, Edmonton, Lethbridge, Red Deer, and even Banff, all advanced compelling arguments for being designated the provisional capital of whatever province might be created. The negotiations began, with Haultain presenting a territorial draft bill for the creation of one large western province with control over land and resources, a secular school system, and an end to the Canadian Pacific Railway's considerable tax-exemptions.

Curiously absent from the federal side in these negotiations was Laurier's senior western minister, Sifton, who was seeking medical treatment in the U.S. The assumption was that the prime minister would not make a final decision until Sifton's return. But the assumption was wrong. Haultain was presented with draft legislation which bore little resemblance to the territorial plan. Ottawa proposed two new provinces (to be called Alberta and Saskatchewan), the federal government would retain control of crown lands and resources, the public school systems would operate under church, not provincial control, and the CPR's tax exemptions would remain.

Haultain was astounded — as was Sifton, who returned to Ottawa some days later. Laurier's western lieutenant had risen to political prominence as an advocate of secular schooling and provincial rights, and now his government was proposing church schools beyond the control of the new provinces. He promptly resigned from cabinet and began rallying opposition within the Liberal caucus. Faced with a revolt, Laurier looked for another compromise. He accepted a Sifton plan which allowed for Catholic school boards, but controlled, certified and inspected by the new provinces.

Sifton did not, however, return to Laurier's cabinet. In a move which would have profound implications for the new province of Alberta, he was replaced as minister of the interior by Edmonton's Frank Oliver. The *Calgary Herald* speculated that Oliver might not be too blatantly pro-Edmonton, and suggested that his appointment was not necessarily bad news for Calgary. Much to Calgary's annoyance, Edmonton was immediately named the interim capital of Alberta.

The *Herald* also noted, more accurately, that while "rival gangs of politicians are shouting themselves hoarse in Ontario over the educational affairs of Alberta" the residents of the new province had other issues on their minds. "Is it just possible," asked the newspaper, "that Alberta would be more thankful to these enthusiasts if they would urge more even-handed justice for the West in the way of distribution of the natural resources of the country, a more equitable boundary division, capital location, and other features of substantial value to the new province?" These were questions which would echo throughout Alberta's first century.

Others also took issue with the federal plan. Medicine Hat was shocked to discover that it would not, like most of the district of Assiniboia, become part of Saskatchewan. The Western Stockgrowers Association was alarmed to find the central boundary of the two new provinces — the 110th meridian — divided the grassland prairie and its membership. It also divided the community of Lloydminister, which very much concerned the Rev. G.E. Lloyd and the other founders of the Barr colony.

Haultain continued to have serious objections. Two provinces meant two governments and two sets of expensive bureaucracy. Ottawa promised to offset this with generous grants, but Haultain pointed out that this in no way compensated for the creation of two additional second-class provinces, which like Manitoba would not control their own land and natural resources. In a confederation of equal provinces, was this not simply unjust? The West, he argued, wanted "autonomy" and equality, not compensation. Despite the complaints Laurier ploughed ahead and the legislation creating the two new provinces was passed into law on July 20, 1905. Inauguration ceremonies were set for Edmonton on September 1, and at Regina on September 4.

Klondikers assemble on Edmonton's Jasper Avenue in 1898. The "Great Back Door Route" to the Yukon goldfields was heavily promoted as "the shortest, cheapest, and best" way to get to the Klondike, and the two-year boom associated with the Klondike gold rush was still celebrated by Edmontonians a century later. But of the hundreds of adventurers who set out from the city en route to the Yukon, most failed to reach their destination and 70 are thought to have perished in the attempt.

Provincial Archives of Alberta B-5184

A nomadic way of life gives way to settlement

OTTAWA CONFIDENTLY PREDICTS THAT RESERVES WILL SOON BE SELF-SUPPORTING, BUT ALBERTA'S NATIVE PEOPLE FACE A FUTURE OF MARGINALIZATION AND NEGLECT

When the then governor-general of Canada, Lord Minto, paid a visit in 1900 to the Blackfoot and Sarcee people of southern Alberta, a number of Calgarians tagged along, including reporters from the city's newspapers. They were astonished by the pride and demeanour of the native people who turned out to welcome the Queen's representative, in particular the mounted escort which rode alongside the vice-regal party. "They were as varied as the wild flowers of the prairies," enthused the *Calgary Herald* correspondent. "Some wore immense head-dresses of many coloured plumes and the tails of animals. Several had the most beautiful shields attached to the tails of their steeds... It is impossible to give an adequate idea of the brilliance of this group."

For later generations who have become familiar with and appreciative of traditional aboriginal culture, the surprise of the Calgarians — who lived scant miles from the Blackfoot and Sarcee — seems very odd indeed. But in the quarter century after the signing of the treaties covering most of the area south of the Athabasca River, natives and newcomers had become almost strangers to each other. Devastated by the inrush of settlement and the loss of their traditional life, the original Albertans had retreated to the reserves assigned by the federal government, becoming increasingly isolated and impoverished.

In the 1880s the federal government had confidently predicted that the reserves would be self-supporting within a decade, and had begun to supply the machinery, livestock and seed necessary to turn nomadic hunters into farmers. The plan saw some initial success, although it was seriously hampered by bureaucracy and inefficiency (poor quality livestock, and seed which often arrived too late for planting). But before commercial farming really had a chance to take hold, a new federal Indian commissioner, Hayter Reed, embraced an emerging sociological theory that argued the best way to create sturdy, self-sufficient farmers lay in "peasant agriculture." To learn the true value of farming, native people must do it the hard way, with homemade tools on small plots. So in a sharp about-face, Ottawa ordered the removal of all mechanical equipment from native farms, to be replaced with scythes and homemade pitchforks. Root crops were to be preferred to grain. No band would be allowed to negotiate credit or be allowed to sell farm produce off the reserve.

Reed's philosophy was abandoned in the 1890s, but the damage had been done and the discouragement it bred lingered on. The story of native Albertans in these years can best be seen in the numbers. By the time of Lord Minto's visit there were only 3,500 people in the Treaty Seven area of southern Alberta, a decrease of 50% since 1880. Disease, in particular tuberculosis, took a dreadful toll. Dr. Peter Bryce, chief medical officer for the federal Indian

Glenbow Archives NA-75-2

Girls at the Old Sun residential school on southern Alberta's Blackfoot reserve. Native residential schools were already a subject of furious public debate, and as early as 1909, Frank Oliver, Ottawa's minister of the Interior, admitted that conditions at many church-run schools were sub-standard. Tuberculosis was rampant and many native families sensibly shunned the schools. The Old Sun school (where enrolment fell to 12 students) was closed in 1909.

Department, estimated a quarter of native children who attended government schools died of the disease. "Of one school with an absolutely accurate statement," he wrote, "69% of the ex-pupils are dead."

In the north of the province the Woods Cree, Chipewyan, Slavey and Beaver people fared better during these hard years. Twenty groups had signed Treaty Eight by the turn of the century, albeit with concerns over their continuing rights to hunt and fish. One of the factors that helped northern people overcome their doubts was the presence among the government's treaty commissioners of an old and trusted friend — Father Albert Lacombe, the legendary Oblate missionary. "I urge you to accept the words of the Big Chief who comes in the name of the Queen," he told them. "Your forest and river life will not be changed by the treaty."

For the next generation Father Lacombe's confidence proved to be well founded. Not only did northern native people maintain much of their old lifestyle, the prices for muskrat, lynx, mink, beaver and other animal furs increased steadily in value. Free traders arrived who competed with the Hudson's Bay Company, and they paid in cash, as opposed to the credit system long used by the Bay. Little would change in the lives of the Treaty Eight native people until the 1920s, when arrival of the airplane and the settlement of the Peace River country brought the outside world closer and eroded their protective isolation.

Glenbow Archives NA-3700-3

Crowfoot, head chief of the Blackfoot in the 1860s. Handsome, courageous and intelligent, Crowfoot epitomised the best qualities of native leadership in the twilight years of the nomadic life.

The arrival of Europeans and the settlement of Alberta brought to an end a nomadic way of life and a unique history that had existed for at least 12,000 years. It was a catastrophe for native people, and a challenge the federal government was ill-equipped to understand, let alone meet. At the beginning of the 20th century Ottawa remained convinced that its policy of regarding native people as wards of the state was not only unavoidable, but successful and beneficial. It was a mindset which would change only slowly.

In 1910 a deputy superintendent-general of the federal Indian Department reported with profound self-satisfaction:

"It seldom happens that all essentials to the well being of the aboriginal race prove so uniformly favourable as has been the case during the year now ended." It is unlikely that native Albertans shared his rosy view. That year the native population of the province fell to around 9,000, with 293 births and 315 deaths. It would be another generation before modern medicine, improved housing and other measures began to reverse that decline, and fully half a century of benign neglect before native Albertans began to take a more active and public role in the life of their province.

15

'Off to the land of plenty.' That was the caption the photographer attached to this photo of a family of settlers preparing to set out from Edmonton at the dawn of the 20th century. Good soil and dependable water drew hundreds, and then thousands of 'sodbusters' to central Alberta.

Provincial Archives of Alberta B-669

During the first years of the new century Edmonton had grown into a bustling agricultural centre. Surrounded by fertile parkland prairie it offered farmers better soil and more dependable water than the grasslands around Calgary, and as a result was attracting many new immigrants. Still, Calgary had the railway and the cattle money. Edmontonians had to travel to Calgary to get anywhere (a situation which would repeat itself towards the century's end). Being designated the provisional capital of the new province was a great opportunity, but just how large a crowd could this farming town muster for the inauguration? According to the 1901 census, the combined population of Edmonton and neighbouring Strathcona was only 4,176. Putting on a show for the expected dignitaries would be a challenge, but the planning had begun before the Alberta Act had even passed in Ottawa. Edmontonians were united in their determination to make the most of this opportunity.

One thing which was sure to impress visitors was a display of the new electric lights. The city announced that electricity would be free during inauguration week, and coloured lights were attached to Alberta College (the centre of the festivities), the fire hall and the Alberta Hotel. Alderman William Griesbach, a highly respected Boer War veteran who had seen something of the outside world, raised eyebrows among his colleagues with a suggestion that council members should wear top hats and frock coats for the various official ceremonies. "Some of the aldermen bucked and declared with oaths and curses they would not wear such a contraption," he recalled in his memoirs, *I Remember*. "However, a certain amount of pressure was applied and J.J. Mills, the clothier, came up to the next council meeting and measured everybody."

These preparations did not go unnoticed in Calgary. "They are getting very toney up in Edmonton," observed the city's *Eye Opener* newspaper, "with their fair and inauguration festivities in sight. Many of the smart young ladies have taken to wearing open-work shoes to display pretty hosiery - a charming idea. It is now in order for the men of Edmonton to start wearing open-work hats, for the purpose of displaying the wheels revolving in their heads."

The official party arrived the night before the inauguration, travelling from Calgary (of course) in a special train which would serve as their accommodation during the festivities. They were led by the governor-general and his wife, Earl Grey and Lady Grey, together with Sir Wilfrid Laurier and Lady Zoe. The Calgarians in the party included Senator James Lougheed, Chief Justice Arthur Sifton (brother of Clifford), and territorial MLA R.B. Bennett. They were entertained that evening at a concert in the Thistle Rink (at 102 Street and 102 Avenue) organized by Vernon Barford, the renowned Oxford-trained organist of All Saints Church. A 41-member choir and fifteen-piece orchestra belted out an enthusiastic rendering of *God*

The debate over which city should be capital of the new province ignited a rivalry between Edmonton and Calgary that was destined to play a pivotal role in the development of Alberta. This 1905 window display at the McDougall and Secord store in Edmonton advised: "Now, don't be naughty Calgary. Let your sister have it. You're not old enough to handle it safely. Run and play with your CPR."

Provincial Archives of Alberta B-6736

18

Prosper Him Our King and a dozen other melodies.

Despite a weather forecast in the *Calgary Herald* that mischievously called for snow in Edmonton, inauguration day dawned bright and sunny, perfect late summer weather. Even the Calgarians present were impressed by the numbers of people who pressed into the city for the parade and official ceremonies. The crowd was variously estimated at between 12,000 and 20,000. It seemed the entire district had turned out. William Griesbach described the parade through the town and down McDougall Hill to the exhibition grounds: "There were bands, floats from patriotic societies, and contingents from various sporting clubs marching in the procession. It was concluded by a very excellent float advertising Ochsner's Beer. Bottles of cold beer were handed out to any thirsty individual who held up his hand."

Behind the floats and various official marchers came the residents of Edmonton, but for the most part the procession was made up of farmers and their families from the surrounding district. "The horses were taken out of the plough and the vehicles were democrat wagons or ordinary farm wagons," wrote Griesbach. "The farmer and his wife sat in the front seat and the horses with their bewhiskered fetlocks trotted along, occasionally becoming sufficiently interested to shy at a banner or some unusual sight." The smaller children crowded into the back of the wagon, "while behind it rode the half-grown sons of the family on half-broken horses, some with saddles and some without." All very impressive.

When everyone had assembled on the exhibition grounds, under a large pavilion erected for the occasion, Earl Grey inducted George Bulyea, a former school teacher and the territorial minister of public works, as Alberta's first lieutenant-governor. Prime Minister Laurier gave a mercifully short speech, after which C Squadron of the North-West Mounted Police charged across the exhibition grounds and pulled up before the pavilion in a flurry of colour and dust. The NWMP artillery boomed out a deafening salute, and Alberta came officially to life. It was, everyone agreed, quite the most marvellous event ever to take place.

Alexander Rutherford and his family in 1900. The son of Scottish immigrants, Rutherford became Alberta's first premier and founder of the University of Alberta. The popular Strathcona lawyer was universally known as "Uncle Sandy."

September 1, 1905. The inaugural day parade makes its way down Jasper Avenue in Edmonton. The entire district turned out for the celebration, with some 12,000 people gathering at the foot of McDougall Hill to hear Governor-General Earl Grey proclaim Alberta officially a province.

Provincial Archives of Alberta B-6717

"Calgary's prospects were never brighter than they are today," reported the *Herald* in 1905. "The country around us in all directions is filling up rapidly. Between four and five thousand new settlers came into central and north Alberta during the month of April alone." There can be no doubting Calgary's sense of outrage and loss at being denied the status of Alberta's capital city, but in the first decade of the new century Calgarians discovered there was more to life than politics. There was also business, and in this arena the city excelled.

The CPR and ranching were the mainstays of the Calgary economy. The city's "Big Four" tycoons - George Lane of the Bar U Ranch, meat packer Pat Burns, rancher and brewer A.E. Cross, and rancher and politician A.J. McLean - all made their fortunes in the cattle business. Mount Royal, the CPR's original upscale subdivision for its managers, was joined by Elbow Park, Elboya and Windsor Park, as Calgary's new entrepreneurial class built substantial homes. The city's original sandstone buildings were joined by yet more impressive structures — a new City Hall, the James Short School, the Grain Exchange, the Lyric Theatre — as frontier character gave way to urban sophistication. The proliferation of bowler hats was frowned upon by some, but the whole city took pride in its streetcars, piped water and electricity.

Actually the electricity was a bit of a problem. The city had bought the Calgary Gas and

Uncovered: the secret passion of a lonely visionary

HAULTAIN'S FRIENDS OFTEN WONDERED JUST WHAT MADE HIM SO MELANCHOLY, BUT THE TRUTH ABOUT HIS PRIVATE LIFE REMAINED A SECRET FOR SIX DECADES

One dignitary who was not in Edmonton for the inaugural celebrations, or for the creation of Saskatchewan four days later in Regina, was the man who more than any other had promoted the cause of western "autonomy" and made it all possible: Frederick Haultain. In a deliberate act of political spite he was not invited. The former premier did not, however, disappear from public life. He remained active in Regina politics (as the leader of the Provincial Rights Party, which would eventually become the Conservative Party of Saskatchewan), and was appointed chief justice of Saskatchewan in 1912. Five years later, in a delayed acknowledgement of his achievements, he became Sir Frederick. In 1938 the lifelong bachelor married a childhood friend, the widow Mrs. W.B. Gilmour.

But those who knew Haultain always noted about him a lingering sadness, which was generally ascribed to the setbacks he had suffered in his campaign for western autonomy. For a lawyer and

Glenbow Archives NA-510-1

A young Frederick Haultain. As premier of the North-West Territories, Haultain played the leading role in securing "autonomy" for Alberta and Saskatchewan - although he would have preferred one large province between Manitoba and British Columbia.

man who had held high office he was also often curiously short of money. Only his old territorial government colleague Walter Scott, Saskatchewan's first premier, sensed there was, perhaps, something more seriously awry in Haultain's personal life. "Doubtless every man has his handicaps, which seem the worst to him in the world," Scott wrote in 1918. "I often puzzle and wonder over Haultain... He was surely hobbled by some handicap."

The answer to this puzzle lay in the papers of Charles Herbert Mackintosh, a former lieutenant-governor of the North-West Territories, but did not come to light until discovered in 1970 by University of Alberta historian Lewis H. Thomas. At the heart of Haultain's melancholy was a woman, Marion Mackintosh, the third of seven daughters of the pompous and arrogant lieutenant-governor.

Haultain met Marion in 1893 when her father arrived in Regina as the imperial representative. She was about 18, half Haultain's age, and a great beauty.

Waterworks in 1900 (the first city-owned utility), and five years later replaced its aging steam pump with an electric one that could handle 2.5 million gallons a day. There was also a gravity-fed system from the Elbow River. So most of Calgary could rely on running water, most of the time - but the supply of electricity remained erratic until the end of the decade, when the Calgary Power Company built a hydro-electric powerhouse at Horseshoe Falls on the Bow. It was capable of producing an impressive 14 megawatts of power, which was finally enough to match the needs of Calgary's rapidly developing economy. The payoff was not long in coming. A reliable electrical supply convinced the CPR to build a large new maintenance facility, which provided 1,200 jobs and almost doubled the railway's workforce in the city.

The increasing use of electricity brought its share of problems, particularly for those not used to this modern convenience, or who were perhaps downright sceptical of it. Hotels, for example, routinely offered advice to guests who might be unfamiliar with the operation of electric lights. "This room is equipped with Edison electric light," read one such sign. "Do not attempt to light with a match. Simply turn key on wall by the door. The use of electricity for light is in no way harmful to health, nor does it affect the soundness of sleep."

Calgary's first "large motor omnibuses" were shipped from Glasgow, Scotland and began service

The premier was immediately smitten, but although he was accounted a confident political orator, and among men a fascinating and witty conversationalist, he was curiously silent and painfully shy with women. It took him two years to pluck up the courage to ask Marion to dance. Thereafter the relationship blossomed, although according to Haultain's biographer, Grant MacEwan, not along the lines the premier would have wished. Marion seems to have regarded him as a fatherly friend and mentor. She certainly did not return his deeper affections.

In 1896 Marion married a young Englishman, Alfred Castellain, one of many well-bred younger sons of the minor nobility who washed up in the West looking to make the fortune they could not inherit. Castellain set up business in Regina, but met with little success and within a few years went broke. He sold up and returned to England with his new wife. Which might well have been the end of any continuing friendship between Haultain and Marion, but when the premier visited England in 1901, for the coronation of Edward VII, he decided to visit the couple. He found an impoverished Marion, and a young daughter, abandoned by her husband and living on the inadequate charity of her in-laws. She was at first reluctant to take the help of her middle-aged friend, but eventually did, beginning a curious relationship which would last almost four decades.

Shortly afterwards Marion returned to her family in Ottawa, where she met another potential suitor, an American from Sioux Falls, South Dakota. Quickly in love again, she wrote to Haultain asking his advice. She was considering a divorce from Castellain and a move to South Dakota to be with her new beau. What did her old friend think?

Haultain's correspondence to Marion has not survived, but he appears to have advised her against divorce, which was a serious move in the early years of the century.

Marion, however, ignored his advice, obtained the divorce and left for Sioux Falls. This second love subsequently also abandoned her and her daughter. She was alone again and ill, and her family would not help. True to form, Haultain did. He financed Marion's return to England and resumed his support. In 1905 Marion announced that she could no longer accept Haultain's financial help — unless they were married. And so they were, secretly, in Ontario the following year. She was 29 and he 48.

Much to Haultain's disappointment, Marion would not return with him to Regina. She convinced him that her medical condition required yet another trip to England and treatment at an expensive hospital. Haultain returned to Regina alone, where he began building a law practice. In 1910 Marion's father apparently wrote to upbraid Haultain for not taking better care of his daughter (a hypocritical charge considering that Haultain had long been Marion's sole reliable support). It is the former premier's heartfelt defence, in a letter to Mackintosh, which survived to reveal his secret marriage and long commitment to a woman with whom he never lived and who never appears to have returned his affections.

Marion eventually returned to Canada and died at Guelph, Ontario in 1938. She was buried at Beechwood Cemetery, Ottawa, under the name Marion St. Clair Castellain. Her marriage to Haultain was never made public, and a few months after her death he married for what everyone assumed was the first time. The architect of Western self-government spent his last few years in retirement in Montreal. He died in 1942 and was buried at the University of Saskatchewan, but it would be another three decades before his first marriage and secret attachment to Marion Mackintosh finally became public.

Inside Calgary's first streetcar, 1909. The proliferation of bowler hats was frowned upon by some traditionalists, but the whole city took pride in Calgary's growing sophistication and an urban infrastructure which included piped water and electricity.

Glenbow Archives NA-644-23

in 1907. The covered vehicles were powered by impressive 40-horsepower engines, ran on solid rubber tires and could carry 20 passengers at a mind-boggling 18 mph. "It is expected that the introduction of these new and powerful omnibuses into western Canada will be the beginning of a revolution in methods of travel," trumpeted the *Herald*. Two years later the city bought the first motorized fire truck in Canada. Operating the truck was cheaper, it was argued, than the upkeep for Jimmy, Squibby, Dick, Frank, Bob, Brownie and Old White Wings, the fire department's prize-winning team of horses. They were put out to pasture. That same year the first streetcar line was opened from downtown to the Exhibition Grounds. It carried 35,000 passengers in its first week, and after six months returned a healthy profit of $7,000. Within a year Alberta Electric had a dozen cars operating along 13 miles of track. It was an enormous success and a source of great civic pride.

By 1912 Calgary's population was nearing 50,000 — an astonishing ten-fold increase in a single decade — and its self-confidence was fully restored. Edmonton might be the capital, but Calgary considered itself the province's principal city. As Calgary lawyer and future prime minister R.B. Bennett put it, Calgarians had the confidence and ability "to make things happen."

Civic pride could also manifest itself in other ways, particularly where Edmonton was concerned. In the winter of 1907 the Calgary newspapers devoted extensive coverage to the case of an Edmonton visitor to the dining room of a Calgary hotel, who had allegedly cursed his waitress over the poor quality of cuisine and service. As he left the hotel a friend of the waitress had given him what all agreed was a well deserved thumping. Rather than charging the assailant, Calgary police charged the victim, one William Boyd, with using insulting language. An equally unsympathetic magistrate fined him $5 and sent him packing.

Edmonton's greatest booster pulls off a dramatic coup

FRANK OLIVER PERSUADES OTTAWA TO NAME HIS HOMETOWN ALBERTA'S CAPITAL, AND THEN FIXES ALBERTA'S NEW POLITICAL MAP TO ENSURE THE DECISION STICKS

Frank Oliver, the Edmonton booster who secured capital status for the city —and as a result forever changed the character of the new province — was a curious mix of puritan morality and political chicanery. He was born Francis Bowsfield in 1853 near Brampton, Ontario, but as a teenager was so incensed at the remarriage of his widowed father that he took his mother's maiden name and left the family farm. He found a job in the printing works of Toronto's *Globe* newspaper and became a passionate disciple of its editor, the crusading Liberal George Brown. By 20 he was working at the *Manitoba Free Press*, and shortly after began a business carting supplies between Winnipeg and Fort Edmonton. In 1878 he set up the first store outside the fort's walls, and then founded the community's first newspaper, the *Bulletin*, in an old smokehouse behind the Edmonton Hotel.

Short, wiry and with a ferociously bushy trademark moustache, Oliver became a driving force in the development of the city. Its concerns became his concerns, and the opinionated, belligerent Oliver became the voice of Edmonton. As a militant westerner he supported the Metis cause to the very brink of rebellion in 1885. He railed against Ottawa, the Hudson's Bay Company and the railways for what he saw as their lack of enthusiasm in promoting rapid settlement. His outspoken support for western self-determination led him, naturally, into politics and the territorial government at Regina.

His equally militant teetotalism ensured his defeat after one term, but it made him available to run as a Liberal candidate for the Alberta constituency in the 1896 federal election. Oliver's victory in that contest now put him in a position to exercise far more influence on the development of the West than might otherwise have been the case. As Clifford Sifton's successor as minister of the interior he was in a position to promote the interests of his staunchly Liberal home town - which he did without shame.

Not only did he persuade Laurier to name Edmonton the provisional capital of the new province, but with the aid of Strathcona Liberal MP Peter Talbot he undertook perhaps the most breathtaking gerrymander in Canadian history, personally drawing up the new map of provincial constituencies so that Liberal Edmonton and northern Alberta had more MLAs than Conservative Calgary and the populous south. It was brazen, outrageous — and thoroughly successful. It made Oliver as despised in Calgary as he was lionized in Edmonton, yet by guaranteeing Alberta two major centres rather than one he had shaped the political and economic structure of the province for the century to come.

Oliver was influential in another important way. As minister

Provincial Archives of Alberta , B-8347

Frank Oliver. Edmonton's greatest champion, he secured "provisional capital" status for his town, and then organized the province's political map to make sure it stuck.

of the interior he reversed Sifton's policy of favouring farmers above all other immigrants, particularly those from Britain's impoverished inner cities. As a result the second half of the first decade of the 20th century saw an increase in the number of immigrants to Toronto, Montreal, Winnipeg and Vancouver, but also to Calgary, Edmonton, Medicine Hat, Lethbridge, Red Deer, the mining communities of the Crowsnest Pass, and a host of other smaller centres.

This first burst of urban growth arguably transformed the province (and the country) as much as the great influx of agricultural settlers. And for many who recalled it in later times, the years immediately before The Great War were a golden age of opportunity and expansion. "We did not go out to the North-West simply to produce wheat," said Oliver. "We went to build up a nation, a civilization, a social system that we could enjoy, be proud of, and transmit to our children..." And to a remarkable degree, you would have to say he succeeded.

The intoxication of the inaugural celebrations could not disguise the fact that in 1905 Edmonton had a long way to go to match Calgary's size and comparative sophistication. Jasper Avenue was a ramshackle collection of wood-frame hotels, livery stables, real estate offices and stores. The sidewalks were wooden, and still boasted hitching posts. Fort Edmonton, far from being the historic landmark its replica would one day become, was a dilapidated reminder of faded glory. As a *New York Times* correspondent had written just four years earlier, to the casual observer the community was "a city of broken dreams, a run-down elephants' graveyard for failed prospectors."

But not for long. There was now a bridge over the North Saskatchewan (the Low Level), and the CPR was talking about finally building another one (the High Level) to connect its 14-year-old Strathcona terminus with the city centre. The Canadian Northern reached the city at the close of

1905, ending the humiliating dependence on travel through Calgary. Edmonton's population was still only 7,000, but that was triple the number of residents only five years earlier. Settlers were pouring into the region and Edmonton was clearly on the verge of a boom.

The problem, in a word, was leadership. City council was still meeting in the old Number One Fire Hall, which continued to serve its original purpose and also as a police station. Sadly, the surroundings appeared to suit the rather unprofessional demeanour of the aldermen. Edmonton historian Tony Cashman recorded one occasion during which council paused to examine the evidence seized during a police raid on a bootlegger. By morning a very jolly group of aldermen had managed to polish off all the evidence, and another bootlegger had to be found to refill the bottles. Justice was preserved, but council's reputation suffered as a result.

More serious was the inability to upgrade Edmonton's telephone system (once a source of much pride, but now sadly outdated and unable to cope with growing demand), pave streets. build schools and service new subdivisions. By the fall of 1907 some 5,000 people, almost a third of the city's population, were living in tents. There were people camped out on the river flats, beyond the Canadian Northern tracks in the east end, and all along the bluffs overlooking the North Saskatchewan. The more enterprising campers pitched their tents below what would soon become the Macdonald Hotel, so they could make use of the ready supply of coal to be found in the hillside. Most embarrassing of all, neighbouring Strathcona had a streetcar

The first train into Edmonton. It crossed the new Low Level Bridge on October 20, 1902, with engineer James Entwistle at the controls. He would later give his name to another community, to the west of the capital.

Provincial Archives of Alberta B-6210

27

system up and running while Edmonton continued to rely on horse and buggy transport.

Unfortunately the city was broke. Despite a rapidly increasing tax roll, the municipal treasurer reported that council was out of cash and the banks would not lend it any more. The new mayor, 27-year-old Boer War hero William Griesbach, was popular and decisive, but clearly out of his depth. He tried to solve the immediate financial crisis by issuing $697,000 in debentures, but the issue was a flop, trading for only 93 cents on the dollar. Griesbach had simply created another way for the city to get deeper into debt, and taxpayers were outraged.

When Griesbach's one-year term of office was coming to an end, the city's business community attempted to draft former mayor John McDougall. He had come to Edmonton in 1883 as a fur trader, and with partner Richard Secord had become the city's first business success story. The pair branched out into land development, and after selling their fur business (to the French fur-trading house of Revillon) they established a very profitable mortgage lending operation. The wealthy McDougall at first declined a return to politics, but the deepening crisis and the entreaties of his friends finally convinced him to run in the municipal election at the end of 1907. He won handily and in January of the following year succeeded Griesbach.

With a wealth of experience and, for once, the full support of council and the Edmonton taxpayers, the gruff, no-nonsense McDougall went to work. He had a new telephone system in place by the spring, and then convinced Edmonton voters to back the purchase of Strathcona's streetcar company and expanded the system to the north side of the river. By November the renamed Edmonton Radial Railway Tramway had seven streetcars and tracks serving all quadrants of the expanding city. The central portion of Jasper Avenue (about one mile in length) was paved, and telephone and electrical lines were strung to accommodate the subdivisions rapidly filling with new arrivals. This, Edmontonians agreed, was more like it. The city was beginning to look like a provincial capital. In little more than a year McDougall had fulfilled all their expectations, and

then some. The grateful citizenry presented him with a sterling silver casket, inlaid with local gold (panned from the North Saskatchewan).

By 1910 Edmonton was experiencing a land boom that would continue almost until the outbreak of the Great War. The city was expanding rapidly in all directions, and almost everyone with a few dollars to spare was investing in land. The Edmonton Board of Trade reported that of 200 businesses operating in the city, 80 were real estate offices. Clearly the old fur trading depot was undergoing a significant transformation, and not only in land development. There was the new Bijou Theatre, where for a dime residents could take in one of the amazing, new moving pictures. They came by the thousands to view a newsreel of the funeral of King Edward VII, a mere month after the actual event. Together with the railways and telephones. it was further evidence that the outside world was now a lot closer to the old frontier town.

Edmonton's modernization did result in some problems, of course, including a handful of noisy, and quite obviously dangerous, automobiles that could now be found rushing along city streets. One early lead foot was the city's medical officer, Dr. Whitelaw, who attracted the attention of the constabulary for travelling at an estimated 17 mph along Jasper Avenue. At his trial the good doctor strenuously denied the charge, arguing that his vehicle could not possibly have been traveling at such a phenomenal rate of speed. Unimpressed, the magistrate fined him $10. "If this goes on," said a downcast Whitelaw, "we will all have to get speedometers installed."

The tent city on the outskirts of Edmonton about 1907. By the fall of that year, some 5,000 people - a third of the city's population - was living under canvas. Former mayor John McDougall reluctantly agreed to run for office and tackle the city's growing problems, which he did in very short order.

Provincial Archives of Alberta A-1372

Edmonton's Malcolm Groat (with beard) being driven in one of the first automobiles in the province. The first "horseless carriage" in Alberta was a steam powered Locomobile purchased in August 1903 by Billy Cochrane of High River. H.W. White of Calgary made the first Calgary-Edmonton automobile trip in a 29-horsepower Ford in the spring of 1906 - by which time there were 41 vehicles licensed in the province.

CHAPTER TWO

The Call of the Land

THE GREAT TIDAL WAVE OF SETTLMENT
BEGINS TO TRANSFORM THE FRONTIER

In the first years of the new century expanding world markets for Canadian exports and the aggressive settlement campaign waged by interior ministers Clifford Sifton and Frank Oliver turned the country from an Imperial backwater into a magnet for immigration. It also helped that Washington, declaring America's western frontier fully settled, stopped distributing free land. Farm prices south of the border immediately zoomed to as much as $100 an acre in Kansas and $200 in Illinois. Despite Canada's harsh winter weather, conveniently overlooked in advertising by the government, railways and land companies, the country which had until recently been leaking population to the U.S. now became the rising star of settlement. One and a quarter million immigrants arrived in the first decade of the 20th century, and the number of Albertans swelled by an astonishing 550% to 375,000.

Interior Minister Clifford Sifton knew what sort of settler he wanted for the West: "None but agriculturalists. We do not recognize labourers at all." As a result he cast his net very wide, for the first time actively encouraging massive immigration from beyond the British Isles. People flooded in from the U.S. and from across Europe. Ukrainians, Russians. Poles, Germans, Austrians, Dutch, and thousands of American farmers who sold their land and moved north to homestead again, armed with experience, equipment, and often a healthy bank balance. It was an amazing spectrum of humanity that would forever change the character of the Dominion. But that was neither Sifton's goal nor his primary concern. "We desire, every patriotic Canadian desires, that the great trade of the prairie shall go to enrich our own people in the East, to build up the factories and the workshops of eastern Canada, and to contribute in every way to its prosperity," Sifton told a Winnipeg audience in 1904.

Sifton was particularly interested in Americans. "The first great demand," he said, "is for persons with some capital." And Americans usually had it. He despatched 18 salaried agents to the U.S.. and the government ran ads promoting "The Last Best West" in 7,000 American rural and farming newspapers. The challenge was to persuade Americans that Canada was not one great iceberg, and that it had, in fact, potentially four times the wheat-growing area of the U.S. Government advertising extolled western Canada as "the largest continuous wheat field in the world." Parties of American journalists were invited to see this marvellous land for themselves, and having been lavishly wined and dined by Sifton's agents they invariably left singing its praises.

The Galician Hay Market in Edmonton, 1903. Clifford Sifton wanted rugged farmers like these, and so for the first time encouraged large-scale immigration from beyond the British Isles.

Provincial Archives of Alberta B-5584

was the immigration of 55,000 American settlers in 1905 alone.

The U.S., alarmed by the loss of experienced farmers, fought back. In Montana, with the aid of irrigation, large tracts of new land were opened for settlement. Florida and New England launched advertising campaigns extolling their climatic advantages. In South Dakota a booklet entitled *Saved from the Clutches of the King* told the story of a fictional American rescued from imperialist Canada. In North Dakota a popular snippet of doggerel warned:

> If Medicine Hat were blown away,
> Clear down to the equator, say,
> Then all the beastly cold would flit
> To some place where they've need of it.

There was concern, too, in Britain at the influx of Americans and other foreign immigrants - especially to Alberta: "the pick of the basket among Canadian provinces." The speech, entertainment, sports, and even the architecture of the rapidly developing province were becoming decidedly American. "Baseball and trotting races are prominent among popular sports, while cricket and rugby football, the ball games of the Empire, find little favour," worried one published report in London. In a remarkable early piece of spin-doctoring, Sifton's masterminds at the Department of the Interior turned such concerns on their head by promoting the view that the fault lay in the lack of immigrants from Britain. In an interview with the *London Star*, one successful English immigrant provided by Sifton's agents warned "Americans and foreigners are fast piling up fortunes in Alberta because the Englishman won't come to his own colony." But despite such concerns Americans remained the largest immigrant group to Alberta in the first decade of the new century (80,000, or 22%), followed by the British (19%).

The interior of the immigration hall in Edmonton. For a week new arrivals were guaranteed a bed and the use of cooking utensils, but not much in the way of security or privacy.

Most immigrants faced some degree of discrimination. The *Calgary Herald* was typical in its views when in 1901 it wondered how Galicians (Ukrainians from the Austro-Hungarian Empire) and other central Europeans could possibly "assume the same political position as their English-speaking neighbours?" But the new Canadians' hard work and obvious commitment to their adopted country rapidly eased tensions. By 1906 Alberta had some 45,000 Galician settlers, and even the *Herald* no longer automatically viewed them with suspicion.

The same could not be said of Alberta's early Asian and black immigrants, who were not so quickly accepted. Oriental immigrants would face decades of official discrimination and hostility, and the possibility of large-scale immigration from Oklahoma of a people known then as "Creek-Negroes" (blacks who had intermarried with native Americans and who were attempting to flee racism at home) sent the province into a near-panic. A petition with more than 3,000 names was sent to Ottawa, warning of "the serious menace to the future welfare of a large portion of western Canada, by reason of the alarming influx of negro settlers." Ottawa contemplated a temporary ban on black immigration, but instead relied on a more furtive policy of discouragement and bureaucratic foot-dragging. Nevertheless, by 1911 there were around 1,000 black settlers in Alberta, mostly farmers who had arrived from the U.S. The majority homesteaded north of Edmonton around Wildwood, Breton, Barrhead, and in particularly the thriving black community of Amber Valley — east of Athabasca — which was home to 350 people.

Edmonton's Frank Oliver, Sifton's successor as interior minister, was more supportive of immigration from Britain, even the urban poor that Sifton had disdained. Numerous charitable organizations began sponsoring the immigration of poor families in search of a better life. The Salvation Army sponsored as many as 500 immigrants at a time, paying for their trans-Atlantic passage and railway tickets. Britain's *Daily Telegraph* was particularly enthusiastic, raising $50,000 from its readers to send several hundred poor families to Canada. (Ironically, eight decades later the newspaper would become part of the publishing empire of Canadian Conrad Black.)

The immigrant class ocean fare was around $15, which was three dollars less than the train

Herbert Darby, his family, and his wife's sister, were among the first black immigrants to what would become Alberta, settling in Vulcan in 1903.

fare from Quebec City to Winnipeg. The trans-Atlantic passage was often rough, with vomiting passengers packed together like sardines. "I became so sick I thought I was going to die," recorded Welsh immigrant John Roberts. "Then I got worse and was afraid I wouldn't." Once ashore, the new arrivals were grilled by immigration officers who were required to fill out a form that asked "Is the applicant honest? Sober? Industrious? Thrifty? Of good morals? Is wife a good housekeeper and tidy?"

The cross-Canada railway journey to Alberta was no less arduous than the ocean crossing, with the trip taking a week in a colonist car, sleeping on wooden seats and boiling tea on a stove at one end of the car. Basic food essentials — bread, corned beef, apples — could be replenished at the longer stops. Once in Calgary, Edmonton, or one of the province's other larger centres, the new arrivals could bed down at the immigration hall, which provided a sleeping cubicle and the use of cooking utensils for a week, but not much in the way of security. English immigrant Gladys Rowell later wrote that "mother had our fortune, less than $200, tucked into a small pouch pinned to the top of her corset."

For immigrants planning to homestead, the final destination was the Dominion Lands office - where any male over 18, or "any person who is the sole head of a family," with proof of identity and a $10 fee could become the proud owner of a quarter section of land. In theory anyway. In practice you had three years to "prove up" your land, which meant clearing at least 30 acres or having at least 20 head of stock, fencing at least 80 acres, building a dwelling and farm buildings, and actually living on the property for six months of the year. Do all that, and you were awarded clear title to the land.

If you had money there was also plenty of land for sale. Land that had been allotted

to Boer War veterans and Metis in settlement of the Riel Rebellion could be bought at steep discounts. The Canadian Pacific also sold land from its vast holdings, and there was also land from earlier, less successful attempts at settlement which had passed into the hands of speculators. All of this now came on the market, creating the biggest land boom in Canadian history.

Occasionally there were ugly scenes at land offices with fights and the less robust being manhandled out of their rightful place in line, but in general the distribution of government land was conducted with typical Canadian orderliness. The scene outside the Dominion Land office at Sixth Street and Victoria Avenue in Edmonton on September 1, 1908 was typical. A lone Mountie and a flimsy wooden fence kept about 250 people in order as the office opened to accept claims on a new allotment of crown land. The *Edmonton Bulletin* recorded the event. First in line was Steele Murdoch, a local tinsmith. Number 13 was Margaret Conklin, a widow from Chicago. "There was

Saskatchewan Archives A-4557-2

the tall, lanky Dakota man with his heavy coat and upturned collar and pea straw hat. and the bright active young fellow from eastern Canada," reported the newspaper. "There was the unmistakeable Londoner, the fair-haired Norwegian and the swarthy native of southern Europe." There were also 30 young men from the Pembina River, a number of whom had been squatting illegally on their chosen quarter sections for over a year. Land agent K.W. McKenzie told the *Bulletin* reporter that if the young men behaved themselves and if they had already cleared land and built dwellings, their applications would certainly succeed. And they did.

Among the immigrants were a number of groups who. in addition to land, were looking for the freedom to practice their faith. In the spring of 1909 these included a curious group of five families who arrived in Edmonton from Toronto. Expelled from the Methodist church some 16 years earlier, they called themselves the Christian Association and they had come to Alberta

The crowds outside the Dominion Lands offices across Alberta were usually orderly, but occasionally things became unruly - as in this scene from 1909.

Alberta's tough and intrepid pioneering missionaries

By the middle of the 19th century Christian missionaries began arriving in what would become Alberta. Catholic, Anglican, Presbyterian and Methodist, they faced enormous challenges and hardships. Included in their ranks were the Sisters of Charity of Montreal (the famed Grey Nuns), and the Sisters of Providence, both of whom staffed the schools and hospitals which were established during this early period. Perhaps no group of missionaries was so influential as the priests and lay brothers of the order of Oblates of Mary Immaculate. Organized in France in 1816, the Oblates arrived in what would become Alberta around 1847. Many were the sons of the French gentry and had little experience of the unforgiving wilderness, yet they proved as intrepid as the fur traders, and had a reputation for being as tough and disciplined as the Mounties. Most famous among the pioneering Oblates were Bishop Emile Grouard (1) and Fr. Albert Lacombe (2), both of whom had communities named after them. Rev. William Bompas (3), the first Anglican bishop of Athabasca, travelled many thousands of kilometres in northern Alberta and the Arctic and was accounted "as great as any Oblate". For new settlers, the building of a church (or several) was an immediate priority (matched only by the urgency in erecting a school), and by the time of Alberta's inauguration substantial churches were appearing in larger towns. The foundation stone for Calgary's Anglican cathedral, for example, was laid amid much pomp and ceremony (4) exactly a year before the creation of the province.

looking for independence and isolation. By the time they arrived in the capital all the suitable land had been taken up, so they assembled 18 teams of oxen and wagons to make the trek to the Peace River country.

And a trek it was. After leaving Edmonton on April 20 they made Athabasca Landing in a week, but after that the journey became progressively more arduous as the group slogged along, cutting their own trail, moving boulders and fording streams. Eventually it was decided to ship women, children and some older men by boat to Grouard on the west end of Lesser Slave Lake. The rest toiled on through the bush and after some weeks the group was eventually reunited. They pushed on into the South Peace, and on July 14 - almost three months after leaving Edmonton - they reached the Beaverlodge River Valley. It was not yet surveyed, but it was exactly what they had been looking for. They immediately set to building homes, and from the open meadows along the river they harvested 250 tons of hay to get their livestock through the winter. They had found their remote corner of Heaven.

A horse was a vital necessity on a homestead, and settler William Ryhason and two friends owned one between them. When it came to making the 95 km journey from their farms (near Frome) to Westaskiwin, the men devised an ingenious method for sharing this four-legged resource. All three would set out at the same time, two walking and the third on the horse. After a few miles, the rider would dismount, tether the animal to a tree, and begin walking himself. When the two pedestrians caught up, one would ride the horse for a few more miles before tethering it again. When the last walker arrived he would then use the animal to catch up with the first - and the whole process would begin again. In those days walking long distances was commonplace. Grande Prairie's Harvey Switzer once walked the 385 km. to Edson. "We were in top-notch physical condition and could walk four-miles-an-hour for hour after hour," he wrote years later. Johnny MacFadden, an Ontarian of Scottish descent, was said to have walked the 320 kms. between Calgary and Edmonton in just four days.

Eastern Europeans, though harder pressed by poverty, seemed generally more appreciative of the potential bounty of new land. Kost Zaharichuk, of Smoky Lake, came from Bukovina with

Immigration pamphlets often oversold the delights of the prairie climate (rarely mentioning winter), but the phenomenal productivity of Alberta's farmland was not exaggerated. In this photo, taken in 1909-10, a Mrs. Blenner-Hasset and youngster Clark Allan stand in the middle of an impressive oat crop.

Success on a new homestead demanded hard work, and ingenuity in making the best of whatever was available. In this photo, above, taken near Edson in 1910, women are cooking outdoors on a newly-cleared farm. Below, John Bolten's family watches as he breaks sod with a team of oxen near Ranfurly in 1906.

only $10, and the first autumn earned 10 sacks of potatoes by working for a German farmer in Fort Saskatchewan. It would be enough to keep his family through the winter. "My wife couldn't believe it and came 50 miles on foot to see for herself. She knelt over those potatoes and prayed for an hour. She thanked God for not letting us starve to death in Canada."

Settler A.D. Adshead described the aftermath of the most severe hailstorm he ever saw: "The poor little chicks in the coop were all drowned, or chilled to death. In the garden, upon which we depended for our winter vegetables, not a potato to be seen, of the cabbages, only a few torn pieces of leaves driven into the ground, and what of the flourishing grainfield that but an hour since had proudly lifted its leaves to the sun? Only a black field of earth was left, with nothing on it except a surface indented all over with holes like huge smallpox marks, where the lashing hail had been driven deep into the soil after having cut to pieces the grain so that not a vestige was visible. And what of the luxuriant prairie grass? Nothing left but the top of the sod, not a pound of hay could we cut there now for winter use for our cattle. We counted dozens of dead ducklings floating on the creek, and the horses came up to the barn with lumps on their backs as big as walnuts."

A young Mary Cross rides a hay wagon at the A7 Ranch, near Willow Creek in 1910. Behind the idyllic scene, the adults were most likely working up a sweat.

Glenbow Archives NA691-18

The tenacity of the men, women and even the children who settled Alberta's farmlands is almost beyond belief for the relatively pampered generations who followed. The work was hard, the winters long — but the chance to own your land was worth a world of toil and trouble. Over the years many hundreds of recollections and personal histories from those times have been published and collected by the Provincial Archives of Alberta. The following extracts speak volumes about the character, determination and sense of humour of Alberta's early pioneers.

As the women enlarged the clearing for a garden, the pile of logs grew. Then Veronica's mother saw the possibility of a log house. She resented living like an animal in a lair and had cried bitterly over it. She longed for the clean, white-washed home she had left behind. From then on she worked with the vision of a log house uppermost in her mind. Before the men returned in the fall, the house had been built. Veronica recalled how hard her mother worked. Before she was finished building the house, both her shoulders were a mass of raw, bleeding flesh. But she refused to give up, and in time all four walls were standing. Thus, without spending a penny and improvising as she went, Veronica's mother built them a home in which they lived for many years.

Siding 16 - Wetaskiwin to 1930

A wagon hauling supplies along the muddy Athabasca Trail, north of Edmonton, in the early years of the 20th century. By the end of the first decade a railway line would replace the venerable fur trade portage between the capital and Athabasca Landing.

Wesley Maxfield was 15 when in November 1906 he agreed to help three ranchers herd 500 sheep east through the Neutral Hills. His sister Minnie remembered that the ranchers promised to see him safely home. "Wesley wanted to go, so mother agreed. The winter set in so severe and quick, and the ranch was so short of help that they could not spare the man (to see Wesley home). There was no way of hearing from him, and when a rumour reached us that a boy was missing on Sounding Lake, hope of his return began to fade. All the sheep perished and the ranchers were so busy trying to save the cattle that everyone was busy at the main ranch. Eight miles away was a smaller herd being fed by a man who lived in a little shack. About February 1 the man died of pneumonia, and Wesley was asked if he could do the job. He wasn't very anxious to be away out there, all alone for weeks on end, but he consented. He managed very well all winter, though, and one day in May rode home, safe and sound - and much more grown up."

Chatter Chips from Beaver Dam Creek

As a youngster, John Nyman of High River went to work on the Bar U Ranch. "Being a slim lad of eleven years, too young to fork hay or handle cows, he was put on the wolfing crew. His job was to crawl into the den with his six-shooter and kill the wolves in there. They seldom caught an old wolf at home, but when they did, John would shoot it and crawl and wriggle backwards out of the den coughing and choking from the dust and gunpowder fumes."

Along the Burnt Lake Trail

American settlers were quicker at learning the ropes. R.W. Elmer, who moved from Oregon to Didsbury in 1907, survived a "harrowing experience" in which four unruly broncos clobbered him with hooves and harrow teeth, breaking his collarbone, after one horse stepped into a badger hole. But an equine injury he took more seriously: "In the fall my best horse ran into the barbed wire fence and the wire girdled a front leg just above the knee. There remained only two inches of skin intact at the back of the knee. I threw him down in the stall, tied him well and with common darning needle and white thread, put in 32 stitches. Quite a mess. He brought a big price next spring."

Salt and Braided Bread: Ukrainian Life in Canada

Arthur Miller was working as a cowhand and coal miner when he slipped while trying to jump aboard a wagon. "I fell under, the rear wheel going over my leg and breaking it above the knee. Fred helped me onto the load. I lay on my stomach and drove the team eight miles to the ranch... The next morning I was loaded in a lumber wagon on a mattress and as they had to walk the horses it took all day to get me to Stettler." There he lodged with an English nurse who took in patients. "The doctor came and they had to cut my overalls off as my leg was so badly swollen. The doctor told me to take hold of the bed and hang on while he set the leg. He wrapped a two-by-four with cloth and fastened it to my ankle and below and above the break and around my chest. I had to lie flat on my back for eight weeks. When the swelling went down he put a cast on."

Chatter Chips from Beaver Dam Creek

"I started to break with four horses tandem and a short handled wooden beam John Deere walking plough. The land was heavy and sticky and hard to break and at times you would have to clean the mouldboard three times on the half mile. Nothing seemed a burden to me that summer. My boots hurt my feet walking in the furrow and one day at noon after I got hitched up I thought I would try it in my bare feet and the cool ground felt so good that I never had my boots on again that summer when I was ploughing. If I wasn't out in the field at 6 o'clock in the morning I thought the day was lost, and at night I went to bed, not tired, but wishing that it was morning so that I could get up again. That year I got eighty acres ready for crop."

Jean Bruce in The Last Best West

A motley crew at the bar of Edmonton's Alberta Hotel in 1905.
Men far outnumbered women in the province at inauguration and
drinking was the universal pastime for single men, eventually
resulting in an energetic movement to ban the sale of alcohol.

Second only to land, the opportunity for education was a great draw for Alberta's settlers. After raising a church, or several, the next building erected by any self-respecting community was a school. As a result, by the time Alberta became a province in 1905 there were already an astonishing 562 schools within its borders, with 34,000 pupils being instructed by 1,200 teachers. Alberta's first premier, Alexander Cameron Rutherford, in addition to being a lawyer had served for almost a decade as a school trustee and was in no doubt of the importance of education to the new province. "Education," he wrote, "is the basis of intelligent citizenship and... the foundation of all good government."

The number of schools was, however, a little misleading. Any three rate-payers could petition to form a school district, in an area not exceeding five miles in any direction and with a minimum of eight school-aged children. Rural schools often began by operating only from June to September. Money was tight and raising sufficient funds to operate a year-round school was difficult. Weather and roads were also issues, with many children travelling on rudimentary tracks that could be impassable in winter and hazardous due to flooding in spring. And in the fall, of course, the harvest often took priority for older children. The hiring of teachers was also a challenge. The pay was poor, the hours long, and those working in rural areas often found themselves alone and isolated. Yet a small army of dedicated teachers, especially young women, trooped to the prairies to take on this arduous challenge, fired by a sense of adventure and the firm belief that they were doing important work.

Some, like Pamela Appleby, came from Britain. Many years later she recalled (in *Syrup Pails and Gopher Trails: Memories of the One-room School*) that it might have been the promise of the vast unknown which lured her from her ordered classroom in London to a frontier teaching job. Or it might have been the opportunity to own a horse, something she had always wanted. As the new teacher at Hillsgreen School, 96 km. northeast of Calgary, Appleby discovered she was expected to share a bed with the daughter of the secretary-treasurer of the local school board, and that not all of the pupils crammed into the school's single room had books. There was also the small matter of her salary. The board could not afford to pay more than a fraction of it. But she did get the horse,

An unidentified mother and her children in the Bowden area. For the settlers who began raising families on Alberta's new homesteads, access to education for their children was an urgent priority.

48

a sturdy mare called Bessie, purchased with the last of her savings. The horse, she remembered, was a great comfort through some very tough times.

Weather was a particular hazard, naturally. At St. Paul, for instance, the teacherage (the shack which served as the teacher's home) was across the river from the school. When spring rains damaged the bridge, he was obliged to borrow a pig trough form an adjacent farm and pole it back and forth across the stream for a week. In the winter months, somebody — either the teacher or a reliable older student — had to get to school early and start the stove. "I would walk through deep snow (a mile and a half) very early to light the fire," Evelyn Lagerquist wrote of her school days in *Buffalo Trails and Tales*. As others arrived "We would sit around the stove with all our coats and rubbers on. For that I got the big sum of $1.25 a month." Ink also had to be thawed, along with water for the wash basin. Even with the stove lit, on cold days those students farthest away would have to work in their coats and mittens.

The standard rural schoolhouse measured about 20 feet by 30 feet (the Department of Education provided blueprints) and could be built for less than $1,000 — including paint. Just inside the door would be small cloakrooms, one for the boys and another for the girls, with shelves for a washbasin and to store the children's lunch (lard pails being the favoured containers). There would also be the inevitable pot-bellied stove, perhaps with pipes strung across the ceiling to help spread the heat around. The education department also provided plans for privies, one for each sex, which were to be situated a discreet and sanitary distance from the schoolhouse. Since horses were the main method of transport well into the 20th century, the school would also often have a small barn. (For unruly boys, the threat of having to clean the manure from school barn was an effective aid to discipline and a salutary punishment.)

As settlement progressed, these schools often had to accommodate as many as 50 students, between the statutory ages of five and 16. Not that all children, or even most, attended school for all

Miss Boler and her class in the one-room school at Harvey School District 1597. The standard schoolhouse measured 20 feet by 30 feet, and could be built for less than $1,000.

of those years. "I was 11 years old before I went to school," Harry Buxton of Three Hills reminisced in *As the Years Go By*. "But mother tutored us at home, so when I finally did get to school I took two grades at a time until I caught up." The lone teacher was faced with a range of ages and intellects, not to mention the significant number of students for whom English was a second language. The fact that most children could get a sound basic education in these conditions is surely a testament to the dedication - not to mention ingenuity - of Alberta's first generation of school teachers.

Looming over the provision of education in these years was the daunting figure of the school inspector, the physical embodiment of the distant education ministry and a person of substantial authority. All schools were inspected at least once a year, and in the country this involved the testing of students in reading, spelling, composition, arithmetic, geography, history, and science. The inspector also looked over the buildings, equipment and financial records of the school. He had the authority to sort out any problems he encountered. The most common being attendance, which determined the size of the government grant and which was often chronically low.

Some school districts were named after their location, naturally, but that was not a requirement. Netherby, north of Hanna, for example, was named after the English birthplace of several local settlers, Springbank for a brook on the outskirts of Calgary, Priddis for the settler who donated land for the High river area school, and Princess and Patricia in honour of the royal family. Other names were more quizzical. Gumbo school district, for example, was named for the prairie mud, Big Rock for the erratic boulder at Okotoks, and Bingo, near Coronation, for a popular local canine.

Conditions for teachers in the towns and cities were a little better. Milton Ezra Lazerte graduated with honours in mathematics and physics from the University of Toronto. In 1910 he got his first teaching job in the little town of Hardisty, in east-central Alberta, at the princely salary of $75-a-month - which as a graduate was substantially more than the $40 to $50-a-month being paid to those with two years of teacher training after secondary education. The school board had also arranged for Lazerte to eat in the town restaurant and sleep in a room above it. Unfortunately the food was bad and the room worse,

Lunch outside the Pine Creek school in 1902-03. These boys have their food wrapped in newspaper, but lard pails were the favoured containers of the day.

50

so Lazerte rebelled. Anxious to hang on to such a qualified young man, the town worthies found much better accommodation behind the fire hall. Although there was a catch. Lazerte would be required to help man one of Hardisty's two fire trucks. He lasted a year, before moving to Medicine Hat as principal of the new Alexandra High School.

Schools in Alberta's booming cities were considerably more grand than those in the country. Edmonton's original one-room school, on McKay Avenue, had been expanded, and the city had spent $5 000 to build the handsome four-room, College Avenue School. But it was clear more substantial structures were needed for the city's exploding population. By 1909 Edmonton could boast several large, multi-storey, brick schools. The Alex Taylor School on Jasper Avenue, the Norwood School, and most impressive of all was the Queen's Avenue School (at 99th Street and 104 Avenue), which housed its principal and other staff in a 62-foot tower. Across the river, Strathcona built several similar schools, including the Queen Alexandra School - where in 1908 the first 45 students of the new University of Alberta were temporarily housed in the third-floor assembly hall. Not to be outdone, in 1908 Calgary opened the impressive, sandstone Central High School - and had to expand it within two years. Alberta's first school dedicated to the training of teachers, the Calgary Normal School, opened in 1906 with an enrolment of eight men and 18 women.

The first class of students at the new University of Alberta, 1908-09. The original intake was housed in the attic of Strathcona's Queen Alexandra School. The first building on the university's own 528-acre campus opened in the fall of 1911.

51

A network of steel connects the young province

AN EXPANDING RAILWAY SYSTEM BECOMES ALBERTA'S LINK TO THE OUTSIDE WORLD, AND IN SMALL TOWNS THE ARRIVAL OF A TRAIN IS GUARANTEED TO DRAW A CROWD

Thomas Grant Wolf arrived in Calgary from Gibbon, Nebraska. He was looking for land to homestead, but where in this vast and unfamiliar new province would he find what he was looking for? Wolf came up with an ingenuous way to prospect for suitable farmland: dismantling a bicycle and fitting it with four wheels that would run along railway tracks. He set off for Edmonton, stopping along the way to examine likely homesteads and inventory the towns and villages. At Millet, 30 kilometres south of the capital, he found two parcels of land he liked and bought them. Wolf then made the long trek back to Nebraska, collected his family, and returned to put down roots in Alberta.

Wolf's method of exploration may have been unorthodox, but his reliance on the railway was not. In the years before the automobile and truck, the railways were Alberta's link with the outside world and the first transportation system

Without earth-moving equipment, creating the grade for a railway line meant horses- and lots of them. These teams are at work in Central Alberta around 1910.

Provincial Archives of Alberta A-6256

within the province itself. The railways made rapid settlement possible. New towns sprouted along the right-of-way — Carstairs, Ponoka, Wetaskiwin, Camrose (originally named Sparling) — and as the network expanded, convenient access to the railway made or broke communities. In a world where isolation was an ever-present fact of life, the railway was the most visible connection to the wider world. In small towns across the province in the early years of the century it was common for a crowd to gather to watch the train arrive, with its always fascinating cargo of mail, freight and passengers. "The daily train is the link with existence," declared a report in the *Calgary Herald*. "In the evening the people come down to the platform to see it come in."

As the century opened Alberta's rail network consisted of the east-west CPR line through the southern grasslands, a spur line to Fort Macleod, and the 300-km-track from Calgary to Edmonton. (The passenger train north made the nine-hour trip on Mondays, Wednesdays and Fridays, and returned the following day. There was no service on Sunday.) The Canadian Northern reached Edmonton in 1905, built a branch line to Morinville the following year, and by the end of the decade rails finally replaced the old fur trade portage to Athabasca Landing. The company also built a series of "coal railways" to take advantage of the fuel to be found in the Red Deer River Valley and along the eastern slopes of the Rockies.

The Grand Trunk Pacific arrived in Edmonton in 1909, and pushed on west to Edson. Both northern rivals began building their own lines to Calgary to compete with the CPR. The result, by the end of the century's first decade, was an

extensive railway network across the central and southern parts of the province. It would remain the main transportation network for at least another forty years. In addition to the east-west railway lines, in the heyday of steam there were no less than three north-south lines connecting Edmonton and Calgary (two owned by Canadian National and one, the shortest, by Canadian Pacific). There were also two lines running north from Edmonton, one to the Peace River country, the other to Lac La Biche. By 1920, sprouting from these were

2,650 miles of branch lines (which would eventually be expanded to 3,730 miles). Most Albertans lived on or near towns served by this network, which often provided the only link to larger centres such as Red Deer, Lethbridge, or the unimaginably large cities of Calgary and Edmonton.

For the movers and shakers of the time, railway travel was a transcontinental affair conducted with style. Each night the Trans-Canada Limited pulled into Calgary's CP station from Vancouver, making a 15 minute stop before pro-

A Grand Trunk Pacific railway construction camp near Jasper in 1910. The GTP had arrived in Edmonton the year before, part of the growing network of railways that would become Alberta's basic transportation system for half a century. At the peak of the railway construction boom there were 4,000 workers in 50 camps like this around the province.

ceeding to Regina, Winnipeg, Toronto and Montreal. (Edmonton was serviced by CN's Continental Limited.) In the golden era of rail travel it was one of a dozen daily, main-line passenger trains linking Calgary to the rest of the country. The Pullman Company operated the upscale sleeping cars for virtually every railroad in North America, but Pullman was considered inadequate for CP, which had its own sleepers. Other onboard amenities included a dining car, smoking lounge (where there was a bar service), a ladies' lounge, and bathrooms for both sexes that included showers. There was also the observation car, which boasted large, "vista glass" windows that "reflect the sun's glare, but let in health-giving ultraviolet rays." The top-line locomotives, some weighing in at 300 tons, could travel the distance between Calgary and Montreal in about 62 hours. All for a return fare of $275 - or roughly three months income for the average Canadian.

The predominance of women in education was firmly established. As teachers they outnumbered men four to one, but in the first decade of the 20th century two thirds of high school students were also female. The major reasons being the demand for skilled labour, jobs which were invariably closed to women, and the low pay in the teaching profession. In 1907 the average salary for an Alberta teacher was $600, which prompted school inspector P.H. Thibaudeau to observe that any young man who was content with such a pittance must be seriously lacking in "one or all of the three Gs: Go, Grit, and Gumption."

That same year, in an effort to keep boys in school longer, Edmonton's first full-time school superintendent, James McCaig, successfully argued for the introduction of more vocational training - woodwork and metalwork — into the city's secondary schools. Despite his innovations and an impressive list of credentials (a BA and MA from the University of Toronto, a law degree, teaching experience in Ontario, superintendent of Lethbridge schools, and service as an Alberta school inspector), McCaig came to grief in 1911 when he was accused of using obscene language and "indulging in intoxicants." One citizen had apparently tailed him for a month, making note of every time he entered a bar.

A school board investigation into his conduct dragged on until 1913, when he was fully exonerated and even given a $500-a-year raise. Nevertheless, McCaig suddenly and mysteriously resigned in October of that year, and it was several weeks before the reason became apparent. "McCaig Kissed Miss Lobb; Is Fined $27.35," sang the headline in the *Edmonton Capital*. The illustrious superintendent had pleaded guilty to common assault on a young colleague, Zaida M. Lobb. His career in ruins, McCaig retired to Lethbridge, where he died in 1922.

Pamela Appleby fared a great deal better at the Hillsgreen School. Mounted on her mare, Bessie, she explored the Red Deer River valley and came to cherish her frontier home. She also loved the country dances, which commonly went on until dawn so that the partygoers could travel home in daylight. She eventually found a welcoming family to board with (they also had accommodation for Bessie), and in the winter months her pupils would drive her to school by horse and sleigh. The school board even managed to pay the money it owed her ($300), which

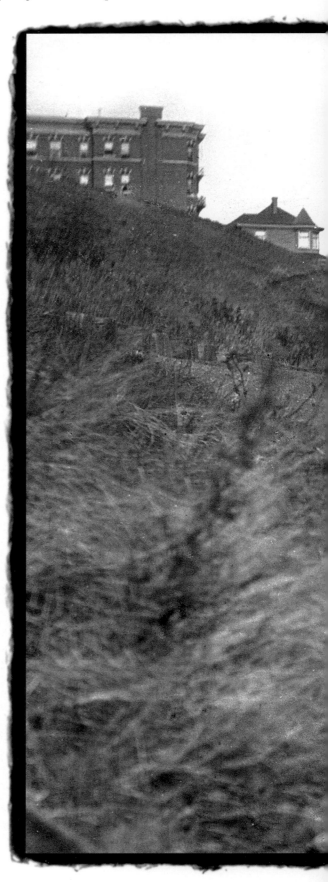

allowed her to buy a fur coat. Her work at the Hillsgreen School was so successful that she was eventually offered a job in Calgary, but chose instead to stay in a part of the province she had come to love. She eventually married Reginald Harvey, another immigrant teaching at a neighbouring school near Munson.

A steam locomotive was always an awe-inspiring sight, particularly for youngsters. This pair watch the passage of a train below Edmonton's Le Marchand Mansion apartments, above what would one day become the city's Victoria golf course.

CHAPTER THREE

'The Empire of Fulfillment'

IN THE MIDST OF THE PROVINCE'S FIRST GREAT BOOM
ALBERTANS LAY THE FOUNDATIONS OF A UNIQUE SOCIETY

Despite the isolation and harshness of frontier life, and perhaps because of it, the ability of early Albertans to entertain themselves was prodigious. The range of events, dances, picnics, debates, concerts, spelling bees and socials, and the numbers of people who attended, are a testament to the communal nature of life before radio and television. If you wanted to have fun, you had to make it.

During the summer months community picnics, some very large, were the main event. In *Green Fields Afar*, authors C. and J. Middleton write about one such event near Carstairs: "Well over a hundred people attended the picnic and we had an abundance of entertainment. One of the cowboys had brought a couple of bucking horses and several had a try at riding them. An obstacle race was a lively spectacle. Foot races were arranged for the younger. A quartet off to one side pitched horse shoes with strained attention and careful measurement after each end. On a platform, a young Englishman named Hepburn sang comic songs and did a nonsense monologue. Mr. Johnston and several others made speeches, without saying anything of importance - an ideal accomplishment before a mixed crowd - and the ball game was exciting... But the greatest interest of all was in getting acquainted with one another. Then came supper on the grass, with a boilerful of hot coffee to wash it down."

When it came to siting such picnics, water was always a draw. A river, stream or lake provided the perfect venue, although as Morden Lane recalled in *Hand Hills Heritage*, taking a dip was hardly the liberated exercise it would become. "At the early day picnics at Hand Hills Lake I don't think I ever saw a swimming suit. The ladies wore dresses [into the water] and the men wore overalls and usually something over the top half, too. The lunches were feasts and there were plenty of lovely shady bowers to set up tables and plenty of private groves in which to change. I don't believe I have ever seen a nicer bathing beach than the south end of Hand Hills Lake, with its gently sloping clear firm sand, the view, the fresh water smell, and the impression you got that the soda in the water was turning your skin whiter."

Rural Albertans, and that was most of them, relied upon local talent and local diversions to while away the long winter months. Dances were the great attraction, with dozens being held every weekend in church and community halls across the province. The monthly dance at Greencourt, in the Lac Ste. Anne district northwest of Edmonton, was particularly popular and well organized. Several hundred people would gather in the 40 ft. by 120 ft. hall, which boasted a maple wood floor, to dance to music provided by at least a three-piece band (usually two fiddles and an accordion). Attendance was $1 for the men, and nothing for the ladies. There was no alcohol, officially anyway, and

Ukrainian settlers dancing in the Hilliard-Chipman district (opposite and below) in the early years of the 20th century. As Alberta's new communities developed, people made their own entertainment - and there was no lack of it.

Provincial Archives of Alberta G-4358

food and coffee were served at midnight and 4 a.m. Entire families would attend, and when the little ones were tired they were rolled up in blankets and slept in a corner of the hall.

Not all entertainment was rustic, with Alberta's larger communities aspiring to all manner of cultural entertainment. Medicine Hat in particular was a hotbed of the performing arts. The city frequently hosted travelling companies performing contemporary and classical fare (Gilbert and Sullivan operettas were a favourite), first in Cotler's Opera House and later in the new, purpose-built community hall. The Hat also boasted an array of its own musicians, choirs and theatre companies. In 1904, for example, W.J. Brotherton (the local jeweller) directed an oratorio which featured a choir of 35 voices. That same year a group from St. Barnabas Anglican Church staged an ambitious "Evening With Dickens" that consisted of songs, choruses and sketches based on the works of the doyen of Victorian authors.

As in everything else, Calgary and Edmonton attempted to outdo each other on the cultural front, with Calgary being the clear early winner. The Calgary Opera House and Hull's Opera House were at the pinnacle of Alberta's entertainment scene. In addition to visiting productions, the Calgary Operatic Society was already half a dozen years old as the 20th century dawned and staged grand operas to packed houses. At Hull's Calgarians could take in performances of *Hamlet, Othello* and *The Taming of the Shrew*, not to mention a visit by Drakero, the famed Filipino contortionist.

The Edmonton Operatic and Dramatic Society wasn't formed until 1903, but it had a considerable advantage in the person of Vernon Barford, the classically-trained organist of All Saints (Anglican) Cathedral. Barford, a one-man Edmonton musical institution who played the piano at dances and organized music festivals for nearly six decades. directed the society's first performance, *The Chimes of Normandie*. Despite some opening night problems (the costumes, rented from Chicago, were impounded by customs inspectors and the star tenor fainted at the end of the second act), the audience at Robertson's Hall (the upper floor of a wholesale warehouse on Jasper Avenue) was reportedly much impressed. The Thistle Rink, on 102 Street, doubled as Edmonton's other major cultural venue, until local entrepreneur Alexander W. Cameron opened a string of

Community picnics were hugely popular in the summer months. This photograph shows a group of Mormon settlers enjoying a picnic near Magrath.

Glenbow Archives NA-131-1

With china and a white tablecloth, this group of British immigrants brought a little bit of the old country to this picnic in the Ranfurly area of east-central Alberta.

theatres - the Empire, Kevin and Lyric - in addition to the Edmonton Opera House (an $8,000 building on Jasper Avenue). After a disastrous fire destroyed the Kevin, Cameron rebuilt the facility as the Dominion Theatre, with its grand lobby also serving the neighbouring Opera House.

Despite all of the building and the seeming vitality of the performing arts, the new century had barely begun before that quintessential modern entertainment, the moving picture, made its first appearance in Alberta. In *Frontier Days in Leduc and District,* C.H. Stout recalled the momentous event.

"One night about 1900, a small crowd sat spellbound in R.T. Telford's new hall on Telford Street as soldiers marched and rode on trains and French dandies flirted on the streets of Paris. The figures they saw moved on a big screen stretched across the stage, and while these walked and ran at bewildering speed, they were lifelike and exciting. It was the first motion picture show seen in Leduc and tickets for the one-night stand were 50 cents. Folks talked about the new sensation for days, forgetting the eye and ear strains caused by the flickers and the operating machine."

The first moving image seen by many Albertans was film footage of the 1901 funeral of Queen Victoria, who had died in January of that year. "Don't fail to see it," encouraged an ad in the *Calgary Herald,* "as you will witness with your own eyes the Grand Military Funeral of the Greatest Ruler the World has ever seen. The views are taken from Hyde Park and as the long procession passes within a distance of 30 feet of you, King Edward and the German emperor at his side, riding a white horse, are life size and are followed by the nobility of Europe with all the Pomp and Splendour of the Great European Courts." The grainy, jerky footage (still seen today in television documentaries) was a sensation.

Card games, like dancing, were frowned on by some urban moralizers, but both flourished as popular pastimes. This group is enjoying a game at the Olson home near Calmar, south of Edmonton, around 1912.

One of the reasons for the popularity of picnics, dances and the like in early Alberta was a looming demographic fact of life. There were many more men than women, and competition for the fairer sex was fierce. By the end of the first decade of the 20th century this great dearth of women had been somewhat mitigated by new arrivals, but in 1911 it was calculated that in the new province's towns and cities men still outnumbered women three to one - and on the farms it was much worse. A 1909 editorial in the *Lethbridge Herald* summed up the problem: "Without the sustaining influence of the fairer sex, the boldest pioneer will weary, then wander; the porcupine will occupy his cabin and the coyote saunter down the trail. Alberta needs women more than men or money."

Victoria Maclean, the former editor of the *Edmonton Sun*, beautifully encapsulated the human dimension of this lopsided reality in the second volume of *Alberta In The 20th Century*: "The settler with a wife had someone for whom to put up a Christmas tree, someone to nag him about gambling and whiskey, someone to chivvy him off to church. Without a wife and children, he had less incentive to half-kill himself clearing, fencing and breaking the land. Across the West, weary bachelors fell asleep at the table in their lonely shacks and soddies, tinned beans untouched on a cold woodstove."

Some women came to the new province on their own, as teachers, nurses, or like Gib Hocken as an orphan. At seven years of age she was one of a party of 30 young girls sent from a London orphanage to new homes in the province. There were thousands more across the prairies. Gib was adopted by a Bowden couple named Fordyce who had already produced 14 of their own children. Only five had survived. Child mortality rates were ferociously high.

But in the early days most women came to Alberta with their parents or husbands, German,

British, Ukrainian, English, Scandinavian, or from a dozen other origins. For wives, the journey to Alberta was sometimes the lesser of two evils. Too many had heard stories of husbands who had promised to return once they had found a job or land, yet never to be heard of again. Victims of accident or illness perhaps, or simply lost to distance and time. So when Elizabeth Hanson's husband suggested she stay at home in Edinburgh, while he prepared the way, she would have none of it. Historian Elaine Silverman recorded Hanson's response in her book *The Last Best West: Women on the Prairie, 1888-1930.* "I wasn't going to be left stranded in the old country with two babies and another on the way. But oh dear, when I saw what I had landed at! It was a wild country in those days, not unruly, not unsafe, but nothing was completed. It was a raw, man's world, not for women."

Those who settled the land faced profound challenges from the moment they began the bone-jarring trip to the homestead, which was often no more than a surveyor's stake at the end of a primitive track. In his memoir *Pioneer Tales*, A.D. Adshead remembers arriving with his wife at their homestead near Olds. "The shades of night were closing in when we neared the farm and my wife nudged me and whispered 'Where is the house? I don't see any house.' I pointed out the low sod shack, all covered with snow. 'But it not any bigger than our old pig pen in Ontario,' she said."

Whether they came from a Ukrainian village, Munich or Missouri, the checkerboard homestead system meant that farms were far apart and female companionship often distant. Settling south of Castor, Benedikte Ausenus didn't see another woman during her first two years on the homestead. And when the men were away cutting timber for fence posts, or hauling supplies from the nearest town, there was no company at all. "These trips lasted from three days to a week," recalled J. Miller of Crossfield in *Prairie Sod and Goldenrod*. "It was always quite eerie in the evening with only a small farm light showing across the distant prairie, the coyotes howling and no close neighbours. Somehow I was never afraid and used to go outside, the better to hear the coyotes. I still like to hear them howl; they were company when no one else was around."

Toughness of mind and a resilient spirit were as valuable as a

Fiddler Phil Wienard of High River. In the years before radio, musical entertainment of all sorts, from opera to barn dances, thrived in communities large and small.

Calgary's Stampede was an instant and enduring hit. Some 80,000 people are estimated to have watched the first parade (below) through the city. The inclusion of hundreds of native Albertans was thought controversial by some, but they turned out to be the star attraction.

Glenbow Archives NA-4035-96

strong back. Monica Hopkins and her husband settled on the rolling foothills southwest of Priddis. A clergyman's daughter, she later recalled in *Letters from a Lady Rancher* that the only thing she knew about married life, let alone ranching, was "glossing and pressing men's shirts." There wasn't much call for that, but she eventually learned all about rendering lard, churning butter, raising chickens, salting pork, branding cattle and planting a garden. And bugs. She learned all about the bugs. "The flies are particularly vicious. We get two varieties here, and they are perfect brutes. One is called a bulldog and is about the size of a wasp. It takes a chunk of flesh when it bites; the horses go nearly crazy when one is flying around them. The other is called a deer fly; it is about the size of a house fly and leaves a poison behind when it has bitten. I always come up in a kind of blister after I have been attacked." She also had observations on mosquitoes. "I have

John Walter's steamboat loads up in Edmonton for a Press Association picnic up-river on the North Saskatchewan. The idea of pleasure cruises from the capital's riverbank would be revived much later in the century, with mixed results.

never seen such huge brutes. As a last resort I got a large bran sack, put my legs inside it and tied the top around my waist. With my legs fairly safe, my arms were going like flails all the time."

Social histories often record that in the early decades of the 20th century it was unusual for women to work, which would no doubt come as some surprise to those women who worked alongside their husbands and fathers on the family farm, cooked, cleaned, tended gardens, and canned, bottled and preserved enough food to last through the long winter. And we should not forget child-rearing, which in an age of large families was almost a full-time occupation in itself. Neither was work outside the home that unusual. Young farm women often found work as domestic help, to supplement the family income, and if the family ran a business the unpaid assistance of unmarried children was not only expected but often vital to its survival.

The loss of a husband meant some women ran farms on their own, while others took in washing, mended clothes, sold butter and eggs, and generally did whatever was necessary to feed their families. In *Crowsnest and its People*, John A. Lloyd recalled his grandmother's efforts to support the

Theatrical performances, both amateur and professional, enjoyed enormous popularity before the Great War. These women, from the Ladies Aid of Wesley Methodist Church, Lethbridge, were staging a performance of Mohawk Crossing in 1914.

family. "It fell upon my grandmother's shoulders to make a living for her young family, and this she did by taking a job at the pit head. The job - shovelling coal out of the mine cars that came up from underground. Because she was only a women she got about half the wages of the men who did the same work alongside. She was not a big woman, but she must have been strong; she was able to lift 11 stone (154 lbs) on a shovel to waist high... Money was still scarce, and so she also took the job of caretaker at the local school."

With examples such as John Lloyd's gran, it is perhaps not surprising that Alberta women became politically active and took a leadership role in demanding social change and equal rights. Large numbers joined the Women's Christian Temperance Union to agitate against the sale of

Vaudeville was the most popular form of entertainment before the movies took hold of the public imagination in the 1920s. Amateur nights often took the place of the professional acts, and generated as much hoopla as 'Canadian Idol' would nine decades later.

Wedding day on the Prairies. This photograph of Mr. and Mrs. Ed Hartt is thought to have been taken by his sister, Ella Hartt, a pioneer photographer who was also a nurse.

Glenbow Archives NC-39-95

68

alcohol - a particular flashpoint in a frontier society in which single men predominated. The newspapers of the day also abound with accounts of campaigns to shut down the brothels of Edmonton's 96th Street and Calgary's Nose Creek. Women in smaller communities could be more direct. In Big Valley when the men would not evict the prostitutes from town a group of wives simply set fire to the local bawdy house and burned it to the ground. As it turned out, such incidents were just the opening salvo in a battle that would have a profound impact on the subsequent history of the province, and on Canadian society in general.

Doing laundry near Balzac in 1905-06. For Alberta women before the Great War, work outside the home was uncommon - while work inside it was unending.

Members of the Edmonton Ski Club, originally formed by Norwegian enthusiasts, are pictured here below the ski jump they built on Connors Hill on the edge of the North Saskatchewan valley.

Glenbow Archives NC-6-654

Albertans' long love affair with the automobile begins

They were noisy, unreliable, expensive and clearly dangerous, but by 1910 almost 700 Albertans owned an automobile and the number was doubling every year. The province introduced its first Automobile Act in 1906 and five years later was charging a substantial $10 licence fee, plus a dollar for a set of plates. Of the 1,700 vehicles registered in Alberta in 1911, half were in Calgary, where the increasing prevalence of automobiles caused a typical debate. You either loved them or hated them. "It is the poetry of motion, the ideal mode of travelling," enthused the *Calgary Herald*. The *Eye Opener's* crotchety editor, Bob Edwards, on the other hand wanted them banned from St.

George's Island Park - so that women and children would not "have their humble pleasures spoiled by the selfishness and arrogance of automobile fatheads." Alberta even had its own car, the Glover (1), which boasted a fifth wheel designed to help it negotiate notoriously poor prairie roads. Poor or not, a spin in the countryside, followed by a picnic (2), rapidly became a popular way to spend a summer afternoon. The new cars came in all sorts and sizes, from the substantial and stately vehicle being driven by this unidentified Edmonton woman (3), to the ubiquitous Model T Ford. Launched in 1908, it rapidly became the most popular car in North America. Particularly in Alberta, where it could scramble up hills and along muddy tracks - most of the time. This 1913 Model T (4) clearly needed a little assistance in negotiating an overgrown trail on the outskirts of Edmonton.

Provincial Archives of Alberta B-5820

Glenbow Archives NA 1328-1261

If the first decade of the 20th century was characterized by heady optimism, astonishing growth and the establishment of self-government, the early years of the second heralded a boom the likes of which Albertans would not experience for another 60 years. It was an era of flamboyant boasts, great dreams and boundless faith in the future. In the words of the *Calgary Albertan*: "Every new Albertan sunrise spreads its life-giving rays upon a more active and promising province." The newspaper predicted with confidence that "before some of the people who read this article have gone to their long rest" the province's population would surely crest five million.

The *Albertan* was, in fact, positively restrained compared to some, including the new premier, Arthur Sifton (brother of Clifford, the Laurier minister of the interior who revolutionized attempts

Mair Polet, the wife of a Villeneuve railway engineer and surveyor, in her state-of-the-art 1906 kitchen. Somebody still had to chop the wood.

An unusual photograph of Muriel Genevieve McIntosh, the 17-year-old daughter of American immigrant parents, on her horse Creamo, near Strathmore in 1908. With cigarette, liquor bottle and leather chaps, she was far from typical of Alberta women of the time.

Glenbow Archives NA-4054-1

A Medicine Hat butcher's shop just before Christmas 1912. As with the rest of Alberta, the Hat boomed in the pre-war years and prosperity and plenty were everywhere apparent.

Glenbow Archives NA-2479-2

to populate the West), who predicted a population of 20 million and called the province the "wonder child of Canada." A promotional pamphlet of the era pictured a stylized map of Alberta as a talking head, murmuring the words "I am the Great Alberta, the Empire of Fulfilment, the land where opportunities are unlimited and the climate ideal…"

The mood was infectious. Edmonton, proclaimed the *Journal*, "must inevitably become the largest city in Canada. There is no other way." Calgary, of course, was having none of that. The *Herald* took to referring to the city as "metropolitan" with institutions and attractions that "would do credit to the largest city in the Dominion." Nor was such municipal hyperbole limited to the two larger cities. According to the *Medicine Hat News*, that city was fast becoming the "Minneapolis of Canada."

The general consensus, backed by statistics and much solemn prognostication, was that for Alberta there could be no looking backward, no cloud on the horizon. Prof. James W. Robertson confidently wrote that "hard times will never affect southern Alberta. The interests of this district are now so diversified that there is no possibility of a pronounced depression." Another academic

Pool halls were enormously popular during these years, and just about every community of any size had one - or more. It was generally considered to be a man's game, but that clearly didn't deter these ladies photographed in the Whitecourt pool hall in 1913.

77

treatise described the future of the southern prairie, enhanced by irrigation, as "one of dense population accommodated with numerous trolley lines."

Such predictions may now seem laughable, mere windy boosterism, but at the time no one was laughing. The numbers suggested the boosters were right. By the 1911 census Alberta's population had grown to a substantial 374,000, and over the next four years would jump to half a million. Upwards of 40,000 people were arriving in the province each year. In 1912 alone some 30,000 Americans made the trek north to set down roots in Alberta. In words that would be echoed six decades later, a visiting Toronto journalist pronounced the entire province to be "one enormous construction site."

That last was a clear exaggeration. In 1914 nearly two-thirds of Albertans were farmers, but the rural scene held more than enough superlatives of its own. Cultivated land had quadrupled since 1906, to 2.5 million acres, and now included the rapidly developing Peace River country.

Workers outside the Alberta Foundry and Machine Company plant in Medicine Hat. It was one of many industries that located in the thriving community, producing munitions during the Great War and later on tractors.

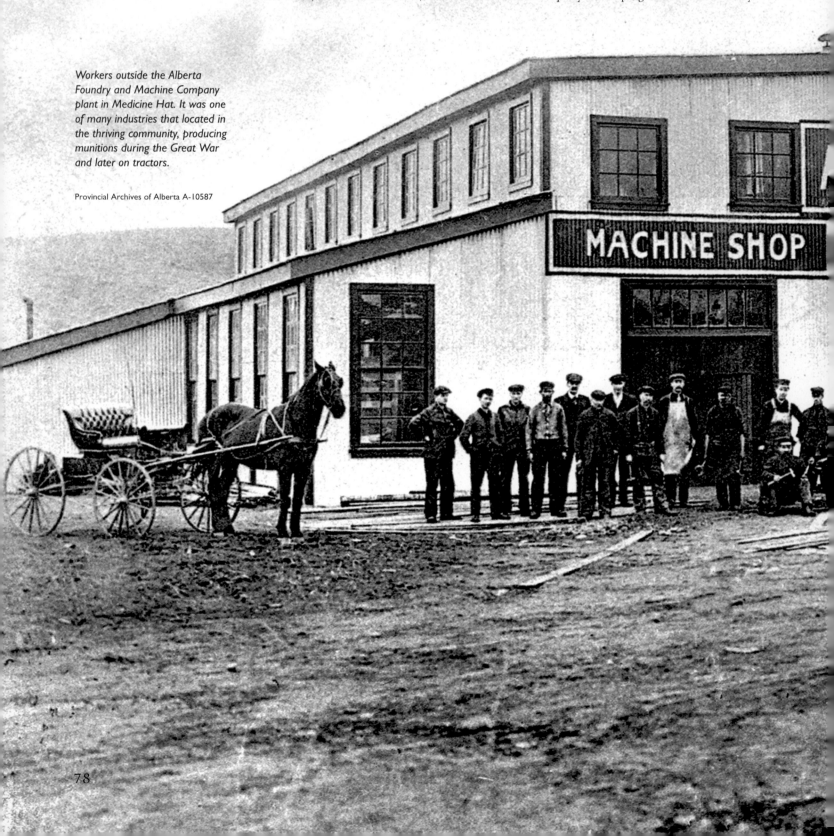

The province's agricultural exports topped $60 million annually, an enormous figure for the times. More than half of that sum was generated by wheat, which was selling for a remarkable $1-a-bushel. And with the opening of the new Panama Canal (in 1914) and the subsequent reduction in shipping costs, Alberta's grain exports to Europe were sure to grow.

Add to this the output of Alberta's 154 coal mines, which produced more than 3 million tons a year, and had 86 billion more in reserve - reportedly enough to supply the needs of the entire world for 1,000 years! Tens of thousands of square miles of easily accessible forest extended along the eastern slopes of the Rockies, there was natural gas around Medicine Hat, and rumour had it there was oil beneath the ground south of Calgary - although no one was quite sure of the demand for that.

In 1914 the *Edmonton Bulletin* interviewed one of the many American immigrants, this one a farmer from Iowa who had settled near Westlock. He told the reporter that he had not been able

to buy his own farm at home and had made a poor living on rented land. "I determined to strike for the Canadian frontier where I could at least fight out the battle on land of my own. I came overland behind a mule team. All I owned on earth was in the prairie schooner with my wife and babies. I homesteaded 160 acres. I added to my original purchase from time to time, until I now have 3,000 acres. There is no mortgage on any part of it. For some of my land I paid $2 an acre, for some $10. I would not sell it for $50." In the corner of the farmer's yard the reporter spotted a mound overgrown with weeds and wildflowers. It was, he was told, the remains of the sod shanty the family called home when they came to Alberta - a mere five years earlier.

A large farm, to be sure, and the American had arrived with equipment, experience and a little money, advantages that not all settlers possessed. But his story was not untypical. The world wanted what Alberta produced, and with hard work and a little luck it really was possible to succeed. For many of the immigrants who had poured into the province in the first decade of the century, the impossible dream had been realized.

The province's towns and cities were experiencing heady growth. According to the census, Calgary and Edmonton both now had populations of over 50,000. Not that this was enough. The boards of trade in both cities pooh-poohed the Ottawa-run census and claimed more than 70,000 residents each. Lethbridge and Medicine Hat had both tripled in size to around 9,000. Substantial four and five-storey buildings were becoming commonplace, and in 1915 two new eight-storey hotels - the Macdonald in Edmonton and the Palliser in Calgary - signalled the arrival of real urban

The inrush of settlers and the rapid growth of Alberta's communities created a real estate boom in the pre-war years. Real estate offices sprang up everywhere, usually serving the surrounding community. This one, located in south Edmonton, features on its window an appeal to German immigrants.

Barber shops were a feature of most communities, large and small, in an era when most men sported facial hair. This photograph is of Tom Spink's shop in Bowden in 1912.

sophistication. All of this activity was a bonanza for the construction trades. In Edmonton members of the Carpenters and Joiners Union earned a minimum of $3 for an 8-hour day. A year later that was hiked to $4. At the time $1 bought 10 packs of Player's Navy Cut cigarettes, a year's subscription to the *Lethbridge Herald*, or a night in Calgary's Albion Hotel - with "steam heat in every room."

A few voices wondered if an economy built on inflation, speculation and high prices could be stable over the longer term, but they were dismissed as "Knockers" - a term of the utmost derision and not something any Albertan wished to be labelled as. They were, as it turned out, right to be concerned. The era of prosperity and growth, which had begun in the 1890s with the end of a global recession, was beginning to slow down. For the first time in a generation foreign investors were growing wary of Canada, and the West in particular. Credit had been over-extended, and now dried up. In 1913 the first unemployed appeared on the streets of Calgary and Edmonton. Within a year Edmonton was struggling to provide relief for 4,000 jobless. Sawmills suddenly

The main street of Stettler about 1910. These years were in many ways a golden age for Alberta's towns, which thrived as the farmland around them filled with homesteads. In addition to businesses supporting local agriculture, Stettler also boasted what was claimed to be the largest cigar factory in the West.

Provincial Archives of Alberta A-6098

found themselves with large inventories of unsold lumber. The Canadian Northern Railway teetered on the edge of bankruptcy. The 1913 harvest had been a bumper one, which was just as well because many farmers had borrowed heavily to buy equipment and land. Still, in the winter of 1913-14 some farmers were forced to look for work in the towns and cities. The *Calgary Albertan*, which had so recently been trumpeting endless sunshine, now talked ominously about a "depression." It was, in truth, a recession, a boom and bust cycle which would become all too familiar to later generations.

Alberta's first great boom was over, but the province would continue to grow and prosper - and the summer of 1914 proved to be glorious indeed. Many who had lived through those heady days would remember the early years of the 20th century as a Golden Age, an exhilarating and optimistic time. But their rosy hindsight would be heavily influenced by a looming, man-made cataclysm in Europe which would engulf even this far-flung corner of empire; a Great War which would call thousands of Albertans to far off battlefields where they would serve with bravery and grim determination, but from which many would not return.

The newsroom of Edmonton's Daily Capital newspaper in 1913. Newspapers proliferated in these years, with Edmonton and Calgary having several. Competition was fierce, and within a year of this photograph the Capital would succumb to pressure from the more established Bulletin and Journal.

Alberta appeared like one vast construction site during the pre-war boom, employing thousands of tradesman and labourers. The photo opposite shows sewer construction in Edmonton, while the one below, taken in 1907, records the brute force often necessary to hoist a beam into position in the days before cranes became commonplace. The dog seems oblivious to the action going on around it. One of the largest construction projects of the period was the raising of Alberta's Legislature Building, a $4 million embodiment of civic pride created above the site of the original Fort Edmonton. Based on the Minnesota state house, the legislature took four years to build. In the 1911 photo at right, architect Allan Merrick Jeffers (front row, far right) is shown with some of the skilled stonemasons who worked on his building.

Patrick O'Byrne: Calgary's meat packing phenomenon

THE IMPOVERISHED SON OF IRISH IMMIGRANTS BECOMES A BUSINESS ICON, BUT HE STILL KEPT A DAIRY COW IN THE YARD OF HIS SANDSTONE MANSION

Like so many young men and women of his generation, Patrick O'Byrne came to Alberta looking for opportunity and found it. Raised on a rocky homestead north of Oshawa, Ontario, the son of Irish Catholic immigrants knew all about hardship. He had dug potatoes, cut timber and done a dozen other things looking to better himself. He had tried farming in Manitoba, but he discovered he had a knack for business and could make more money buying and selling his neighbours' hay and beef. He moved again, this time to Calgary, where he rapidly established a thriving business supplying beef not only to Albertans, but also into British Columbia and as far as the Klondike. As Pat Burns he is remembered as the quintessential Calgary business tycoon: successful, outgoing and generous, but despite his wealth never drifting far from his humble origins. The opulence of the magnificent $40,000 sandstone mansion he built in 1901 was legendary, but so was the fact Burns kept a dairy cow in the back yard.

By the early years of the new 20th century he had discovered the benefits of what later economists would call vertical integration. He bought ranches, raised his own cattle, and operated slaughterhouses, tanneries, and a string of retail stores selling his products. He branched into the dairy business, at one point owning 65 creameries and cheese factories, and then into the wholesale fruit business. In the years after the Great War he diversified into oil and mining, and opened offices in London, Liverpool, Seattle and Yokohama. Burns innovative practice of feeding his cattle through the winter, while other ranchers in southern Alberta let their animals fend for themselves on the open range, allowed him to survive the legendary winter of 1906-07, which decimated herds and effectively brought to an end the golden age of Alberta ranching.

There seemed no end to Burn's success in business. Details of his private life are sketchy, but it's clear that this part of the Burns' story was, by contrast, rather sad and lonely. A sister and brother died young, and his marriage in 1901 to Eileen Ellis seems less than satisfactory. Eileen, the product of a wealthy Penticton ranching family, was tall, educated and urbane. Burns was short, plump, illiterate and somewhat lacking in the social graces. Eileen eventually moved to California, and later still to Victoria, where her husband continued to support her in comfort until her death from cancer in 1923. The couple's only child, Patrick Michael, died in 1936 of an apparent heart attack. He was just 30.

Burns himself died only five months after his son, aged 80. Although he sold his meat-packing interests in 1928, the Burns brand name continued in Alberta into the 21st century. The name Pat Burns also continues to be much venerated in his adopted city, but it may be the grand old man of Calgary business never quite got used to his new persona. According to biographer Grant MacEwan, he continued to use the name Patrick O'Byrne on his marriage certificate and other legal documents.

Glenbow Archives NA-1149-1

Pat Burns in later life. A multi-millionaire philanthropist and the dean of Calgary cattlemen, he typified a whole generation that reached for the Alberta dream.

The interior of Pat Burns' meat packing plant in Calgary. His first operation, on the banks of the Bow River, burned down, but he rebuilt and eventually created Calgary's first multi-national business, with offices in the U.S., Britain and Japan.

CHAPTER FOUR

'The war to end all wars'

OF THE 49,000 ALBERTANS WHO FOUGHT IN THE GREAT WAR
HALF WERE WOUNDED, AND 6,000 WOULD NEVER RETURN HOME

In Alberta, as elsewhere across the senior dominion of the British Empire, the glorious weather of summer 1914 was enjoyed to the full. The bloom was clearly off the province's first great economic boom, but the future remained bright and in communities large and small the picnic season was in full swing. The newspapers carried stories of the escalating political tension in Europe, but few Albertans paid much attention to that.

When Britain declared war on Germany on August 4th, 1914, the Canadian Parliament did likewise. From St. Petersburg to Berlin, Paris, and London, few leaders saw the general mobilization of troops as a catastrophe in the making. In Alberta and across Canada most people accepted what they read. The

Germans would have to be taught a short, sharp lesson, but it would all be over by Christmas - in all likelihood before any Canadian troops saw action. The enthusiastic support for the war was almost universal among the majority of Albertans, who were British by birth or descent. Courtesy of telephone and telegraph, the news of the outbreak of hostilities reached the province on the evening of August 4th. In Lethbridge it was relayed to a crowd outside the offices of the *Herald*. "They listened in tense silence until the dispatch was finished," the paper reported the following day, "and then one yell rent the air, hats were thrown sky high and for a moment people went mad." The scene was repeated in communities across the province. In Calgary, as dusk settled on the city, people streamed downtown and a Scots piper led the crowd up and down 9th Avenue. In Edmonton thousands of cheering people blocked Jasper Avenue and two bands led a parade which circled the downtown streets until dawn.

Nineteen-year-old Calgary accounting clerk Wally Bennett and his pals enlisted immediately "thinking the war might be over before we got there." Harold Peat, a 21-year-old Edmontonian, was less optimistic about the war being over that quickly, but just as enthusiastic. "I was going whether it lasted three months, as they said it would, or five years, as I thought it would."

A machine gun company of the Canadian Corps, holding the line in shell holes during the Battle of Passchendaele, November 1917.

Peat was small and originally refused by recruiters, who were overwhelmed by thousands of strapping young Albertans eager to enlist. Determined not to be left out, he pretended to be Belgian and told another recruiter that wanted to avenge two brothers already killed in action. By August 27th he was a member of the 101st Edmonton Fusiliers and on a train bound for the Canadian army's assembly point at Valcartier, Quebec. He would be seriously wounded in action at Ypres, Belgium, but he would survive.

Volunteers from Alberta's farms poured into the larger towns. Day after day the newspapers printed long lists of those who joined up. On August 6th the *Journal* noted that eight young men from Peace River had arrived in Edmonton to enlist. Some 500 Mounties changed their police uniforms for military khaki, and 10 Edmonton women volunteered to serve as nurses with the troops off to Europe. They were led by Flora Wilson, a veteran of the Boer War and the recipient of three medals for bravery. At Medicine Hat 26 volunteers left to join the Calgary Rifles. The *News* reported that "Acting Mayor Boyd presented each with a bill of large denomination as a token of pride and esteem from the citizens." A week later another contingent of 100 left the Hat for Valcartier. Some 49,000 Albertans would eventually serve in uniform. The province would eventually provide 24 battalions for the Canadian war effort, four of which would remain almost permanently in the front line (drawing replacement troops from the rest). Almost half the Alberta contingent would be wounded, and 6,140 were killed.

After a winter training in England, in March, 1915 the first Canadians went into the Allied line at Armentieres, a little coal mining town on the French-Belgian border. Among them was Pte. Harold Peat. "We of the 1st Division were the greenest troops that ever landed in France," he later wrote. In those first days Sgt. Wilfred Wilson, a Calgary real estate agent who served with the 10th Battalion, made an odd discovery about the enemy, whose trenches were sometimes only yards away. "Are any of you fellows from Calgary or Vancouver?" came a query from the German lines. "It was some surprise," wrote Wilson. "Wasn't it funny that we should be fighting against Germans who had been in our own part of the country, some of them undoubtedly men we had

The terrace restaurant of Edmonton's almost-completed Macdonald Hotel. As the war approached, Albertans enjoyed the summer and generally ignored the reports of looming conflict.

Provircial Archives of Alberta A-6741

Glenbow Archives NC-6-1392

Soldiers take a tea break at Sarcee Camp outside Calgary (above). The recruits were eager to get to Europe and into action - fearing the war would be quickly over. By 1915 the news from the front was far less optimistic, but recruits - like these men of Edmonton's 51st Battalion marching along Jasper Avenue (below) - still volunteered in large numbers.

Canadian troops newly-arrived in trenches near Armentiers, France, early in 1915. Their baptism of fire would come within a matter of weeks.

often seen on the streets of Calgary?" It was technically illegal for German-Canadians of military age to travel to Germany to enlist, but some did. Usually via the United States, which would not enter the war for two years.

The Canadian troops were beset by poor equipment, boots that sometime disintegrated in the mud and the notorious Ross rifle - which made a wonderful hunting weapon, but had a nasty habit of jamming during battle. When Capt. Frank Pott led his Medicine Hat contingent into the line he was surprised to discover that the trenches were no more than waist high, leaving his men exposed to German shelling. "It was no picnic," he wrote home. "We suffered badly from want of water. I had only a drop left and dared not use it as I had to keep it for the wounded." He had 20 spades sent up from the rear and his men were eventually able to dig trenches that offered more protection. "We were shelled all the time, but we got used to it by then," he wrote. It was his last letter. Shortly after he wrote it Pott was killed in action.

On April 15th the Canadians were moved to a bulge in the Allied lines near Ypres, surrounded on three sides by an enemy dug in on higher ground. There were rumours that the Germans opposite had been experimenting with poison gas, but even if it were true no one had a clear idea of how you defended against such a weapon. Late on the afternoon of April 22nd the Germans began an artillery bombardment and opened the valves on nearly 6,000 cylinders of chlorine gas, releasing a yellow-green cloud which drifted across No Man's Land into positions occupied by the Canadians and French Algerian troops to their left. The scene was captured by Pte. W.R. Gayner of Calgary in a letter which was later printed in the *Herald*. "The air seemed electrified and filled with flying fragments of metal. A shell exploded on top of us, killing right and left, flinging me high into the air to come down buried by debris but miraculously unharmed... Then came the gas. Choking, blinding chlorine. The French, poor devils, gave way exposing our flank, and at last the order came to hold our end at all costs. We lined the ditch alongside the road leading up to the trenches, and through the hedge poured in a flanking fire upon the advancing Germans. With the gas swirling round us we stood, a mere handful holding an army, if only momentarily."

Blackfoot Mike Foxhead (shown here between two friends), defied the instructions of his chief and volunteered. Despite the concerns of many elders, native Canadians joined up in proportionately larger numbers than any other group. Foxhead was killed in action in France.

A doctor with the Canadians suggested to the astonished troops that if they breathed through rags soaked in urine it would offset the worst impact of the gas. It worked to some extent, although not everyone got the message. Amazingly the green Canadian troops did not run, and much of the gas eventually began to dissipate as it drifted farther into the now-vacated French lines. The Germans advanced to within four miles of Ypres and there seemed little to stop them going the whole way, but surprised by the ferocity of the Canadian fire on their flank and perhaps unaware of the extent of their success - they stopped and dug in. Just before midnight 15,000 Canadians, including Calgary's 10th Battalion, fixed bayonets and, shoulder to shoulder, counter-attacked through the darkness. The fighting lasted through the night and the following day. By the time the 10th was withdrawn from the line on the morning of April 24th, 642 of

Lt. Harcus Strachan, a rancher from Chauvin, Alberta, leads a troop of the Fort Garry Horse back to Canadian lines after an attack on German artillery. Strachan's bravery would win him the Victoria Cross.

the battalion's 816 men had been killed or wounded.

The Second Battle of Ypres would continue until the end of May and the Germans used gas again in an attempt to dislodge the Canadians. This time everyone knew the value of rags or towels soaked in urine or trench water. The Allies retained their toehold in Belgium, in no small part due to the courage of the rookie Canadians. "The Canadians had many casualties," recorded British commander-in-chief Sir John French, "but their gallantry and determination undoubtedly saved the situation." The bloodbath at Ypres cost the 1st Canadian Division nearly two thirds of its fighting strength, but senior British officers would no longer complain about the unruly and undisciplined colonials. At Festubert later in 1915 and at St. Eloi and Mount Sorrel in the spring of 1916 the Canadians would consolidate a reputation, freely recognized by the German commanders, as crack troops.

This cheery bicycle messenger of the Canadian Corps makes his way through the mud of a Canadian camp behind the lines in 1916. The Flanders' mud would hardly have been conducive to cycling.

Little cheeriness in this front-line Canadian trench. The soldiers endured cold, damp and the constant threat of shelling and sniper fire. A hot meal and a bath seemed like the distant delights of Heaven.

National Archives of Canada PA-1326

98

In September 1916 the Canadians found themselves on the Somme battlefield, site of the worst slaughter in a terrible war. During the opening attack on July 1st the British had suffered the worst single-day military disaster in the country's long history - more than 55,000 dead and wounded. By the time the Canadians entered the line British losses numbered nearly 200,000. During three months of fighting on the Somme, at Courcellete and Thiepval, the Canadians would count their success in yards and their losses in the thousands. The enthusiasm and optimism of 1914 had long since been replaced by the brutal reality of trench warfare. "You know how anxious I was to get to the front line," Pte. W.H. Gilday wrote to his sister in Rosebud Creek. "Well, now I am just as anxious to be far away. I am afraid my nerves won't stand battles." He described the initial Canadian assault on the Somme on September 15th. "You think they run, holler, yell and such like, but that is not the case... We walked very grim and quiet; until I struck the barbed wire my mind simply stood still. I wish I could tell you everything that happened, but you would never realize how things are."

At the end of November the Allied high command finally withdrew to new defensive lines on the Somme. A new breakthrough was being planned between the northern French towns of Lens and Arras along a seven-mile escarpment that hinged on the village of Vimy. The Germans had held the high ground since October 1914 and had turned it into an underground fortress and the keystone of their entire Flanders defensive system. The French had twice tried to take it in 1915,

Six machine-gunners from Calgary's 50th Battalion. They are (l-r back row) Cpl. David Dean, Pte. A. Foulds, Sgt. H. Mackenzie, and Cpl. E. Ede. Kneeling in front are Pte. W.R. Edgar, and Pte. Hugh Everest.

Heavy naval guns firing over the Canadian lines at Vimy, spring 1917. In preparation for the attack at Vimy, the Canadians perfected devastating counter-battery fire which destroyed much of the German artillery.

at a cost of 300,000 casualties. Now the Canadians were asked to try again - but this would not be a repeat of the murderous Somme debacle. The Canadian Corps commanders, Sir Julian Byng and his Canadian deputy, Lt. Gen. Arthur Currie, asked for and received permission to make this an entirely Canadian operation. During the winter of 1916-17 (Europe's coldest in 35 years) the four divisions of the Corps would train for months in the most meticulously researched and planned offensive of the war to date.

There could be no surprise at Vimy. From their vantage point atop the ridge the German troops could see for miles and would be fully prepared for any attack. Arthur Currie, who masterminded the operation, came up with an innovative answer to this problem. If the Germans could see everything, his men would go underground. Through the winter Canadian and British engineers built six miles of underground subway, some 50 feet below ground, which carried men, ammunition, telephone lines, fuel, water and food to the front line. Several had narrow-gauge railways. There were dressing stations and cavernous rooms for storage. One, Zivy Cave, was big enough to hold an entire battalion of men beyond the reach of German shells.

During 1915-16 the Canadians had perfected the use of trench raids — night attacks on enemy lines. At Vimy these raids involved up to 1,000 men and had all the trappings of an assault, from artillery barrages to teams of stretcher bearers. By the time of the actual

Pack horses, left, taking ammunition to the guns of the 20th Battery, Canadian Field Artillery, at Neuville St. Vaast, before the assault on Vimy Ridge. There could be no surprise at Vimy, and fighting continued through the winter of 1916-17. Below, Canadian soldiers tend to the temporary grave of a fallen comrade, killed in the months preceding the attack on Vimy Ridge.

Two Canadian soldiers posing in gas masks examine a Lee Enfield rifle. The sturdy Enfield (designed by a Canadian) was standard issue for British troops. It was much preferred to the Ross rifle originally supplied to the Canadians, which was a fine hunting weapon but didn't stand up to the rigours of the battlefield.

assault the Canadians knew every inch of the German defences, in detail, while the Germans were kept permanently unsettled by the raids. The rules governing the deployment of artillery were rewritten by Andrew McNaughton, a 30-year-old McGill engineering graduate from Moosomin, Saskatchewan. Instead of just pummelling the German trenches, McNaughton's guns also concentrated on silencing the German artillery - with deadly effect. But Currie's real piece-de-resistance was a scale model of the battlefield built behind the Canadian lines. His men trained on it hour after hour, until they knew the terrain and their objectives by heart.

The battle for Vimy Ridge began at 5:30 a.m. on the morning of April 9th, Easter Monday, with the most intense artillery barrage of the war thus far. British Prime Minister Lloyd George recorded that he could hear the faint thunder of the guns at home in London. "At the break of day the whole country seemed on fire," gunner Fred Simm of Lethbridge wrote home to his father. "I can well remember sitting in place on the gun seat ready for the word, half a minute to go - then 'Let 'er rip boys.' Each gun firing four rounds a minute, with six guns to the battery, and we were only one battery in hundreds doing the same stunt. It was some fireworks."

And it worked. Under the protection of the Allied barrage the four Canadian divisions swept over the German outer defences and by lunch time were in control of most of the ridge. Pte. John Pattison, a 42-year-old gas fitter for the Calgary Gas company, was one of many Albertans who took part in the assault at Vimy. On the heights he single-handedly attacked and silenced several machine guns, first with grenades and then with his bayonet. For his bravery he was awarded the Victoria Cross, but was never to wear it. Pattison was killed at Lens seven weeks later. The Calgary

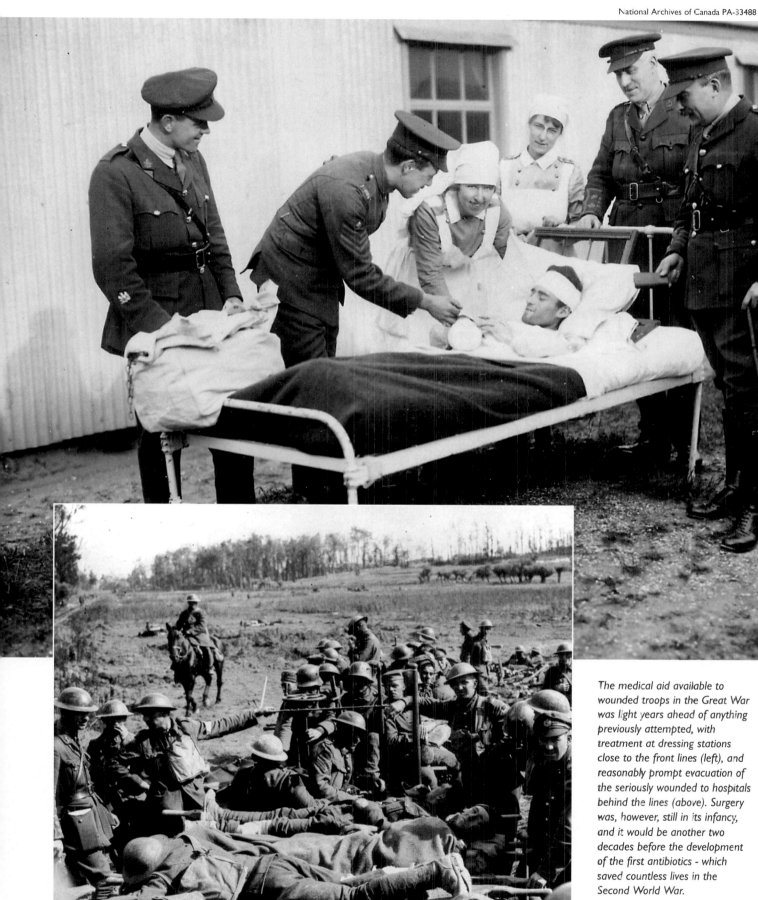

The medical aid available to wounded troops in the Great War was light years ahead of anything previously attempted, with treatment at dressing stations close to the front lines (left), and reasonably prompt evacuation of the seriously wounded to hospitals behind the lines (above). Surgery was, however, still in its infancy, and it would be another two decades before the development of the first antibiotics - which saved countless lives in the Second World War.

bridge which crosses the Elbow River at 2nd St. N.E., near the Stampede Grounds, was named in his honour. His eldest son, Henry, enlisted shortly afterwards, at age 17, and following tradition wore his father's VC.

It took several more days of tough fighting to clear the German troops from the strong points at the north end of the escarpment, but by the end of the week the Canadians had established a new Allied front line on the eastern side of Vimy Ridge. News of the battle was greeted with astonishment. In a war with few success stories, it was a singular victory, gaining more ground and capturing more guns and prisoners than any previous British offensive. The *New York Times* called it "a day of glory," and the French termed it "Canada's Easter gift to France." An unnamed Albertan serving with the Canadian Scottish summed up the attitude of the soldiers themselves. "They said in Lethbridge we were a bunch of booze fighters, but we showed them today what we could do."

The price of victory was onerous: 10,602 Canadian casualties, with 3,598 dead among them. After the battle, Bob Forrest, serving with Calgary's 50th Battalion, looked for 17 comrades from Okotoks who had been with him as the Canadians began their assault on Vimy Ridge. He wept to discover he was the only survivor. "If I get back home, some of their mothers will ask me how they got killed," he said. "How can I make them understand we all had to keep going no matter where and how our buddies fell?"

Edmontonians had their own problems in the summer of 1915, when the North Saskatchewan River rose three metres in ten hours on June 28. The river waters eventually crested 12 metres above normal level, inundating homes and businesses in communities on the riverside flats in the centre of the city. The boatman below is making his way through Rossdale after managing to rescue some household belongings.

PRISONERS OF WAR FUND

On the home front Albertans were eager to pitch in to help the boys overseas. On 40th Avenue in Calgary's Elbow Park, a wagon from the Samaritan Club (top) collects cans and bottles for a prisoner of war fund. In this photograph a group of schoolchildren in Lethbridge pose while knitting socks for soldiers serving in France.

The Great Western Garment Co's factory in Edmonton. During the war years it became the largest supplier of military clothing to the Canadian forces.

Glenbow Archives NC-6-62221

imy consolidated the reputation of the Canadian Corps as an elite force and placed it in the forefront of the battle for the lowlands of Flanders which raged throughout the fall of 1917. There the Canadians fought for control of another ridge, although the modest incline of Passchendaele hardly deserved the name. It became a byword for mud and slaughter, with 16,000 Canadian casualties, but German commanders later admitted it marked the beginning of the end for their hopes of victory. The Germans marshalled all their remaining resources for one last major assault, and on March 21st 1918 attacked on a 50-mile front in northern France. The British Fifth Army was all but destroyed and German units advanced far enough west that long-range artillery could reach the outskirts of Paris, before the offensive ran out of steam.

The Allied counterattack would be led by the Canadians and Australians, but the Canadians were so well known as crack assault troops that the Corps, now commanded by Canadian Sir Arthur Currie, had to go to extraordinary lengths to hide its presence. But in this they were successful. The attack began at dawn on August 8th, as thick mist covered the battlefield. The Canadians advanced so rapidly that they got in front of their own artillery barrage. Calgary's Fighting 10th estimated 40% of its casualties were as a result of friendly fire. Nevertheless, the German commander, Gen. Ludendorff, called it "the blackest day of the German army." The Canadians were elated. Pte. Sam Hemphill, a 21-year-old meat

Canadian troops enter the ruined city of Cambrai on October 9, 1918. There was fierce fighting on the approach to the city, but after the 31st, the Alberta Battalion, took the villages to the north of the city – the German army simply melted away, setting fires as they left.

National Archives of Canada PA-3270

108

packer from Edmonton decorated for his bravery that day, wrote "When you'd been at Ypres and you'd been around the Somme, when you got 200 yards or 100 yards you thought you'd made a wonderful advance. But here we'd gone miles!" Hemphill reported that his unit, now far behind the German lines, captured raw recruits who had just stepped off troop trains. "They had on brand-new uniforms. They had never been dirtied."

By the middle of October the Canadians had taken the city of Cambrai and the Germans were in full retreat. At the end of the month the Corps took the strategic industrial city of Valenciennes, near the Belgian border, and a few days later were in the outskirts of Mons, a Belgian city which had been in German hands since August, 1914. On the morning of November 11th, as the Canadians entered the centre of the city, the news arrived that an armistice had been signed and would take effect at 11 a.m. "Nobody said a word for quite a while," recalled Calgarian Joseph Heffernan. "Then a few cheered a bit feebly. I think most of us were kind of in shock." As Edmonton's 49th Battalion marched into the city Belgians threw flowers in their path and church bells played Tipperary. Pte. F. R. Hasse was bone tired and unimpressed. "The only road worth taking from here is to Jasper Avenue," he declared. You could hardly blame him. Of the 4,050 soldiers of the 49th who served in France, a thousand would never see Jasper Avenue again, and fewer than 800 would return home unwounded.

In the last hundred days of the war, advancing from Amiens to Mons, the Canadian Corps had suffered more than 45,000 casualties, but the four Canadian divisions had defeated more than 50 German divisions - a quarter of the entire German army. "No other force of equal size ever accomplished so much in a similar space of time during the war, or any other war," wrote Arthur Currie. On December 13th soldiers of the two senior Canadian divisions, hundreds of Albertans among them, led the victorious occupying force across the Rhine and into Germany. It was an honour they had earned.

Alberta soldiers line up for ballots at a polling station behind the front lines to vote in the 1917 provincial election. When their votes were counted, they had elected Nursing Sister Roberta McAdams as their Soldiers' Overseas MLA. She was only the second woman elected to any Canadian legislature.

At the news that an armistice had been signed on November 11, 1918, victory parades and celebrations erupted all over Alberta. Revellers at Nanton (left) crowd aboard a car. One passenger, towards the rear, is wearing a mask, presumably as protection against the Spanish Influenza epidemic which had already hit the province. The more organized victory parade at Vulcan a few days later (below) involved floats decked out as warships.

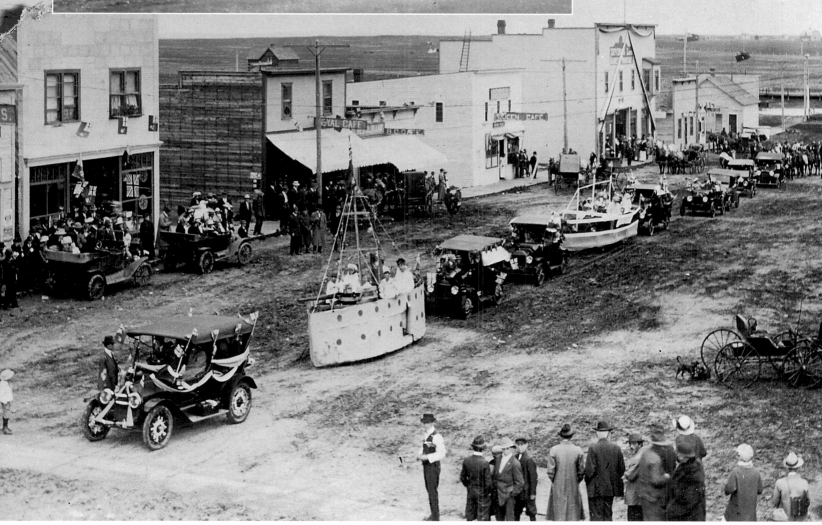

The prohibition movement politicizes Alberta's women

IN 1916 THE SIFTON GOVERNMENT MOVES TO BAN THE SALE OF ALCOHOL, AND AT THE SAME TIME DECIDES TO EXTEND THE FRANCHISE TO WOMEN

In March 1915 a long-running crusade to ban the sale of alcohol in Alberta found a curious ally in Bob Edwards, the whiskey-loving editor of the province's best-read newspaper, the *Calgary Eye Opener*. Perhaps the one thing Edwards liked better than a drink was his independence, and when a delegation of hotel owners offered him $15,000 for his support against a liquor ban he was incensed. According to Robert Gard in his book *Johnny Chinook*, Edwards told the businessmen "I've never sold the old rag yet and I never will" - and threw them out of his office. When a group sup-

porting the ban soon arrived asking for his support, Edwards wanted to know what they would offer him in return. "We haven't got a dollar, Bob," replied their leader. Which decided the matter as far as Edwards was concerned. The *Eye Opener* would support prohibition.

Edwards did not actually see the publication of his lengthy, and somewhat half-hearted, endorsement of a liquor ban. He was in hospital recovering from one of his regular binges. But in a front-page article the *Calgary Albertan* called Edwards' editorial a "fatal blow to the opponents of

The well-stocked interior of a Calgary liquor store, in the fall of 1907. The argument over prohibition divided Alberta society between the "drys" and the "wets".

Glenbow Archives NB-28-29

112

A foursome enjoying a drink at Chevigny's store in Plamondon. Alberta's French community was a good deal more liberal in its attitude towards liquor than its Anglo-Saxon, Protestant neighbours.

Relaxing with a drink in a North-West Mounted Police canteen. The reluctance of the Mounties to enforce provincial liquor laws led directly to the creation of the Alberta Provincial Police.

Prohibition." And perhaps it was. In July a referendum solidly endorsed a ban (58,295 to 37,509), with Lethbridge being the only major centre voting against. Alberta officially went dry on July 1st, 1916, and would remain so until the spring of 1923.

In the long run, far more important than the liquor ban was the politicization of a growing number of Alberta women. Drinking to excess - the world "alcoholism" had yet to come into vogue - was a particular problem in Alberta's towns and cities, where men often outnumbered women by four to one and the sobering influence of marriage, or even female company, was in short supply. Nor was heavy drinking limited to single men. The habit, once ingrained, was hard to kick, and

the toll on families was cause for much public concern - particularly for women, who bore the brunt of it. Whether it was through the Women's Christian Temperance Union (WCTU), the Moral Reform League, the United Farm Women of Alberta or their church, the movement to ban alcohol became the first political experience for thousands of Alberta women. And the one thing they learned was that changes to the law generally came through the ballot box, and women did not have the vote. Once they decided they ought to have it, the changes came thick and fast.

In 1914 the Equal Franchise League presented a petition bearing 3,767 signatures to Edmonton city council, which then had the city charter amended to grant voting rights to all adult

The redoubtable Nellie McClung (right), pictured in 1916 with the famous British campaigner for women's voting rights, Emmeline Pankhurst. McClung was elected to the Legislature in 1921.

Women outside Hawey's Jasper Confectionary store, on Jasper Avenue in Edmonton, after casting ballots for the very first time in the 1917 provincial election.

women. Calgary and Lethbridge soon followed, and within four years women would be able to vote in municipal elections throughout the province. The push for the right to vote in provincial elections was taken up by the formidable duo of Nellie McClung and Emily Murphy, both immigrants from Manitoba. McClung was a teacher and writer active in the WCTU, while Murphy was a journalist and self-taught expert on women and the law (her three brothers were all lawyers). When a demonstration at the Legislature and a 12,000-signature petition didn't persuade Premier Arthur Sifton to act, McClung and Murphy paid him a private visit. He noted that they were "very determined women." On February 26th, 1916, Sifton introduced a bill to act on the Prohibition referendum, and also a bill to extend the provincial franchise to women.

The 1917 provincial election was the first in which Alberta women could vote, and also be candidates. Louise McKinney won the Claresholm constituency, becoming the first female legislator in the British Empire. Two months

later she was joined by Roberta MacAdams, chosen by Alberta soldiers and nurses stationed overseas as one of two MLAs under the Alberta Military Representation Act. In February 1918, a week after being sworn in, MacAdams brought a bill to the legislative assembly to incorporate a welfare organization, the War Veterans' Next-of-Kin Association. It was the first law introduced by a woman to be passed anywhere in the Empire.

In the 1921 provincial election Nellie McClung herself was elected to the legislature (as an opposition Liberal), along with Alix-area farmer Irene Parlby, who joined the new United Farmers' government as Alberta's first female cabinet minister. Emily Murphy was appointed a police magistrate in 1916, and the following year was promoted to provincial magistrate. On the bench she joined Alice Jamieson, who had become a juvenile court judge in 1913 and is widely believed to have been the first female judge in the western world.

CHAPTER FIVE

The dry times begin

A WORSENING DROUGHT AND UNREST AMONG FARMERS SIGNALS THE END OF ALBERTA'S FIRST POLITICAL DYNASTY

The 1930s have become synonymous with drought and suffering on the Prairies, but for much of the southern Alberta the dry years actually began in 1917, before the Great War had even ended. Capt. John Palliser, the 19th century explorer, had written off much of what would become southern Alberta as semi-desert useless for farming. His words were echoed some years later by William Pearce, who in a survey for the federal government argued that southeastern Alberta in particular was fit only for ranching. In the rush to settle the new province these bleak assessments were ignored, but by the end of the second decade of the 20th century it seemed as if the words of Palliser and Pearce had returned to haunt the farmers who had struggled to prove them wrong.

"After eleven years of constant toil I have come to the end of the road," farmer James Roebuck of Whitla told Premier Herbert Greenfield in July 1922. "My money and children have gone and now my wife says this is her last year on this desert. Six years in succession without a crop, and only two crops since the country was settled in 1909. I think that has been a fair trial." Many dry belt farmers agreed. By 1926 some 6,400 farms had been abandoned as almost 17,000 people moved on. The Tilley East area (1.5 million acres around Empress, Jenner, Alderson, Redcliff and Suffield) was among the hardest hit by years of drought and summer heat. At the end of the Great War it had 2,386 farm families, but by 1926 that had dwindled to less than 500.

The problem was weather. Up until the end of the Great War, Medicine Hat's rainfall during the May to August growing season had averaged eight inches, which was little enough. In 1919 the entire year's precipitation was less than eight inches. Until 1915 the mean daily maximum temperature in the Medicine Hat area had been around 25C. For the next 15 years it averaged 30C, and in some years more. In 1917, for example, the average July daily maximum temperature

A thresher stands half buried in windblown soil. The weather turned nasty, and so did the mood among Alberta's frustrated farmers.

was 33C. The weather could also play wicked games. Around Winnifred in 1925 good spring rainfall encouraged a promising crop, but in July the temperature jumped to 38C, accompanied by high winds. The crops simply shrivelled and died.

When the 1920s began, William Frederick Ewing was seven years old. His mother had died in the influenza epidemic of 1918, and his father was struggling to hang on to the family cattle operation near Lethbridge. "We had no rain and no feed for the cattle. You could sell anything you could put a string around and call it feed. That winter, for instance, they had some moisture just east of Calgary and some people baled grass off the tops of the sloughs - right off the ice. They'd sell that for $65 or $70 a ton. It was just belly wash, there was no food value in it. The cattle would eat it and they'd die.

"Between borrowing money to buy the feed and then losing the cattle, when spring came we had nothing. Dad walked out with his saddle and the clothes on his back. In those days when you went bankrupt you lost everything, including your name. My father had to pay back everything he owed. He couldn't own anything because his creditors could seize it. So we got a place in my stepmother's name, and my father broke horses and did custom work hauling grain and ploughing land. I was barely nine then. I wasn't old enough to really know what was going on. I went along for the ride and hoped the next meal was there." (From *Lethbridge: A Centennial History*, City of Lethbridge and Historical Society of Alberta.)

Considering the situation it is perhaps not surprising that Charles Hatfield generated much public interest in southern Alberta during the early 1920s. The 40-year-old California-born Quaker said he could make it rain whenever he wanted, and even offered a money-back guarantee. Hatfield arrived in Alberta with a wad of press clippings purporting to show his success in making it rain in places as far afield as Australia, England and South Africa. But his most prodigious feats were said to have been in California, where it was reported that in 1916 he had been responsible for a dam burst and the destruction of over a hundred bridges. In 1921 the rainmaker struck a deal with farmers in the Medicine Hat area. If Hatfield could produce at least four inches

Farmers in the Lomond area taking part in a government-sponsored rabbit hunt. Rabbits became a staple of the prairie diet during these hard times.

Trick photography provided this image of a giant grasshopper. Humour aside, swarms of the insects became a serious problem on both sides of the Canada-U.S. border.

of rain between May 1st and August 1st, he'd be paid $8,000. Cynics recalled that the area's average rainfall during May, June and July had traditionally been just over six inches, so Hatfield had a pretty good chance of walking away with the money.

The rainmaker raised a 24-foot steel tower at Chappice Lake, north of the Hat, and topped it with shallow pans containing secret chemicals which, he promised, would draw moisture from passing clouds. Within a week the area had an inch of rain, and by the end of May almost two inches. Crops sprouted and things were looking positive, but June was mostly hot and dry and the crops withered. By the end of the month the rain tally was only 2.42 inches. July was better, with a little over two inches of rain, but by that time the crop had already been burned. No matter, a deal was a deal and the three-month total of 4.25 inches meant that Hatfield received his money. The *Bassano Mail* newspaper was not impressed. "If he could have made a nickel's worth of rain why did he not do so in the torrid weeks when crops were burning up...? His scheme is on a par with the gold brick and Spanish treasure games. The world progresses and suckers are born every minute."

As a result of such criticism Hatfield eventually refunded $2,500, but as if to prove the *Bassano Mail's* point he was re-hired by desperate Medicine Hat area farmers to produce rain in 1922. When they changed their minds Hatfield left in a huff for Italy, where he proposed to offer his service to alleviate a drought in the area of Naples. He also announced that he would make his services available to the Pope, and might even be persuaded to share his secrets with the pontiff. There is no record of any such interest from the Holy Father, and Hatfield seems to have drifted into well-deserved obscurity.

The answer to the woes of Alberta's dry belt farmers was actually already apparent in the 1920s, by which time Lethbridge was already proclaiming itself Canada's leader in irrigation, with 130,000 acres being fed by the St. Mary's River. By 1926 there were 950,000 acres of farmland earmarked for irrigation around Lethbridge, Brooks and Medicine Hat, although only a quarter of that was actually irrigated - the major reason being the very different methods needed for irrigation farming. Many a dryland farmer discovered to his sorrow that wet land wasn't wheat land.

The Duke of Sutherland's farm, near Brooks, with workmen channelling irrigation water. By the middle of the 1920s it was clear that irrigation could save much of southern Alberta's drought-ravaged farmland.

Provincial Archives of Alberta P-768

It was much better suited to crops such as sugar beet, sunflowers, alfalfa, corn and vegetables. Irrigation farming was also more labour intensive and farmers discovered that 160 acres was about the maximum a family could handle. There was also the problem of who paid for expensive irrigation projects. Dry land farmers couldn't bear the entire cost and hope to make a living, and by end of the 1920s the CPR, with very deep pockets, was the only business interested in subsidizing irrigation. Some form of government involvement was suggested, and indeed it seemed a logical idea. Alberta was overwhelmingly rural and the farmers the single most influential lobby group. In fact the province had been governed by the United Farmers of Alberta since defeating the Liberals in 1921. But even a UFA government was faced with the reality that irrigation projects benefited only a fraction of Alberta's farmers, and urban Albertans not at all. Increased government involvement would be a very tough sell.

And it was about to become much tougher. As the decade came to a close the world was on the verge of the worst recession since the 1880s, capital was increasingly scarce, and the price of wheat - the engine of the Prairie economy - dipped towards a shocking 15 cents-a-bushel. The problems of Alberta's dry land farmers were about to be overshadowed by a global economic meltdown which would leave its mark on a generation of Albertans.

Children and nurses at a clinic in Coaldale, near Lethbridge, in 1925. The deteriorating health of farm families roused the government to organize travelling clinics such as this.

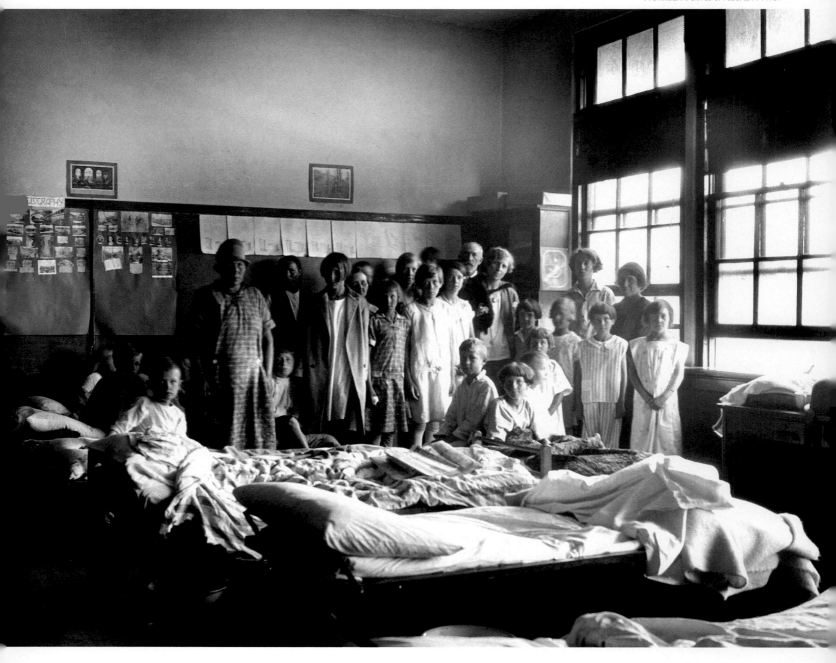

An unidentified farm family near Hanna poses with the body of their child in a rough, home-made coffin. The times were particularly hard on the very young and the old.

Women's fashions underwent a complete change during the 1920s. Hemlines, according to one Methodist minister, were now "a little too far from the ground, and not quite near enough to Heaven." This stylish Calgary woman, opposite page, opted for a typical but revolutionary mid-calf hemline that bears little resemblance to dresses of only a few years before. Even wedding dresses were not immune from the changing style, as with that of Alberta bride Beatrice Irma Broberg, below. In this non-automated era the drudgery of daily household chores remained, but at least a woman could now listen to the radio while doing the laundry.

A heroic mission of mercy through frigid skies

WOP MAY AND VIC HORNER CAPTURE HEADLINES AND THE PUBLIC'S IMAGINATION WITH A DARING MID-WINTER FLIGHT NORTH IN AN OPEN COCKPIT AT FORTY-BELOW

In mid-December 1928, Albert Logan, the respected factor of the Hudson's Bay post at Little Red River, 90 kms east of Fort Vermillion, fell ill with what was thought to be a cold and sore throat. When he did not recover, his wife, a former nurse, correctly diagnosed diphtheria, a potentially fatal and highly contagious disease that destroyed the tissues of the respiratory tract. By the time Dr. Harold Hamman was summoned from Fort Vermillion, Logan was in the final stages of the disease, and the doctor feared a deadly epidemic.

With only a limited supply of old serum with which to vaccinate 200 people, Hamman sent a message to Peace River, to be relayed to authorities in Edmonton. It took Metis couriers Joe Lafleur and William Lambert 11 agonizing days to cover the distance in frigid weather, and the message was finally received in the capital at the end of the month. Alberta's deputy minister of health, Dr. M.R. Bow, asked the Edmonton and Northern Alberta Aero Club if they could help. The club, in turn, asked Wilfrid "Wop" May if he'd make the 600-mile flight to Little Red River.

A graduate of Edmonton's Victoria High School, May was a Great War veteran who had flown with the Royal Flying Corps, the predecessor of the Royal Air Force. May

Pilot May accepts the supply of serum from Alberta's deputy health minister, Dr. M.R. Bow. Charcoal burners were installed in the baggage compartment (shown open) to prevent the vital medicine from freezing.

Glenbow Archives NA-1821-2

Horner, in the front seat, and May prepare to leave Blatchford Field in Edmonton shortly after noon on January 2, 1929. "You can tell the world it was a cold trip," May said on their return.

asked his friend, Vic Horner, another veteran of the war (who had served with the Princess Patricias' Canadian Light Infantry) to be his co-pilot. They would make the trip in a 75-horsepower, open-cockpit Avro Avian, with charcoal burners in the small baggage compartment to prevent the 500,000 units of diphtheria vaccine from freezing. The pair applied anti-frosting paste to their goggles, stuffed chocolate in their pockets for sustenance, and took off from Blatchford Field just after noon on January 2nd.

Increasing snow and falling temperatures forced the plane to land at McLennan that first night. When May removed the vaccine for overnight storage at the town's hotel, he discovered that the charcoal heaters had leaked, and oil-soaked rags on the floor of the plane had begun to smoulder. Had they stayed up longer there was a good chance the plane would have caught fire.

The next morning they continued to Peace River, with the temperature now hitting -36C. The two frozen airmen warmed themselves with tea at the police station while the plane was refuelled. By now the temperature had dropped

to -45, but they made it to Fort Vermillion in three hours, the engine spluttering as they skimmed the tree-tops. After handing over the vaccine to Dr. Hamman, the pair turned around and headed south. Logan had died the previous day, but with the vaccine on hand his would be the only death.

May and Horner recuperated in Peace River for two days and then began the perilous trip back to Edmonton. The mercy flight had been front-page news in the papers, and the subject of hourly updates on the radio. When the little plane finally landed at Blatchford Field it was met by a crowd of 10,000 cheering people. "This feat," effused the *Western Tribune* in Vancouver, "was nothing more or less than a sublime gamble with death or an errand of unalloyed mercy, and must forever be associated with great deeds of men since time began." May and Horner dismissed the fanfare, saying they had simply been doing a job. "You can tell the world it was a cold trip," admitted May. "But here we are, and damned glad to get this far."

After 16 years of Liberal government that mirrored the politics in Ottawa and the rest of the country, in 1921 Albertans turfed the province's first political dynasty in a stunning election upset. It was the first of several dramatic realignments which would punctuate Alberta politics in the 20th century, and the beginning of a tradition of throwing massive support to political parties offering radical agendas and the promise of change. This penchant for dramatic change, broad public agreement, and minimal political opposition, would stand in stark contrast to Canada's rather predictable political landscape and would eventually confer upon Albertans a reputation for unconformity and opposition to the national political consensus. It all began with two intelligent, energetic, and physically-imposing men who typified the successful Alberta farmer, but who came from very different backgrounds. Oddly, what these two shared was a reluctance to enter politics.

Henry Wise Wood was the fifth child of a prosperous American farming family with land in Missouri and Texas. A successful rancher and businessman (he established one of Missouri's first telephone companies), the restless Wood was not content to manage his father's holdings. Like a million other Americans during the early years of the century, he was drawn to the Alberta frontier and in 1905, at the age of 45, he bought a section of land near Carstairs where he settled with his wife and four children. He became immediately active in the Society of Equity, a group promoting the rights and welfare of farmers. Over the next quarter century he would be the most influential voice in Alberta's powerful farmers' movement. He was elected president of the United Farmers of Alberta in 1916 (and re-elected 14 times), and as the organization's intellectual heart he would become known as the "Uncrowned King of Alberta." Uncrowned because when the

Farmers arriving in Cardston in 1924, after abandoning their dried-out homesteads. The exodus was in sharp contrast to the optimism of settlement a decade earlier.

Glenbow Archives NA-114-17

129

Travelling salesmen at Whitelaw, in the Peace River district, in 1928. The pioneering salesmen and their loaded vehicles were by now a common sight throughout much of the province.

UFA won its surprising election victory in 1921, Wood, who had argued against the movement "going political", refused the premiership when it would have been his for the asking. Leadership of the first UFA government fell instead to Herbert Greenfield.

Greenfield was born 1869 in the ancient city of Winchester, England. His father was a moderately successful businessman, and had the elder Greenfield continued to be successful it's unlikely that his son would have ever come to Canada. But his father lost everything in a failed dredging company, and in 1892 young Herbert crossed the Atlantic in search of his own fortune. After working in the small oilfield at Sarnia, Ontario, and as a $7-a-month farm labourer, he married Elizabeth Harris and moved to Alberta in 1904, homesteading near Westlock. Their first years in Alberta might have overwhelmed a couple with less determination. Their first house was destroyed by a bush fire and they spent the next winter in a sod hut used by a trapper. Greenfield and his wife then both worked in a local lumber yard until they had enough credit to buy materials to rebuild

The enigmatic figure of Henry Wise Wood. The American-born farmer was perhaps the most influential Albertan never to hold high public office.

Glenbow Archives NA-627-1

Premier John Brownlee. A reluctant politician, he gave the province effective, competent leadership and finally wrested control of natural resources from Ottawa.

133

their home. From then on they prospered and both became active in the farmer's movement. By 1917 Greenfield was vice-president of the UFA, and after the successful 1921 election was reluctantly persuaded to lead the new government. (Greenfield hadn't even contested the August election, but was successful in a by-election in Peace River four months later.) It was not work the rugged, pipe-smoking farmer relished. "I thought I knew what work was," he complained to an *Edmonton Journal* reporter. "But I didn't. I used to just have time for meals, now I don't even have that. They make me work at meal times, too!"

It didn't help that Elizabeth Greenfield died suddenly during her husband's first year in office. By 1924 there was open revolt within the fractious UFA caucus, and the city newspapers in particular were critical of the government's alleged radicalism. The *Edmonton Bulletin* claimed the UFA favoured Soviet-style communism, and as proof cited a speaking invitation to J.S. Woodsworth, the socialist clergyman and "Bolshevik spellbinder" from Winnipeg who, the paper suggested, favoured public ownership of land "by a Soviet under the Lenin system." With an election looming and defeat a very real possibility, Greenfield resigned as premier and was succeeded by his attorney-general, John Brownlee, who had been his chief aide and mentor since the 1921 election. "Back to the farm for me," Greenfield told reporters, but in fact he quickly remarried and moved back to England as Alberta's agent-general in London. He would later return to the province to become president of the Alberta Petroleum Association and a director of the Home Oil

Alex Ross, a former UFA cabinet minister, presents Alberta's first "Old Age Pension" cheque (for $20) to 101-year-old W. Kennedy Lee in September 1929. The Brownlee government had opposed the national scheme, but changed its mind after it was clear it had enormous public support.

Company. He died in Calgary in 1949 at the age of 80. At the end of the 20th century the Greenfield homestead, 4 km south of Westlock, was still being farmed by his grandson, Frank.

The new premier, John Brownlee, was another tall (six-foot-four), physically imposing character who came to politics reluctantly. He was a thoughtful, even sombre individual, and far from charismatic, but behind his often melancholy demeanour was a serious mind and steely determination. A conservative by nature, the lawyer and former country school teacher had only entered politics after much urging by Greenfield and Wood, but under his shrewd and meticulous leadership the UFA government finally found its feet and many historians would argue provided Alberta with its most effective government of the century. Within a year Brownlee had eliminated the government's deficit and posted the province's first surplus since before the Great War. Construction was also started on Highway 2, linking Edmonton and Calgary. Despite overwhelming opposition from the city newspapers, in the 1926 election Brownlee and the UFA were returned to office with an increased majority.

Brownlee led a vigorous and competent government, but without a doubt his impressive achievements were in relations with the federal government. As attorney-general he had wrung major concessions from Ottawa on westbound rail freight rates, lowering the cost of farm machinery manufactured in the East. He had also pressured the federal government to reinstitute the Crow's Nest Pass freight rate (suspended during the Great War), which guaranteed a fixed rate for carrying Prairie grain. But his greatest achievement was gaining control of natural resources for the three Prairie provinces. Like Manitoba and Saskatchewan, Alberta had entered Confederation as a second-class jurisdiction, denied resource rights given to the older provinces. Ottawa had steadfastly refused to move on the issue for 15 years, but Brownlee recognized the vulnerability of Mackenzie King's minority Liberal government and organized an intense opposition lobbying effort. In January 1926 it paid off, with Alberta and the other Prairie provinces finally being granted the same rights as the others. For Alberta, the timing was perfect.

Figure skaters from Edmonton's Glenora Skating Club in the 1920s. Later in the century, as the fabled Royal Glenora, it would produce a clutch of world champion skaters.

WORKERS OF THE World DEMAND YOUR RIGHTS
More Immigration
More Starvation

Turner Valley proves Alberta's energy potential

The province's first great oilfield seems doomed to failure then Royalite 4 arrives with 'an explosion like a six-inch gun'

In 1924 an Imperial Oil well called Royalite No. 4 had struck natural gas near Black Diamond at a depth of around 2,800 feet. When the gas pressure fell off rapidly over the next few months, Imperial decided to go deeper. Down the tool bit pounded, to 3,730 feet, deeper than any other well in the province - and found nothing but 350-million-year-old limestone. Royalite No. 4 looked like just another in a succession of mostly dry holes which had cost the company nearly $5 million. Imperial had had enough and ordered the crew to stop.

If it hadn't been for a curious and stubborn engineer by the name of Sam Coultis, Alberta's Turner Valley oil field might have continued on the road to oblivion. After the boom of the Great War years, Turner Valley had sputtered almost to a stop. It took two years and $50,000 to drill a productive well in the coulee 30 miles south of Calgary, and with the average well's production dwindling to no more than 10 barrels a day — it was just a matter of time until the field was abandoned. But Coultis urged Imperial to continue at Royalite No. 4. With the well already at record depth, why not invest a little additional time and money and see what was down there? After some argument, the company reluctantly gave the go ahead.

It didn't take long for Coultis's determination to be

Oilers at work at the wellhead. Rig crews usually worked 12-hour shifts for $2 to $3 a day. Some companies, like Royalite, built well-run camps providing food, a bunkhouse and even bathrooms and showers. Workers for less affluent companies often had to build their own accommodation with wood and tarpaper.

Gas being flared at Turner Valley. At night, the glow from burning gas illuminated the sky as far away as Calgary, almost 50 kms distant.

rewarded. On the night of October 12th, after drilling just 10 more feet, there was "an explosion like that of a six-inch gun" as gas and naptha blasted from the well. The flow of gas was established at 21 million cubic feet a day, plus 300 barrels a day of naphtha, an oily liquid that could be turned into gasoline. At that rate Royalite No. 4 was worth $1.5 million a year, and was immediately labelled the "Wonder Well." It was also a monster, defeating the best efforts of the crew to control it and destroying the heaviest equipment available in Alberta. On November 9th it caught fire, sending a plume of flame shooting high into the air. The well was

tamed by December, but its output was so prodigious that it raised new problems. There was simply no market for that much natural gas and up to 90% of it was simply flared off. But with the explosion in automobile use, the market for naphtha was well established and by the spring of 1926 Royalite No. 4 alone was producing more - 217,000 barrels a year - more than all of Ontario's 4,500 wells combined. That same year Calgary's Home Oil No. 1 well drilled down to the 5,280-foot-level and struck natural gas, plus the more useful naphtha at double the rate of Royalite No. 4. Two years later another Calgary oil company, Okalta, brought in a well

The Turner Valley oil discovery created a stock promotion frenzy in Calgary. Every available office space downtown was taken up by brokers, who traded night and day for six days a week. On Sundays Police Chief Al Cuddy personally patrolled the streets to prevent trading on the Lord's Day.

which produced natural gas and naphtha at a staggering rate of 32 million cubic feet a day.

A pipeline was built to Calgary and more uses were found for Turner Valley's natural gas, but at least 200 million cubic feet - the equivalent of an 87-car train of coal - was flared off every day. It was said Calgarians could read the newspaper at night by the glow from the valley. The flares produced so much heat that in the vicinity of Turner Valley crocuses, lilies and wild strawberries matured four to six weeks early. It was only a matter of time before the government was forced to act, and in 1931 it passed legislation restricting the flow of wells in the Turner field to 40% of their capacity, in an effort to reduce the burning of gas. Still, by that year an estimated 600 million cubic feet of gas was being flared off every day. By that time Alberta was producing nearly a million barrels of oil each year, most of it from the Turner field, and had surpassed the production of Montana, Colorado and New Mexico combined.

But the sad fact was that the flaring of such vast amounts of natural gas reduced the pressure needed to bring oil to the surface. Between 1924 and 1931 it is estimated that 260 billion cubic feet of natural gas went up in flames. In later years expensive secondary recovery methods - using water pressure — would be of some help, but only a fraction of Turner Valley's enormous potential would ever be used. From the Ottawa viewpoint, the expert prediction was that "pretty nearly all the authorities agree that the life of our natural oils, while problematical, is ending." In reality the Turnery Valley field, while vast, was just the beginning for Alberta's oil patch — although it would take another two decades to prove it.

Rig captain A.P. 'Tiny' Phillips. The work was hard and dangerous, but the oil patch attracted rugged individualists who weren't much put off by hardship or discomfort.

The years after the Great War were a roller-coaster ride for Edmonton. In 1914 the capital had a population of 72,000, but by 1921 that had fallen to 59,000 (less than Calgary's 63,000) as the building boom evaporated and the price of wheat dropped from $2.31 a bushel to less than $1. The city would recover during the decade, growing to 80,000 residents, and modest development continued. In the photo on the opposite page, workers install a Northwestern Utilities' pipeline which brought natural gas to the city from a discovery at Viking. Below, in an early effort to create a market for northern Alberta's oilsands, a crew uses an experimental "bituminized" paving process on St. Albert Trail in north Edmonton. Nevertheless, Calgarians mocked the capital as the largest city in Canada (in area), with the fewest people. Between 1920 and 1945, the city repossessed properties equivalent to 56% of its total area (excluding streets) in lieu of unpaid taxes. Almost half of that land was forfeited by 1929.

While only the most determined Edmontonian would attempt the drive to Jasper (inset), by the 1920s Calgarians could routinely reach Banff in their automobiles. If it rained, however, digging your vehicle out of the mud (main photo) was also routine.

Glenbow Archives NA-1341-9

142

PATHFINDING CAR
EDMONTON TO VICTORIA
VIA
JASPER AND KAMLOOPS
OVERLAND 4
LINES MOTORS LTD.
DOMINION NOBBY TREAD TIRES

Riding the rails. Like this Albertan climbing aboard a CN boxcar, in the 1930s desperation drove tens of thousands of men to travel the continent in search of work.

Glenbow Archives NC-6-12955b

144

CHAPTER SIX

The Great Depression

THE 'DIRTY THIRTIES' RAVAGE THE ALBERTA ECONOMY
AND PRODUCE ANOTHER GREAT POLITICAL UPHEAVAL

The collapse of stocks on Wall Street on October 24th, 1929, did little to dampen Albertans' enthusiasm for oil stocks or speculation in commodities, especially wheat. The fate of U.S. Steel or General Motors shares was certainly a topic of conversation, but little more than that. No less an authority than the *New York Times* appeared to agree, declaring the top story of 1929 to be the South Polar expedition of Rear Admiral Richard Byrd. Informed opinion was of the view that the new Federal Reserve system south of the border would lower interest rates and prevent any widening of the economic crisis. Meanwhile, the *Calgary Herald* offered tips to housewives interested in speculating on the Turner Valley boom in oil stocks. "On the whole," opined reporter Kathleen Redman Strange, "women seem able to stand the strain of this exciting speculation better than men. I have heard of two men who have literally gone off their heads over their winnings, but never a woman."

But month by month the price of wheat dropped, from 92-cents-a-bushel in August 1929 to 56 cents by the end of the year. With the Prairie wheat pools having paid more for the 1929 crop than they could now sell it for, they were effectively insolvent. The Soviet Union dumped enormous amounts of wheat on the European market, depressing prices further and reducing demand for the 1930 Prairie crop. By December of that year the farm-gate price of wheat had fallen to 15-cents-a-bushel, and what would come to be known as the Great Depression had finally come to Alberta.

The Depression did not arrive with great fanfare or a lot of noise. It crept in like a thief, leaving small signs of trouble that accumulated until even the most devoutly optimistic and upbeat could not deny that something unprecedented was happening. In the spring of 1930 the *Calgary Albertan* reported that city garbage collectors had begun selling the cast-off clothes they collected. School districts around the province discussed providing milk and other food to children over the summer holidays, since so many were now clearly becoming malnourished. Transit systems in the cities noticed a sudden, steep decline in revenues, as people either walked to work or had no work to go to. Automobile registrations fell by 20%, and stores discovered demand for eggs, pork, cheese, and all manner of foodstuffs was declining steeply. "To see so many young men looking for work in town is most regrettable," reported the clearly puzzled *Ponoka Herald*. "The change has come so suddenly..." The onset of winter saw the unemployed going door to door offering to do odds jobs for food.

To the bad economic news was added a deterioration in the weather. The drought which had driven so many farmers from southern Alberta in the early 1920s had eased at the end of the decade, but it now returned with a vengeance. Water levels in the streams and rivers dwindled in some places to 5% of normal. The *Medicine Hat News* reported that things were worse south of the border, where 20 American states registered record droughts, but that produced yet another horror - grasshoppers. Alberta had always had them, but now they moved north in huge numbers, devouring what was left of the pitiful crops. "They ate the handles of pitchforks, the armpits out of shirts on farmers backs, clothes off lines," author James Gray recalled in *Men Against the Desert* (Saskatoon, Western Producer, 1967).

In the summer of 1933 there were signs on the southern Prairies that the drought might be breaking, but in the better weather the grasshoppers thrived, says Gray. They stripped every farm and garden between Brandon and Calgary. Official surveys found 18 million acres of Prairie farmland, one quarter of all the arable land in Canada, were stricken by drought. As many as six million had been seriously damaged by wind erosion as a result of the drought, and 300,000 acres were deemed to have become desert. All in all, land which had previously supported some 900,000 people now struggled to provide a minimal livelihood. The Red Cross estimated that 125,000 Prairie farm families were destitute.

Faced with an unprecedented disaster, the Alberta government, Ottawa and the railways devised a plan to move farmers from the drought-ravaged south and resettle them in the north of the province, chiefly the Peace River country. In a single week in August 1931, the Northern Alberta Railway moved 39 carloads of farm families and their effects. An astonished *Edmonton Bulletin* recorded the exodus. "Long trainloads of bawling cattle crawling across the sun-baked prairie... tired women with lack-lustre eyes and grimy children, looking out of the dusty windows of day coaches... Their cattle are better off than the women. They call the cattle dumb animals, but they at least can bawl their hunger and thirst; the women and children cannot do that - not loud enough to be heard by the world."

By 1934 many of those resettled in the Peace River country had raised good crops and it seemed the program was a success, but there were continuing problems. Banks would not extend them credit without a guarantee from the province, which was not forthcoming. Some crops went unharvested for want of something as simple, and expensive, as binder twine. "They are without twine and they can't get it," complained *Peace River Record* publisher Charles Frederick. "They are homesteaders and they are getting their first real crop off the land they have cleared. This crop would enable them to get off relief, that is if they could harvest it." By the end of 1936, of 1,000 farm families resettled in the Peace River country, 300 had simply given up.

To the economic collapse was added a worsening drought on the Prairies, with topsoil simply blowing away. This monstrous dust storm was photographed near Twin Rivers, on the Alberta-Saskatchewan border south of the South Saskatchewan River.

One family's epic journey from misery to salvation

EMBLEMATIC OF THE SUFFERING OF ORDINARY ALBERTANS IN THE DEPRESSION, THE FEHR'S ARE PART OF THE GREAT EXODUS FROM THE PEACE RIVER COUNTRY

The exodus from Peace River produced what is probably the most famous Canadian photograph of the Depression years. It was taken by a police constable in Edmonton and pictures the Fehr family - Abram and Elizabeth and their seven children - standing beside their 1927 Chevrolet and trailer. In 1933 they had moved from Hague, Saskatchewan, to homestead at Carcajou, an Old Mennonite colony more than 200 miles north of Peace River. After a winter of living on noodles, biscuits and whatever Abram and his brother could hunt, a flood wiped out their farm and sent their neighbours scurrying to higher ground. Facing starvation, the Fehrs made an epic, two-month trek to Edmonton, living on handouts and whatever odd jobs Abram could find along the way. They survived on cold tea, bread crusts, syrup, the occasional cup of milk and wild strawberries the children picked by the roadside. By the time they arrived in Edmonton they were broke and had not eaten at all for a day or two. To make matters worse, the Chevrolet's axle broke. Without money for repairs, Abram welded it with equipment borrowed from a sympathetic garage owner - who was so impressed with the work, he offered Abram a job. He didn't take it. The family was determined to return to Saskatchewan. But while Abram was trying to sell his watch on the street, the Fehrs attracted the attention of Constables Ed Kenny and Ernie Foster. They were particularly concerned about the plight of three-month-old Peter, and after feeding the family at the station house they took them to the Salvation Army. "They gave us the meals, meat and cookies and cake, but I can't eat much," Elizabeth recalled years later, in an interview with the *Canadian Magazine*. "They take away my baby. I worry... Then in an hour and a half there was the baby. Two police and two policewomen and they have it in a white blanket and they dress it so nice and give it a bottle with milk. My blanket was all so poor. Then you know what I do? I cry. And oh, the police were so good, they say 'No cry, no cry.' Then I say 'Thank you very much.' " With a collection from the police station house, some donated clothes and two days food, the Fehrs returned to Hague, 30 miles north of Saskatoon. Elizabeth died there in 1992, and her husband three years later. Most of the family still lives in the Hague area, although John, a tinsmith, moved to Calgary, and Herman, a logger, retired in Burns Lake, B.C. Little Peter took over the family farm, and was always known as the Peace River Kid.

The famous police photograph of the Fehr family after their trek from Peace River to Edmonton in 1934. From left to right are: Abram Jr., 4; Helen, 6; John, 2 (in front of his father); Agatha, 3; Cornie, 10; Herman, 8; and Elizabeth holding baby Peter, aged 3 months.

The economic collapse prompted much political unrest, and not always as mild as this May Day demonstration of Edmonton children demanding free text books from the provincial government.

The economic collapse and the drought produced an army of destitute and desperate Albertans, and sights their grandchildren would come to associate with Third World poverty. Hundreds of the unemployed built shacks on the banks of Calgary's Elbow River, near Victoria Park. In Edmonton the authorities evicted "homeless wanderers" from the large storm sewer which ran from beneath the downtown to the North Saskatchewan riverbank, and then padlocked the entrance. Many of the destitute built shelters along the river, or burrowed into the heavy clay of the bank. George Miwlisch lived for three years in such a hole, reported the *Edmonton Journal*. He equipped it with a door, linoleum floor and even a

Not everyone was fleeing the land during the 1930s. The Daynaka family, who had emigrated from Poland in 1928, are shown here in the spring of 1933 on their way to High Prairie to take possession of a new homestead. It had taken the parents five years work as farm labourers at Ranfurly before they could afford to buy their own land.

Glenbow Archives ND-3-6343

This man, who identified himself to the Edmonton Journal in 1931 simbly as Old Joe, claimed to have been riding the rails for six decades.

Below Edmonton's Hotel Macdonald those without other options used other people's cast-offs to build homes on what was then the Grierson Hill municipal dump. It was home to 30 single men, and one of several such communities in Edmonton and Calgary.

Edmonton Archives EA-160-325

porch, and gave his address as "Seventh Tee, Mayfair Golf Links," which was just above his head. But if a sense of humour was an asset, there was nothing funny about the grinding poverty faced by many Albertans. A letter from the files of Prime Minister R.B. Bennett, a Calgary MP, reported that "officials from the city Health Department have found it next to impossible to prevent men and women carting away spoiled food from the dump at Nose Creek... On several occasions sanitary inspectors herded persons away from the dump, only to find that they had returned later in the day."

Those in the most dire straits were the isolated homesteads which dotted the province. "I am a mother of seven children," one woman wrote in a letter to the *Calgary Albertan*. "My children are in bad need of shoes and stockings. We need a stove and some underwear. We are alone here, in a poor house on a homestead 180 miles north of Edmonton. My husband went away four months ago and has never come back." Such letters became a regular feature of newspapers, and were invariably followed by donations of food, clothing and other necessities. Pressed to the limit, some families simply abandoned their children with city authorities or police. One distraught mother left four young ones with Edmonton Police Service Sgt. Reg Jennings, who was manning the front desk at police headquarters. "My husband left me a year ago," she told the officer. "Here are my children. They are hungry and I have no money to feed them." She then vanished into the street.

The interior of one of the Grierson Hill shacks in 1938. The Edmonton Journal *discovered that most of the men living here supported themselves in one way or another. This particular man wove baskets which he later sold in town.*

155

Outside Calgary's Capitol Theatre in 1930, Boy Scouts unload toys contributed to needy children. There was no lack of volunteer effort to help the families of the unemployed.

Four more were given to the RCMP at Rimbey (the Mounties handled relief in rural areas), with no food at home the parents asked that they be found shelter for the winter.

Ingenuity thrived in an economy where money was in short supply. The pre-Depression boom in automobile ownership, for example, left many farmers with vehicles they could no longer afford to run. Rather than leave them useless, many removed the engine compartment and hitched what remained behind a horse, which was much cheaper to operate. The resulting transportation, the Bennett buggy, came to define an era in which you made do with what you had.

Then there was the gopher business, which provided pocket money for a generation of Alberta youngsters. With most rural municipalities paying a one-cent bounty for a gopher tail, there was cash to be made in hunting the little rodents. A provincial pest-control competition was launched in 1930, which also included bounties on crows and magpies. Three years later the *Ponoka Herald* reported that the provincewide haul in this competition amounted to 48,555 crow and magpie feet, 201,499 crow and magpie eggs, and an astonishing 725,253 gopher tails. Later, more environmentally conscious generations might be appalled at such slaughter, but it did help to round out the food supply. People ate smoked gopher, baked gopher, and even pickled gopher. Author James Gray noted that schoolchildren in Stettler enjoyed bread and gopher for lunch.

Ethel McClymont, born Ethel Denning in Boyle, 144 km north of Edmonton, was one of six children of English parents growing up on a half-section. "We had a mixed farm, with wheat, cattle,

Gopher hunting was popular and profitable pursuit for rural children like these in the 1930s. The government sponsored a bounty program for extermination of agricultural "pests". And the gopher meat was a useful dietary supplement.

Fish still abounded in the North Saskatchewan River in Edmonton in the 1930s, including sturgeon. Matthew Waite and Robert Smith caught this impressive specimen in 1934 at what would later become Rundle Park

pigs and chickens. Mum had a big vegetable garden, and she kept turkeys. We used to have roast turkey every Sunday. The turkeys hid their nests and we had to follow them and gather up the little ones because they'd curl up and die outside. If they were in poor shape we'd put them in the oven to warm them up. I used to go out hunting with a .22 with our little terrier, Tippy. He'd chase the partridge and grouse up in the trees and I'd shoot them. When our mother cat used to catch them for her kittens, Mother would cut off the best parts and give the rest to the cat. We had a trap line to catch weasels. My older brother made a board and skinned them. We got 35 cents a skin for weasels, less for rabbits. We worked hard, but we had a lot of fun."

Gordon Towers, future lieutenant-governor of Alberta, was born in 1919 on a farm 16 km southeast of Red Deer. "We were pretty well self-sufficient, like the majority of people that got through that period. We'd take our wheat to Camrose to the mill, have it ground into flour, and

get our shorts and our bran flakes. My dad also had one of the first grinders in the district, which he'd built at the turn of the century. It ran by a windmill on top of the barn. He would put the wheat through the fanning mill to blow out the dust and seeds, then run it through the grinder twice. That wheat mixed with flour made a very healthy bread, spread with cream from the cows that we churned into butter. We also ate the fat of the roast, hardened and frozen, on bread. I remember having breakfast at six o'clock in the morning. There was no coffee or tea, but you sure could work on that kind of food because it was so basic and so healthy."

The tough times produced hardship, hunger marches and political unrest, but they also brought people together and prompted too many acts of solidarity and charity to list here. Neighbour helped neighbour, and there were few who wouldn't give a little of what they had to help a stranger in distress. In 1932 farmer H.A. Walter of Raley, near Cardston, found himself with a particularly good crop of wheat - a rarity in itself in those times - and offered 100 bushels for the homeless and jobless if a miller could be found who would grind it, a trucker who would haul it, and a baker who would turn it into bread. Within days of the *Lethbridge Herald* printing Walter's story, the Ellison Milling and Elevator Company offered to grind the wheat, truckers D. Morris and D.R. Yates volunteered to haul it, George W. Green and Co. provided sacks, and Western Bakery and Canadian Bakeries both offered to turn it into loaves. Those on relief in the Lethbridge area welcomed the fresh bread.

Even in the hard times there was still time for recreation, and many communities developed parks and other amenities. These Edmontonians are enjoying a game of giant checkers in the city's Riverside Park (later renamed Queen Elizabeth Park).

THE CANADIAN BANK
OF COMMERCE

NEW YORK OUTFITTERS

THE BOY'S SHOP

*Edmonton's Jasper Avenue, looking
east from 102nd Street, in 1930.
Most entertainment still took place
at home, but the downtown streets
remained busy after dark.*

Edmonton Archives EA-10-226

The popular 'Ma' Trainor and her Calgary Hillbillies perform at the studios of radio station CJCJ. Announcer Don Mackay is standing behind Mrs. Trainor.

The 1930s were undoubtedly grim for many Albertans, but this was also the decade in which radio and the movies became an established feature of popular culture. Radio was free entertainment, once you had bought the receiver and paid Ottawa $2 for a licence. In those days much of the content was local and original. Edmonton writer Gwen Pharis Ringwood, for example, churned out radio plays on every subject from Socrates' wife to a series on the lives of Prairie pioneers called *New Lamps for Old*. She was paid $5 a script. There were news reports, lots of them, and musical entertainment from the likes of Graydon Tipp and his High-Class Orchestra, broadcasting direct from Edmonton's Capitol Theatre, or Ma Trainor and her Calgary Hillbillies performing in the studio at Calgary's radio station *CJCJ*.

Louis Trono, the son of a coalminer, was born in 1909 in Bankhead, 8 km east of Banff. He displayed musical talent at an early age. "By the time I was 14, I'd made enough tips from working as a busboy and caddying at the Banff Springs golf course to buy my first trombone. Next year I became the youngest member of the Banff band. I went to Calgary to work with a band that played the first call every night at the Mandarin Gardens, a club that broadcast on CFAC on weekends. Single guys like me were paid $7 a week, married men $14, and we got our meals. In the early days we traveled the whole province in old, beat up cars that were always breaking down. One time we hit a blizzard about 50 miles outside Calgary and had to wait out the storm parked in a snowdrift. It was fifty below, and we had no heaters or windshield wipers. It was fun, but there was no money. When George V died in 1936 there was a month of mourning. Everything was cancelled, including dances. We had no chance to save up money and some of the guys took any jobs they could get, but I didn't do anything else and I got by without going on relief." In 1998, Trono, then 89, was still playing trombone at the Banff Springs hotel.

And then there were the movies. They had been popular since before the Great War, but with the advent of the talkies in 1928 the cinema became one of the few growth industries of the Depression. Despite their toney or exotic names - The Empress, Dreamland, Rialto, Palace -

A group of Smoky Lake swimmers wearing the one-piece, cotton knit bathing suits which became standard wear in the 1930s. It was no longer considered necessary to be completely covered.

Provincial Archives of Alberta A-11872

the original movie houses were generally small and the seats often threadbare, but tickets were cheap and young people in particular flocked to see the latest productions. A University of Alberta survey of Grade 6 to Grade 10 students in Edmonton and Calgary found that 45% attended the movies at least once a week, and many more often. The newspapers reflected the general enthusiasm for what was already an overwhelmingly American medium. "Chalk this up on your calendar," advised the *Edmonton Journal* early in 1929. "*Dynamite*, Cecil B. De Mille's first talking picture, is coming to the Rialto theatre Monday and will be shown for one complete week. The picture, decked with beautiful gowns, pretty girls, thrills, a glass bathtub, and spectacular mine explosion, returns the producer to the highly-coloured type of story with which he made his earlier triumphs."

Tony Botter, the son of a shoemaker at Bullivant's store in Medicine Hat, was born in 1914. "When I finished high school I worked as a movie projectionist. There were three theatres in Medicine Hat then, all owned by the same man, J.H. Yuill. The Monarch was the first-run theatre; it had about 650 seats. The Empress had eight hundred and the Roxy about four hundred. I began

The 1930s were an era of hunger marches and protests by the unemployed. In the summer of 1935 several hundred jobless men left Vancouver aboard freight trains to take their grievances straight to Ottawa. In Calgary they were cheered by citizens and allowed to camp in the civic stadium. The trekkers reached Medicine Hat on June 10 and paraded through the city (below). They would get no farther than Regina, where police attempts to break up the marchers resulted in a riot in which one police officer died and hundreds of people were injured.

as an apprentice and worked in all three theatres, matinees and evenings. By the Thirties we were running only talkies. The theatres had put in new equipment when they got sound in 1929. The Monarch Theatre ran newsreels, with American and Canadian content, about a week behind the news. In the Empress and the Roxy the newsreels would be several weeks old. The noisiest audiences were kids on Saturday afternoons. They'd have special kids' shows with lots of cartoons - Mickey Mouse, Felix the Cat - and the kids would scream so loud you could hear them in the projection room. Saturday serials were continued every week; they used to pack the Roxy with kids watching serials. For young audiences the cowboy shows were really tops - westerns starring Tom Mix, Harry Carey, Hoot Gibson and Roy Rogers. The Marx Brothers were popular, and we sure used to have crowds for Shirley Temple shows." After the war Botter became an electrician, but still filled in at the movie theatres as a projectionist. He retired in 1930.

By the end of the 1930s owners were spending considerable sums of money to renovate and upgrade movie houses. Edmonton's renovated and expanded Empress Theatre, for example, re-opened at the end of 1939 after a $30,000 overhaul. Just in time to screen the latest Hollywood sensation, *The Wizard of Oz*. Other forms of entertainment did not prosper during the Depression. The city's symphony orchestra was disbanded in 1932, and like many once-popular amusement parks, the Borden Park Funland, with its Green Rattler roller-coaster and Tunnel of Love, was demolished in 1935.

Edmonton temporarily lost its professional hockey and football teams, but amateur sport thrived. The Edmonton Athletic Association men's hockey team packed the Northlands' arena (which by now boasted artificial ice), and fans would fill first Diamond Park, and later Renfrew Park, for contests between teams sponsored by the likes of Edmonton Motors and Harry Cohen's Army and Navy store. Most popular of all were the tilts between city and country teams. Wetaskiwin's famous farm boy pitcher Elmer Randall was guaranteed to get a hostile reception from the partisans in the right-field bleachers. Libraries thrived in a situation where, for the first time in history, most people were both literate and strapped for cash. Albertans became Canada's leading borrowers of books, particularly in Edmonton, where the main library loaned almost as many books as Toronto's Central Library - which was twice the size. Also for the first time, restaurants serving appropriately frugal fare, hamburgers, became the most popular eating places.

Soap box Derbys could draw big crowds, and contestants who were well into adulthood, while treasure hunts caught on with younger Albertans who had more energy than money. The *Journal* explained the rules of this strange new phenomenon. "Someone must go out ahead and bury the 'treasure' - which may be rolls and wieners, or bacon and potatoes for roasting. The party sets out with the aid of a chart and finally finds the spot where the 'arrow points' to the 'pirate's chest'. The party then ends in the usual campfire meal and sing-song. Such treasure hunts may be carried out by moonlight, too." Another source of puzzlement was the craze for something called a Yo-Yo, a small spinning wheel attached to a cord. "Each passing day sees an increase in the numbers of youngsters who are becoming Yo-Yo addicts," reported the *Edmonton Bulletin* in 1931. "The popularity of the Filipino toy has spread like wild-fire. Old folks and young folks alike have discovered that the Yo-Yo provides something a little different. It provides relaxation, requires skill in handling, and each Yo-Yo fan feels a personal satisfaction in being able to keep the little wooden wheel spinning without tangling." Yo-yos, treasure hunts and soap box races would all survive the Depression, and like so many other pastimes eventually fall victim to a quintessentially passive entertainment medium which required no effort or interaction: television.

The economic chaos of the 1930s left its mark on an entire generation of Albertans, some more deeply than others, but its impact on the economic life of the province was cataclysmic. In 1929 the value of Alberta's agricultural production was a substantial $240 million, with a massive 16.3 million acres of land under cultivation. The crop of spring wheat alone that year topped 88 million bushels. With yet another $500,000 budgetary surplus safely in the books, Brownlee's UFA government won a substantial majority in the June 1930 provincial election. A year later the price of Alberta wheat had dropped from $1.02 a bushel to 45 cents, 25 cents below the cost of production, and almost a quarter of working Albertans were unemployed. It would get worse, much worse. By the middle of the decade the province would be effectively bankrupt, running a $5 million deficit and relying on the federal government for bailouts. Yet it was not economics or unemployment which would destroy Brownlee, and shortly after the UFA dynasty. It was sex, and a pretty, 22-year-old government typist.

The sad seduction of Miss Vivian MacMillan

A JURY HEARS VERY DIFFERENT VERSIONS OF THEIR FRIENDSHIP
BUT THE TRIAL RUINS BOTH THE PREMIER AND THE SECRETARY

In 1933 Premier Brownlee and his family had rented a summer cottage on Sylvan Lake. On August 3 a letter arrived at the cottage from the Edmonton law firm of Maclean, Short and Kane. Addressed to the premier, it announced "We have been instructed to commence action against you for damages for seduction of Miss Vivian MacMillan." Brownlee's response to this bombshell was typically stoic. He immediately hired two prominent Calgary lawyers to represent him, and then left for Ottawa to work on the Royal Commission on Banking and Currency. With his private life presumably in some turmoil, Brownlee spent

his time drafting the structure of the nation's new central bank, the Bank of Canada. What, if anything, can be read into Brownlee's apparently unruffled response to allegations he had seduced MacMillan is just one of many questions that remain unanswered concerning Alberta's most famous and lurid political scandal.

MacMillan was the daughter of the mayor of Edson. Through her father she had met the premier on a couple of occasions before moving to Edmonton in the summer of 1930 to enrol in a secretarial course at Alberta College. According to testimony at the trial, the move had been

Vivian MacMillan with her parents, Allan and Letha Maude. They first met the premier when their daughter was a 16-year-old Girl Guide.

encouraged by Brownlee, who had befriended the 18-year-old and eventually secured her a job with the provincial government. According to MacMillan, it was the beginning of a three-year affair in which she had been a reluctant participant.

At the trial Vivian MacMillan was shown to be inconsistent on a number of facts, and plain wrong on others. The premier denied all her allegations, and his wife, Florence, and a number of other witnesses provided spirited testimony in his defence. In his instructions to the jury, Acting Chief Justice William Ives (known in legal circles as "Cowboy Billy") noted the circumstantial nature of the case against Brownlee: "The story of the female plaintiff is wholly and entirely unsupported by any other evidence..." In fact Ives had disallowed the testimony of three women who might have corroborated some of MacMillan's story, but in any event after five hours of sometimes heated deliberation the jury decided there was substance to the young woman's basic allegation. It found that the premier had indeed seduced MacMillan in 1930, and awarded her damages of $10,000 and her father (also a plaintiff) $5,000. Judge Ives refused to accept the verdict, on the grounds it was unsupported by evidence, and dismissed the MacMillan's case, awarding costs to the premier.

Appeals and counter-appeals would continue until 1940, with the $10,000 judgement against Brownlee finally being upheld (MacMillan's father ran out of money and dropped his appeal). But by that time there were no winners in a case which had mesmerized Albertans for months, headlining the newspapers day after day. The trial effectively ruined both Brownlee and MacMillan. The premier had resigned as soon as the original jury verdict came down. He eventually became president of United Grain Growers, and later practiced law with his son, Alan, but his public life was over. He died in 1961. Vivian MacMillan received scant sympathy. She went home to Edson, worked as a store clerk, and married twice before moving to Arizona in 1959 for health reasons. She died in 1980 and is buried in Calgary.

Premier John Brownlee golfing at Edmonton's Mayfair Golf Course in the spring of 1930. Within months he would be embroiled in a court case that would destroy his own reputation and contribute to the demise of Alberta's second political dynasty.

Glenbow Archives ND-3-5136b

The most stunning outcome of the Brownlee trial was Albertans' rejection of the UFA. The Depression proved to be the downfall of most governments across Canada, and eventually might also have seen off the competent and successful Brownlee administration. But in Alberta the combination of economic woes and sordid scandal produced the second of those momentous political shifts which have marked the province's history. In sweltering heat at the provincial election of August 22nd, 1935, not a single UFA candidate came close to being elected.

The party which had governed Alberta for 14 years was swept away, not by the opposition Liberals (who confidently expected to win 45 seats), but by a radical new political movement led by William Aberhart, a Calgary school principal and founder of the Calgary Prophetic Bible Institute. Armed with a wacky economic theory devised by British engineer Maj. Clifford H. Douglas, Aberhart's movement promised a "social credit" of $25-a-month to every adult to pay for necessities such as food and shelter. In the midst of the Great Depression it was the straw many were looking for, and Aberhart's Social Credit party took 56 of 63 seats in the 1935 election. Alberta had elected the most controversial government in the country's history.

Aberhart immediately had a pressing problem. Providing adult Albertans with a $25-a-month handout would cost the province $170 million a year, roughly six times total government revenues. There was not enough money in the provincial treasury to meet the civil service payroll, and $15 million in government bonds would come due by the spring of 1936. Alberta was bankrupt. The Socreds' immediate answer to the problem would have appeared predictable and conventional to Albertans in the late 20th century. The Aberhart government fired civil servants and raised taxes. The budget of February 1936 raised personal and corporate income taxes, imposed a 2% sales tax on all but essential items, raised the provincial levy on land, and hiked taxes on beer and liquor (which were now distributed by the province). It was not enough.

On April 1st Alberta became the only province ever to default on a bond issue. Other Alberta securities were promptly delisted by major exchanges around the world and borrowing money became a near impossibility for the province. So at the end of May the province retaliated by arbitrarily cutting in half the interest paid on all Alberta bonds, debentures and other

William Aberhart with his two daughters, Ola and Jean, on holiday in California in 1925. Few would have guessed that he would lead the next political revolution and become the most controversial premier in the province's history.

securities. Politically, Aberhart and the Socreds were promoted as the champions of the suffering West in its struggle with "moneyed interests" in the East. Lost in the rhetoric was the plain fact the province was welching on investments made in good faith by many ordinary people - Albertans among them.

In August 1936 the Aberhart government launched it's most famous, or infamous, fiscal policy. It issued $500,000 in "prosperity certificates" or scrip. For the notes to remain valid the holder had to buy a weekly stamp (sold for 1 or five cents at provincial offices) which was to be affixed to the back. After two years valid notes could be redeemed for regular $1 or $5 bills. To get the scrip into circulation they would be issued as pay, or part-pay, to provincial and municipal employees.

The Social Credit government's prosperity certificates - more commonly know as scrip or "funny money" - first appeared towards the summer in 1936. Former Edmonton mayor James Douglas posed for this publicity photo in which he is using scrip in a city store. The scheme was not a success, and the government redeemed the scrip the following spring.

The government would effectively be borrowing $500,000 at no interest, and the stamps would pay for the cost of printing and administration. The problem was that only Ottawa could issue legal tender, and those using the scrip had to believe that a bankrupt government which had just defaulted on other obligations would at some point redeem the certificates with real money. When it was revealed that the province itself would not accept scrip in payment of taxes or at government liquor stores, the plan was doomed.

The province's four largest municipalities, Calgary, Edmonton, Lethbridge and Medicine Hat, eventually petitioned the government to abandon the scheme. On April 1st, 1937, it did just that, offering to redeem any certificates still outstanding. As it turned out, less than half the original $500,000 had ever been used and only about $12,000 remained in circulation. Many of those were never turned in. No doubt some were kept for sentimental reasons, but ironically Alberta's "funny money" became more popular, and valuable, as a tourist curiosity than it ever had as currency. Visitors paid as much as $5 for a $1 scrip, and as they became increasingly rare the value went up - and up. By the end of the 20th century certificates in good condition and with at least one stamp could fetch $450. More stamps made it more valuable.

The Aberhart government continued to struggle to find the "magic of Social Credit". It passed legislation to control banks, and opened its own - called Treasury Branches. It sought to censor newspapers, regulated wages, and imposed price controls on just about everything bought and sold in the province. Laws were passed to prevent foreclosure on farms. The government also defaulted on one bond issue after another. As a result, reporters from newspapers across Canada and as far away as New York and London jammed the Legislature's press gallery. Alberta's Social Credit revolution was an international story, and deploring the government's activities became the almost daily preoccupation of editorial writers all over the country.

The Accurate News and Information Act effectively put Alberta's newspapers under government control and ignited an all-out war between the Aberhart government and the press. "The newspapers who are the mouthpiece of the financiers persist in publishing falsities that are entirely unfair and untrue," argued the premier. "They determined to confuse all whom they can beguile into reading their spurious articles and they want to give Alberta a black eye in the sight of the world." To say the relationship between press and government had become poisoned would have been a gross understatement. "A majority of the newsmen in the press gallery believed that the telephones in our workroom were tapped," wrote *Calgary Herald* reporter Fred Kennedy. "We had learned long ago to keep all documents related to covering the Legislative Assembly locked away in our desks. At the hotel I was confident that my room was being entered at times by people other than the chambermaids." And Kennedy was the only reporter the premier actually trusted.

All of this provoked widespread opposition to the government, with protest rallies drawing thousands of people, and membership of the Social Credit movement dropped by almost half. Yet there was no doubt that Socred loyalists

A Bennett Buggy near Dapp, Alberta. This improvised method of transportation - the horse-drawn automobile - was particularly popular among farmers when they could no longer afford gasoline. Named after Prime Minister R.B. Bennett, the buggy defined the era.

Glenbow Archives NA-2497-21

still believed in the "magic" of its economic philosophy with a fervour that can only be described as religious. By 1939 four years of chaotic, confrontational government had polarised Albertans as never before and the pundits confidently predicted that a looming provincial election would bring an end to the Social Credit experiment. But the world was changing, and Alberta with it. By the fall of 1939 Germany had invaded Poland and Canada was once again at war.

The first term of Social Credit government had been ruinous. The province had defaulted on every bond issue that had come due, government debt stood at $129 million, with $12 million in unpaid interest, and Alberta's reputation as a place to invest had been ruined. Almost all of the government's important legislation had been thrown out by the courts, the newspapers were virtually unanimous in their condemnation. As for Premier Aberhart, he admitted to his radio audience "I'm dead, but I won't lie down."

Perhaps Albertans appreciated that stubborn streak. There were certainly still many who were willing to accept the belief at the heart of Socred philosophy: that Ottawa, the banks, and the railways were the cause of Alberta's problems. And in addition to the increased unity of Albertans in the face of war, there was also a growing belief that the economic hard times were, at long last, coming to an end. Whatever the reason, the election when it finally came (on March 21st, 1940), was the closest in the province's history. It took 19 days to sort out the results, but when the dust settled the Socreds still held 36 of the Legislature's 57 seats - 10 by less than 200 votes.

The war would quickly replace provincial politics as the major concern of Albertans and the media, and the second Social Credit government was positively docile compared to its tumultuous first term in office. Yet Aberhart was to be subjected to one more public slight by his opponents. Every premier who had won a second term in office had been granted an honorary Doctor of Laws degree by

Calgarian R.B. Bennett visiting the city's Junior Red Cross hospital school for long term patients. After a lifetime of public service Bennett achieved his goal of political leadership, but the times conspired against the first Albertan to become prime minister.

the University of Alberta, and in 1941 the university informed Aberhart that he would be so honoured after delivering the convocation address. Friends bought the premier a gown, and he set about writing his speech. But the university had not reckoned on the animosity of its Calgary senators, who convinced all but one of their colleagues to deny the honour. Among Socred partisans this was seen as yet another blatant example of establishment bias, and the following year they exacted revenge. Most of the senate's powers were transferred to a new board of university governors.

But by now Aberhart's health was failing, he was careworn and perpetually tired. As he left for a family visit to B.C. in the spring of 1943, he told Socred colleague Alf Hooke, "Alf, I did not know a man could feel as weak as I do and still walk around. I am looking forward to a little rest at the coast." He would not return. He died in Vancouver on May 23rd, of liver and kidney failure, at the age of 64. In death, as in life, he would remain a controversial figure. His family, deeply embittered by the criticism heaped upon him in Alberta over the years, rejected the government's plans for a state funeral and buried him in Vancouver.

Aberhart's governments built roads, laid the foundations of a public

The co-op store in Bluesky, east of Fairview in the Peace River area. By the 1930s every town had its co-op store. This one shipped milk and cream to the city.

health-care system, overhauled the province's schools, improved labour laws, and staunchly defended those hardest hit by the Great Depression. But perhaps his most lasting impact was in consolidating Alberta's image as the perennial bad boy of Confederation, constantly at odds with conventional wisdom, and opposed to the creeping extension of Ottawa's political and economic power that would come to dominate so much of the national agenda during the remainder of the 20th century. Aberhart's contrariness lives on as almost the default position of Alberta governments, and indeed has become deeply ingrained in the provincial psyche. One can only imagine he would approve of that.

The Ottawa bureaucracy that everyone came to love

SCIENCE, POLITICAL WILL AND THE HARD WORK OF MANY ALBERTA FARMERS EVENTUALLY RESCUES FROM DESERT A HUGE SWATH OF SOUTHERN PRAIRIE

By the end of the 1930s some 96,000 settlers had abandoned southern Alberta's drylands. The extraordinary reclamation of 77,000 square miles of drought-ravaged land stretching along the U.S. border from southwest Manitoba to Calgary and Lethbridge began in 1935 with the establishment of Prairie Farm Rehabilitation Administration (PFRA) by the Bennett government. Originally planned as a temporary measure, the PFRA was so successful with irrigation projects and the promotion of dryland farming techniques that it became permanent in 1939 and went on to become one of the most effective and practical organizations ever created by Ottawa. It took science, political will and the hard work of thousands of farmers, but the PFRA eventually rescued from desert the entire

Palliser Triangle. Leading the PFRA assault in southern Alberta was Asael E. Palmer, superintendent of the experimental station at Lethbridge.

In his book, *When the Winds Came*, Palmer recounted one typical story of the time; the saving of Alex Flanagan's farm at Hutton, southeast of Drumheller. When Palmer offered to reclaim his farm, Flanagan said he'd already given up. "There's nothing to be done. I've tried everything during the last four years and the soil moves with every breath of wind and cuts off any plant growth that may have started." But with encouragement and the offer of help, the farmer agreed to try again. Before planting spring rye, Palmer advised him

One of the many experimental farming practices in the 1930s involved creating windbreaks with hemp - or marijuana. Mrs. H.E. Spencer is shown here against the backdrop of a hemp windbreak near Warwick, Alberta.

to prepare the fields, 10 acres at a time starting on the wind-ward side of his farm, by ploughing up the hard subsoil under the drifting piles of dust. After seeding, he was to spread a scattering of straw or "trash cover" over the ploughed land, which prevented further drifting. With the help of his son and brother, Flanagan did as he was asked. The soil held, and a heavy shower allowed the rye to germinate. While most crops in the district continued to fail, Flanagan's rye stood waist high. When he harvested he left the stubble high enough to protect the soil, and the following year sowed crested wheatgrass - raising a good crop of hay. Flanagan's farm was on the way back, and as more and more farmers adopted the PFRA techniques, so were Alberta's drylands.

Farmers who moved from Alberta's bone-dry south to the Peace River country in search of water sometimes got more than they bargained for. In 1934 this boy is shown paddling a cattle trough across the yard of the Sheridan Lawrence ranch near Fort Vermillion.

The 2nd Canadian Division sails for Britain from Halifax
in August 1940. On board the unidentified ship were
the Calgary Highlanders and the 20th Field Battery
from Lethbridge. For obvious reasons, sailing orders for
Canadian troop ships were kept deeply secret.

National Archives of Canada PA-11497

CHAPTER SEVEN

The war that united Alberta

A NEW AND MORE TERRIBLE CONFLICT THREATENS BRITAIN
AND ALBERTANS ARE ONCE AGAIN CALLED UPON TO SERVE

On the morning of Friday, September 1st, 1939, Albertans awoke to discover Europe once again engulfed by war and the senior Dominion expected to rally to the side of the Motherland. That Canada would do that was never in doubt, but conspicuously absent was the unbridled enthusiasm that had greeted the onset of the Great War, a mere quarter century earlier. Albertans in 1939 harboured fewer illusions about the world and life in general. Even if you were inclined to forget that the country was still paying off the $20 billion debt incurred in fighting the last war, its human toll was still all too evident among the thousands who had returned home with permanent physical and mental scars.

Canada was even less apt to entertain the possibility of war than Britain or France. In addition to the pervasive desire for peace, many Canadians now inclined towards the isolationist, American view that Europe's wars should be left to Europeans. The prime minister, William Lyon Mackenzie King spoke for many Canadians in 1935: "The idea that every 20 years this country should automatically and as a matter of course take part in a war overseas for democracy or self-determination of other small nations, that a country that has all it can do to run itself should feel called upon to save, periodically, a continent that cannot run itself... seems to many a nightmare and sheer madness."

It was indeed a great deal to ask, but by the end of the 1930s it seemed inevitable it would come to that. Allan MacDonald was a law student at the University of Alberta during those years. and his views - like those of many Albertans - had gradually changed. "In the early 1930s I signed the peace pledge, and wasn't going to fight in any war, because war was unjustified and wars were whomped up by the money barons for their own good. But by 1937, as I grew up a little more, I realized that Hitler was a terrible menace." Macdonald was not alone in that realization. The prime minister's opposition to war evaporated, and in Alberta Premier William Aberhart told reporters, "Canada's place is beside the Mother Country and the Empire in this struggle... This is a war for the preservation of democracy." The belief that this was indeed a just war and unavoidable would come to define the second great conflict of the 20th century and forge a steely determination to see it through — whatever the cost.

Many Albertans joined the war effort for more practical reasons. As in 1914, the onset of recruiting coincided with poor economic times and limited job opportunities. For some, donning a uniform meant security and three square meals a day. "In those days it was so difficult to make any money, just to buy groceries with," recalled Bentley's Bert Baker. "So I decided to join the Navy and I would be well fed, taken care of. And I was. Oh, the glamour of it all. It was glamorous to be a naval seaman. It was great... until we got overseas and got to war."

That the Second World War brought an end to the Great Depression is not in doubt. The numbers tell the story. In the spring of 1939 there were 61,000 Albertans on relief. A year later that had been reduced to less than 40,000, and by the spring of 1941 the number was barely 4,500.

If Albertans in 1939 had a much better idea of what they were in for than they had in 1914, it didn't have a noticeable impact on recruitment. That was just as brisk as it had been 25 years earlier. By war's end 78,000 Alberta men and 4,500 women had entered the armed forces. At 43% of the eligible age group of men, this was only marginally lower than it had been during the Great War. Of the first two Canadian divisions (40,000 men) raised in 1939, two regiments came from Alberta: the Edmonton Regiment and the Calgary Highlanders. Before the end of the year, the Edmontons were en route to Britain. Two armoured regiments were later also raised in Alberta;

Glenbow Archives NA-2864-3448qqq

Two 17-year-old recruits, Ivan Gould (left) and Richard Theriault, are sworn in at Calgary. The two recruiting officers look sceptical, but a lot of 16 and 17-year-old Albertans ended up in uniform.

the South Alberta Regiment and the Calgary Regiment - known as the Calgary Tanks. All four units would distinguish themselves in some of the toughest fighting of the war, but that would not come for many months.

At the outbreak of war a number of Albertans were already flying with the British air forces, among them George Walker of Gleichen, who had joined the RAF in 1937. In September 1939 he was co-pilot of a Whitley bomber dropping leaflets over western Germany, urging the people to rise up against Hitler. He went on to win the Distinguished Flying Cross (DFC) before being shot down over Germany and spending the rest of the war in a POW camp. Also flying over Europe that fall was Hiram Peter "Cowboy" Blatchford, son of a former mayor of Edmonton (after whom the city's original airport was named). On October 17th, flying one of the early Spitfire fighters, Blatchford brought down a German bomber off the Yorkshire coast - the first enemy plane to be destroyed by a Canadian.

The RAF's 242 Squadron, made up largely of Canadian pilots, destroyed 30 German aircraft in the skies over France in the spring of 1940, before being evacuated ahead of a seemingly unstoppable German invasion. They left behind 20-year-old pilot Donald MacQueen of Drumheller, who was killed in action on June 9th, 1940. Calgary's Willie McKnight, also with 242 Squadron, shot down 10 German planes while defending British and French troops around Dunkirk.

As the four-month Battle of Britain began about 80 Canadians were already flying with the RAF, many with 242 Squadron. They were commanded by the legendary Douglas Bader, who had fought his way back to active duty despite losing both legs in a plane crash. The no-nonsense, upper crust Bader initially didn't think much of these scruffy looking colonials with a reputation

There was a good deal less jingoism in 1939 than there had
been in 1914, and this time Albertans knew what they were
in for. Nevertheless, the bond with Britain was still very strong.
This tiny patriot was photographed in Edmonton.

Provincial Archives of Alberta KA-26/3

A parade through Edmonton in 1940 of the various branches of the armed forces, including a contingent of sailors. Some 7,400 Albertans served in the navy, and many saw action in the grim and pivotal Battle of the Atlantic.

for wildness, but after he discovered they'd lost all their kit in the evacuation from France he handed out his own shirts and opened an account for the boys with a local tailor. In one famous action on August 30 1940, the 242nd took on a force of German bombers and about 30 escorting fighters, destroying a dozen enemy aircraft, damaging others, and forcing the retreat of the rest. Bader and his wingman, Willie McKnight, accounted for five of the downed planes.

Twenty Canadian pilots were killed during the Battle of Britain, including a number of Albertans. Willie McKnight survived and is credited with destroying 21 enemy aircraft (twice winning the DFC), before being shot down over the English Channel in January 1941. (After the war Bader visited Calgary to honour his young comrade, and the city's McKnight Boulevard is named after the graduate of Crescent Heights High School.) Cowboy Blatchford survived until May 3rd, 1943. Leading an attack on a power plant in occupied Holland, his fighter was badly damaged and he was forced to ditch in the North Sea. His body was never recovered.

In the North Atlantic, danger came very early for some
Albertans. On the very first night of the war, without
warning, a German U-boat torpedoed the Canadian passenger liner *Athenia*. On board were Mrs. James Orr of
Calgary and her baby daughter, Margaret. "I was not particularly frightened," Orr later told the *Calgary Herald*. "I
felt that if my time had come to die, I was ready, and then,
having Margaret to look after calmed me." She managed
to clamber with her baby into a damaged lifeboat, and
spent the night on the frigid ocean helping other women
to bail with purses and shoes. Orr and Margaret were
eventually rescued and returned to Glasgow. After several
weeks they made another trans-Atlantic crossing, this one
uneventful, and returned home.

*Three Albertans who survived the
sinking of HMCS Athabaskan on
April 29, 1944. They are (left to
right) Donald W. Newman, Petty
Officer William Frees, and
Clarence Statz.*

Early in the war the Royal Canadian Navy took responsibility for convoy security in the western sector of the North Atlantic. It was a role for which it was poorly equipped and barely trained.
About the only thing the navy did not lack was enthusiasm. At the outbreak of war the RCN had
six destroyers, four minesweepers and a motley collection of small craft. In 1940 Ottawa ordered
the building of a fleet of corvettes, originally designed as coastal patrol vessels. Weighing less than
1,000 tons and armed with depth charges and four-inch guns, these sturdy little ships would
become the backbone of RCN operations against German U-boats during the Battle of the Atlantic.

German submarines hunted in what came to be known as wolf packs, lining up across the
path of a convoy. "Wolf pack was right," recalled Calgary sailor Ossie Hodges. In October 1941 he
was part of a convoy escort led by the destroyer HMCS *Columbia*. "There were so many of them.
We were lucky to stay afloat. We'd go to move to the left, and there would be, not one, but a line
of subs pointing right for us. We'd try the other side - same thing. We managed to run through, I

A group of Calgary Highlanders at the city's Mewata Armouries. The regiment was among the first to be shipped to Britain, in August 1940. Many would not see Alberta again until the war was over.

don't know how." Six merchant ships and the Royal Navy corvette *Gladiolus* were not so lucky.

Some 7,400 Albertans would serve in the RCN (and others in the Royal Navy), and the province's newspapers made much of the "Prairie sailor" phenomenon. A headline in the *Calgary Herald* in 1940 announced "Best Sailors Come From Prairies. Never Saw The Sea, But They're Willing To Learn." Commodore Vic Henning of Edmonton thought it might have had something to do with the "similarity between the undulating wheat fields and the sea." Whatever it was, naval uniforms, which had been a rarity in Alberta before the war, now became common. Although Henning recalled that the first time he wore his uniform in Edmonton a child asked: "Gee, mister, are you a member of the Salvation Army?"

Perhaps Canada's single greatest contribution to the war effort, and certainly the most expensive, was the British Commonwealth Air Training Plan, founded at the end of 1939 to train aircrew

for the Allied forces. At airfields across the Prairies, pilots, navigators, gunners, wireless operators and other aircrew - more than 131,000 in all - were trained for combat. They came from every corner of the empire (Britain, Australia, New Zealand, South Africa, Fiji, India), from occupied Europe (Poland, France, Belgium, Norway), and prior to Pearl Harbor included almost a thousand volunteers from the U.S. But by far the largest contingent was from Canada itself: an incredible 72,835. By 1945 fully one quarter of the aircrew strength of the British and Commonwealth air forces would be Canadian. The cost of training all these men would top $2 billion, with Canada footing almost three-quarters of the total bill - an enormous effort from a country of just 11 million people.

A dance for airmen of the Commonwealth Air Training Plan in a hangar at Calgary Airport. Tens of thousands of young fliers were trained at airfields across the Prairies, including many in Alberta.

The Canadian catastrophe at Dieppe

POOR INTELLIGENCE AND A SURPRISE AT SEA BY GERMAN SHIPS LEAD TO THE WORST DAY OF THE WAR FOR CALGARY'S TROOPS

For Canadians, the hit-and-run attack on the French port of Dieppe on August 19th, 1942, remains the most controversial action of the war. If there were convincing military reasons for the assault, they have never been made public. But there were certainly political reasons. The Allies were under intense pressure from the Russians to make at least a token attack on German-occupied Western Europe, and after two years in Britain the Canadian army was lobbying for a more active role in the war. The result was a plan for a nine-hour raid on Dieppe, led by 5,000 troops of the Canadian 2nd Division, among them the Calgary Highlanders and the Calgary Tanks, supported by

British commandos and a small force of U.S. Rangers

The assault was marred by faulty intelligence and bad luck. As the ships carrying the Canadians approached the French coast they encountered a German convoy. Six Allied vessels were sunk in the skirmish, but worse still the gunfire could be heard by the defenders of Dieppe and the element of surprise was lost. Delayed by the action at sea, the troops landed in broad daylight in front of the waiting German guns, which had a clear sweep of the beach. Only half the Calgary tanks made it ashore, the rest either being destroyed at the water's edge or trapped aboard damaged landing vessels. The steep beach itself, made up of deep layers of stones,

National Archives of Canada PA-113248

Survivors of the ill-fated raid on Dieppe scramble up scaling nets to get aboard a rescue vessel (above). As the last one sailed away from the French coast, some 2,000 Canadians were left behind. Those who were successfully evacuated to Britain (opposite page) were the lucky ones.

was quite unlike anything the Canadians had trained on and proved a formidable obstacle to the tanks landing in support of the infantry. That 16 tanks made into the town was a minor miracle in itself.

The scene on the beach was one of absolute carnage. "Anything I saw in the last war - and I saw plenty - not in the slightest can compare with this," reported medical officer Capt. L.G. Alexander of Calgary. "A combination of fire from every direction, both sides, in front, behind, above - and from every conceivable type of weapon." He was awarded the Military Cross for his bravery in treating the wounded under fire. Cpl. J.A. Gregory of Calgary, another Great War veteran, lost an eye and was wounded in the arm during the fighting. "I was all through the last war, at Vimy and Passchendaele, but I never saw anything to match the terrific fight at Dieppe."

The withdrawal began at 11 a.m. Under intense German fire some of the rescue boats were sunk and others forced to retreat. Almost 2,000 Canadians watched as the last over-loaded boat departed. Of the 5,000 troops who had left Dover early that morning, 907 were dead and hundreds

more wounded. In the air the RAF and RCAF had lost 119 aircraft, more than on any other day of the war, including during the Battle of Britain. At sea the toll was one destroyer and 30 other vessels lost. Among the lists of dead and missing were more than 100 Albertans, some two dozen from the Stettler area alone. Worst hit were the men of the Calgary Tanks, only three of whom returned to England. All in all, 1,946 Canadians were marched into captivity from the debacle at Dieppe.

The Allied commander during the assault, Lord Louis Mountbatten said later: "I have no doubt that the battle of Normandy was won on the beaches of Dieppe. For every one man who died at Dieppe in 1942, at least 10 or more must have been spared in Normandy in 1944." A great grandson of Queen Victoria and cousin of Queen Elizabeth, Mountbatten later served as Allied commander in Southeast Asia, and as the last colonial governor in India. A respected public figure in Britain, he was - understandably - less popular in Canada. Mountbatten was killed in an IRA terrorist bombing in 1979.

An Edmonton Junior Chamber of Commerce salvage campaign sponsored by Canada Packers. On the home front people did whatever they could to support the war effort.

Two posters from the myriad of publicity campaigns which exhorted Canadians to support the troops, stay healthy and above all waste absolutely nothing. The country had never before experienced such a level of government regulation and control.

Loyal citizens
do not hoard

RATIONED
SUGAR ½ lb. a week PER PERSON
TEA ½ of the usual PURCHASE
COFFEE ¾ of the USUAL PURCHASE

Meat, sugar, tea, coffee and, above all, gasoline, came under tight wartime controls. Rationing in Alberta was never as tight or prolonged as in Britain, but at least in the cities ration books became a way of life.

The Great War had for the first time united Canadians in a national undertaking, and 25 years later the response was, if anything, more prodigious. In the words of historian Desmond Morton (*A Military History of Canada*, Hurtig Publishers, Edmonton, 1985), the entire country was "directed, regulated, rationed and exhorted" to a degree unimagined in the pre-war years. Unemployment was a fading memory and thousands of women joined the workforce to replace those in uniform. There were programs to round up metal, rubber, fat and bones (to make explosives and glue). It was the greatest recycling effort in Canadian history. Everything from Great War souvenir helmets and shell casings, to cooking pots and wrought iron railings were collected for the war effort. Calgary, Edmonton, Ponoka and Drumheller donated ancient field guns from city parks. One patriotic Edmonton police officer donated 137 antique guns. By the end of 1943, Alberta grain elevator agents had collected from farmers nearly 60,000 tons of scrap metal - everything from tractors to woodstoves.

But what Ottawa needed most was money, and it came up with some remarkably successful ways to raise it. The 25-cent War Savings Stamps were affordable for almost everyone, and a huge hit. Children were encouraged to buy them with their allowances, adults gave them as Christmas stocking stuffers, and they were popular door prizes at a host of community events. The more expensive Victory Bonds could be bought in denominations of $50, $100 or $1,000, and raised $12 billion by war's end. When they were offered for sale, in many Alberta communities - Turner Valley, Raymond, Innisfree and Pincher Creek - they were oversubscribed on the first day. Through nine bond campaigns, Lethbridge was the national per-capita leader no less than five times. To encourage bond sales Calgary's Palliser Hotel broadcast Hitler's ranting speeches over its public address system, and it worked.

There were all manner of campaigns to support the beleaguered mother country: Seeds for

By September 1940 the German blitzkrieg across Europe made the fall of Britain seem possible, followed perhaps by a direct attack on Canada. Alberta was a long way from the action, but that didn't stop the authorities from conducting mock "decontamination" drills - like this one in Edmonton - to prepare for the possibility of a gas attack.

Provincial Archives of Alberta P-5875

Britain, Milk for Britain, Jam for Britain, and even an Overseas Cigarette Fund — all financed from donations, bake sales, whist drives, raffles, dances and concerts. Cities like Red Deer and Lethbridge adopted the warships that bore their names, collecting all manner of home comforts for their crews. Calgary raised $24,480 to buy 272 depth charges for HMCS *Calgary*. Edmontonians raised enough to buy a $25,000 Spitfire fighter, and in 1944 adopted an entire RCAF squadron (to celebrate the occasion Flying Officer Lefty Miller, a former *Edmonton Journal* paper boy, bombed a German airfield with a copy of the newspaper wrapped in a brick).

Ross Munro of the Canadian Press (later editor of the *Journal*) and the *Calgary Herald*'s Dick Sanburn brought news of the war to Albertans. But for the first time radio, and in particular the newsreels at the movie theatres, brought the sounds and sights of warfare to the home front. BBC

radio news reports were rebroadcast to Canadians, including the defiant and pugnacious speeches of Winston Churchill: "We shall fight on the beaches... we shall fight in the fields and in the streets. We shall never surrender." In the early years of the war, when the news was invariably bad, CBC announcer Lorne Greene (later of *Bonanza* fame) earned the nickname The Voice of Doom. War correspondents like the CBC's Matthew Halton, a Pincher Creek native, became household names with their reports from Europe.

And perhaps more than any conflict before or since, this one became synonymous with music. Whether it was Vera Lynn's *We'll Meet Again*, Bing Crosby's *White Christmas*, or Glenn Miller's *In the Mood*, music permeated the war years. Between the outbreak of war in 1939 and August 1940, sheet music and record sales in Alberta doubled. Like the movies, music provided a welcome distraction from the news, the casualty lists, and for those with loved ones in the forces the ever-present fear of a telegram and a visit from a military chaplain or local minister.

It was also a time of shortages. Some were predictable. Metal, rubber, and cloth were all in short supply, as were silk (used for parachutes) and gasoline. But some shortages needed explanation. Dentists became hard to find (many were in uniform), and even if you could find one treatment might be limited because most dentist's drills came from Britain. Teacups without handles suddenly appeared in the stores. There was a shortage of manpower and they were much quicker to manufacture. The same was true of bakeries, which had plenty of flour but few bakers and so switched to the production of basic, unsliced bread.

The rationing of gasoline was a particular irritant for a society already becoming car-dependent. Mike Sokolosky of Castor claimed to have developed a carburetor which would reduce consumption to 125-miles-to-the-gallon, while an Edmonton mechanic went one better and rigged his car to run on natural gas, claiming 200 miles for 38 cents. In the spring of 1942 a nationwide 40-mile-an-hour speed limit came into effect as a method of reducing gas consumption, and within a matter of weeks had reduced Alberta traffic accidents by 50%. That same year, with gas and tires increasingly difficult to obtain, a Calgary doctor came up with a novel idea for saving fuel. Rather than driving to house calls, he hired a secretary and allowed patients to make an appointment to see him at his office. It was an idea which would catch on.

For some Albertans in uniform the reality of the war meant long periods, sometimes years, as prisoners in old German or Austrian military camps. Their lives were characterized by boredom, hunger, and the occasional glimpse of the proceeding war. Manny Raber of Medicine Hat parachuted out of his burning bomber over Belgium in October 1943, and spent months hiding with the Belgian resistance before being captured by the Gestapo in early 1944. At a transit camp near Frankfurt, Raber and other prisoners found themselves on the receiving end of an Allied bombing raid. "Some of the bombs were dropping so close that we could feel the heavy shelter shudder and shake," he later recalled. "A particularly close explosion extinguished all the candles and collapsed a portion of the shelter. Two airmen were killed and several injured in... the longest 40 minutes of my life." When Raber and the surviving prisoners were marched through the rubble of Frankfurt, angry Germans "waved blood-stained sheets and started to thrown bricks at us."

There were also continual efforts to escape, which was considered the duty of all imprisoned officers. The most famous of these, the subject of ex-POW Paul Brickell's 1951 book, *The Great Escape*, and the still-popular 1963 movie of the same name, was a mass escape from prison camp Stalag Luft III on March 24th, 1944. The tunnelling was masterminded by a Canadian, Wally Flood, and the escape attempt involved a number of Albertans, including Edmontonian Gord King, and Calgarians Barry Davidson and Henry Birkland. "We successfully dug a tunnel, [perhaps] the longest ever dug," recalled King in a 1999 interview. It was 40 feet deep and 376 feet long. "It had electricity and lights... There was an air pumper made of kit bags, and it would pump air through a pipe made of coffee tins. My job was to pump this thing."

King and Davidson were among the 124 POWs discovered in the tunnel when a guard saw steam rising from the exit hole and raised the alarm. They were punished by being made to stand naked in the cold for hour after hour, all the time expecting to be shot. But the two survived, while many of the 76 who made it out of the tunnel did not. Only three eventually made their way to safety, 23 were captured and returned to the camp, and 50 were executed by the Gestapo under direct orders from Adolph Hitler. Among them was Calgarian Birkland.

Thousands of American troops arrived in Alberta in 1942 to begin work on a highway to Alaska, which was thought to be threatened by Japanese invasion. Edmonton became the headquarters for the U.S. Northwest Command, with as many as 48,000 American soldiers and civilian employees passing through the city. These American soldiers were photographed at the south end of the city's High Level Bridge, near a sign marking the start of the Alaska Highway.

Provincial Archives of Alberta BL-456/1

Almost 40,000 German prisoners of war were sent to Canada, about half eventually being housed in two large camps at Lethbridge and Medicine Hat. There were several hundred escape attempts, even though it was effectively impossible for the POWs to get out of Alberta. This fleeing prisoner was captured near Taber by a Mountie and members of the Home Guard.

*Rev. J.S. Mulloney of Lethbridge says mass for men of the
1st Canadian Tank Brigade during the campaign in Italy in
1943. The hard-fought Italian campaign was the first-large
scale deployment of Canadian troops in Europe.*

Members of the Loyal Edmonton Regiment help a wounded comrade to an aid station (above). Soldiers of the regiment grab an improvised Christmas dinner in the midst of the street fighting (top right). A crew of the Calgary Tanks take a break from the fighting (bottom right). They are (left to right) Cpl. Mac McWither, Trooper Art Sanford, Capt. G.W. Hamm, Trooper Howard Gill, and Sgt. M.M. McKenzie.

National Archives of Canada PA-114487

In the second major Canadian engagement of the war in Europe, the 1st Canadian Division went ashore at Pachino, Sicily on the morning of July 10th, 1943. Losses were mercifully light, 32 dead and wounded, but it was the beginning of a brutally tough Italian campaign in which Albertans would distinguish themselves over and over again. Over the next two months the Edmonton Regiment was in the forefront of the fighting as the Allies made their way through the rugged Sicilian hills to Messina. It was the Canadian army's first sustained action of the war, and the cost to the Eddies was 54 killed and 108 wounded. The regiment landed on the Italian mainland, at Reggio, on September 3rd, this time accompanied by the Calgary Tanks, their numbers replenished after the catastrophe at Dieppe.

Through the fall the Canadians fought their way up Italy's mountainous spine, with the Alberta units seeing fierce action at Campobasso and Colle d'Anchise. The 1st Canadian Division was ordered to take the Moro River and the town of Ortona, which anchored the eastern end of the heavily-defended German line. At the end of December at Ortona the Loyal Edmonton Regiment (Loyal had been added to its name in recognition of its performance during the first months of the Italian campaign) met the German 1st Parachute Division in one of the most famous and hard-fought battles of the war in Italy. Over Christmas 1943, the fighting raged through the narrow streets and squares of the medieval town. "For some unknown reason," wrote an Associated Press correspondent, "the Germans are staging a miniature Stalingrad in hapless Ortona." Moving forward house by house, the Eddies eventually pushed the German paratroopers into the town's old castle. During the night of December 27th they concentrated their fire on the ruins - and the next morning the enemy was gone. For the Edmonton regiment, the toll at Ortona was 63 killed and 109 wounded.

Also in action in Italy were the men of the 1st Special Service Force (SSF), a unique commando brigade made up of Canadian and American elite troops, many Alberta volunteers among them. The unit was made famous after the war in the movie *The Devil's Brigade* (the name given to it by opposing German troops). The film is a colourful but reasonably accurate account of the assault on a mountain called La Difenza, one of several fortified high points the brigade captured around Monte Cassino.

National Archives of Canada NAC/PA 144106

Among the officers of the brigade was Stan Waters, a University of Alberta undergraduate who left his studies to join the Calgary Tanks. Waters later volunteered for the SSF, and in Italy assumed command of an American brigade after all its senior officers had been killed or wounded (eventually five out of the six SSF battalion commanders were Canadians). In 1973 Waters became commander of the Canadian army, retiring in 1975 as a lieutenant-general. In 1987 he became one of the founders of the Reform Party, and two years later became the only elected senator ever to sit in Canada's upper house. He died of pneumonia in 1991.

In the spring of 1944 the Calgary Tanks took part in the attack on German lines hinged by the fortress-like monastery of Monte Cassino. On May 11th the Albertans attacked in support of the 8th Indian Division, with whom they had trained during the winter. The tanks battered their way across the Gari River and broke through the German lines, but at heavy cost to the Calgary Tanks and the Gurkhas and Pathan infantry of the Indian army. The Indian troops were relieved by the Loyal Eddies and Princess Patricia's Canadian Light Infantry, and in an attack across open fields the Edmonton regiment lost almost as many man as in the entire operation at Ortona. But the German forces were forced to retreat, and on June 4th the Allies reached Rome. The first troops into the liberated city were the Canadians and Americans of The Devil's Brigade.

The Canadians continued the advance through northern Italy with the Eighth Army, the Germans resisting with their usual resolve, until January 1945, when they were ordered to join the rest of the Canadian army in Northwest Europe. In all, 548 Canadians gave their lives during the Italian campaign, many Albertans among them.

Capt. A.W. Hardy of Edmonton, medical officer of the West Nova Scotia Regiment, lies under a tree being tended to by a stretcher-bearer. Hardy was wounded near Santa Christina, Italy.

National Archives of Canada PA-115198

Private H.R. Hansen, of the Loyal Edmonton Regiment, on the outskirts of Ortona. The battle for the town raged over Christmas 1943.

'Everyone worked through the day and night'

ALBERTA WOMEN PLAY A CRUCIAL ROLE AT HOME, AT WORK, AND IN UNIFORM, WHILE THOUSANDS OF WAR BRIDES CROSS THE ATLANTIC TO BEGIN NEW LIVES

German bombing took a heavy toll among the RAF's female air controllers (26 were killed in London during a single raid) and Canadian women trained as operations room staff were in high demand. Phyllis Patterson joined the RCAF in Edmonton and was among an early group of Canadian women to travel to Britain. In New York they boarded the luxury liner *Queen Mary*, which instead of its usual compliment of 2,100 passengers was loaded with 14,000 troops. The great ship was much faster than most other vessels and travelled alone across the submarine-infested North Atlantic, speed its only protection.

"One day the captain informed us that the Germans had announced their sinking of the Queen Mary, so we laughed heartily and felt brave," recalled Patterson. "On the following day the ship lurched sharply, and for a few hours took a zigzag course to lose a submarine that was tracking us. Suddenly we all recognized our vulnerability." The ship travelled far off course to lose its pursuer, and by the time it docked in Britain had nothing but chocolate bars to feed its passengers. "When we docked in Scotland on a dull, rainy afternoon, we heard a thrilling sound, someone singing, lovely and clear, from the dockside. It was Vera Lynn, a tiny figure in a trench coat and beret, standing on the dock in the pouring rain, singing her heart out for us."

Among the Canadians who landed in Normandy after D-Day were nurses of the Royal Canadian Army Medical Corps, hundreds of whom served overseas. Albertan Jessie Morrison later recalled that her unit was issued khaki battle dress and given field training - digging trenches, map reading, and route marches - before being shipped to Arromanches in Normandy in the wake of the D-Day invasion. "That memorable day we were all caught up with the emotion of the event. Strangely, the first thought for all of us was that we wanted to meet together in prayer." Her unit landed wearing full battle dress, minus weapons, and began treating the wounded in an 800-bed field hospital near the ancient city of Bayeux. A few miles from fierce fighting around Caen, she recalled the night sky blazing with shellfire and the ceaseless roar of the guns. "Everyone worked through the day and night until every patient was cared for, and hundreds passed through our hands in a single night," remembered Morrison. They lived on field rations and slept, when there was time, in Boer War tents. Mobile showers came by occasionally, but the nurses usually gave them a pass. "The boys needed them more than we did."

In addition to the women who joined the army, navy and air force, thousands more volunteered to work in munitions, manufacturing and chemical plants, producing everything from shells to aircraft to tanks. In 1942 when Ottawa organized a cross-country registration of unmarried women in their 20s, 45% signed up in Edmonton and Calgary and many were sent to work in central Canada and Vancouver. Thousands of women went to work to replace the men who were in uniform. As the country's main meat processors, Alberta packing plants employed hundreds. As did the dairy industry, which in addition to butter and cheese was converted to the production of huge quantities of powdered egg for Britain. At Edmonton's Great Western Garment Company, the largest manufacturer of military uniforms in the country, almost 90% of the workforce was female.

It was the beginning of a trend. Edmonton hired its first policewomen at the end of 1942, and Calgary soon did likewise. In the fall of the following year the first group of 20 female conductors began work on Edmonton streetcars. As the capital's first and only milk deliverer, 24-year-old Isabel York from Camrose got the same pay as the men she worked with. But for most women that would take another three decades, or longer.

The new competition for female labour made it difficult for Alberta schools, which relied heavily on women teachers, and where the pay was low and the hours long. Many teachers joined the forces, while others found more lucrative employment, and by the middle of the war some 500 schools across the province were seriously understaffed. But the shortage of labour was most acute on the province's farms, where there was no end to the heavy workload women had taken on during the Depression years. Women increasingly took responsibility for keeping family farms going. When Lethbridge dairy farmer Alan Hamilton joined the army in 1942, his 19-year-old daughter, Elaine, took over management of the operation with the help of two younger sisters.

The flow of immigrants to Alberta had been sharply reduced during the Depression, and dried up almost completely during the war years - with one notable exception. During the war Canadians in uniform spent more time away from home than any other Allied servicemen, and during their long sojourn in Britain some 48,000 got married. Between July 1942 and August 1944, 63 British wives and 36 children arrived in Alberta, but as the war drew to a close

Two women cleaning a freight locomotive in Edmonton in 1943. Women took on even the heaviest industrial work, replacing the men who were overseas.

the trickle became a flood as shipload after shipload of war brides, about half with children, crossed the Atlantic to join husbands they hardly knew in an unfamiliar country.

In *Promise Me You'll Take Care of My Daughter*, author Ben Wicks tells the typical story of Iris Hughes, who imagined her new spouse's Alberta farm would be something like those she knew in England, complete with thatched roof and picket fence. "What a culture shock," she remembered later. "The house was of bare boards, banked to the windows with manure and straw to keep the frost out in winter - as it wasn't insulated and every nail hole was as big as a quarter."

Most struggled at first, but with the help of in-laws and neighbours they made the adjustment. Stella Chudleigh's husband, Rufus, had at least given her an unvarnished description of life and climate in Brooks, and she received a warm welcome from his family. "Mom treated me just like another daughter and was very patient with the green, 22-year-old English girl born and raised in town. I soon settled in, in spite of no electricity, gas, or plumbing of any kind. That first summer I had to learn how to wash clothes on a scrub board, clean coal-oil lamps, separate the cream, churn butter, can dozens of jars of fruit and vegetables, and cook on a coal and

wood stove for the hay crews and threshing crews."

For war brides from occupied Europe, Alberta was a haven of peace and security. When her father, a member of the Dutch underground, was captured and sent to a concentration camp, Ann Wood (later of Westlock) took his place. "If the underground took a stand and did some damage, the Germans would just take people off the street and stick them on a tree with a bayonet," she told Wicks. "We had been without food and water a long time when the Allied troops began attacking our city, Nijmegen, early in September 1944. They were bombing and shelling, and as I stuck my nose out of a foxhole a Canadian soldier grabbed me and pushed me back in. That's how I met my husband. Later that month the Canadians took the city, after a long, hard fight, and Ernest stayed through the winter. We had to get three sets of papers, and I married the same guy three times."

War brides and their children gather for a Christmas party at the Salvation Army citadel in Calgary in 1946. Some 48,000 Canadian servicemen were married overseas, and for many of the wives the move to Canada required a considerable adjustment.

Operation Overlord, the D-Day invasion of France, has become a legendary event, the subject of countless books and movies - and rightly so since it changed the course of history and eventually gave birth to a united and peaceful Europe. But often lost in the telling is the fact that Canada was a major player in this momentous undertaking. Fully one fifth of the troops taking part in the invasion were Canadian. Hundreds of Canadian fliers took part in the bombing and reconnaissance missions over France in the weeks preceding D-Day, 16 Canadian minesweepers cleared a path for the invasion fleet, and on the night of June 5th, 1944, the 1st Canadian Parachute Battalion was one of three Allied airborne units which dropped into Normandy to seize bridges, cut communications and create as much disruption as possible.

Fifteen thousand Canadians landed on Juno Beach, and among the first was George Lynch-Staunton of Pincher Creek, an artillery spotter with the 14th Field Regiment (and after the war a provincial court judge). He had barely touched the beach before he was wounded by a German shell, and spent D-Day and the following night lying injured in a shell hole. Eventually rescued and returned to England, he would return to fight in Holland the following winter.

Also among the first Canadians ashore on D-Day was Ronald Sole of Barrhead, a tank driver

Soldiers of the Princess Patricia's Canadian Light Infantry, which included many Albertans, take cover in a field. The enemy positions in front of them are being shelled.

and mechanic with the Fort Garry Horse. The landing craft that delivered Sole and his Sherman tank to Juno Beach was off course and landed three tanks in water 50 feet deep, rather than the 4 feet expected. Sole had insisted on inflating the flotation canvas around his tank, and his vehicle was the only one to make it to shore - where it was quickly disabled by the German guns. "By then our sergeant was wounded and our radio operator was - I guess you could say he was shell-shocked. There was an awful amount of explosions and shellfire." Sole recalled in a 1999 interview.

After abandoning the tank, Sole and his four comrades still had to make it up the beach under withering fire. "I told the others to take the sergeant in and I would draw fire. I jumped to the other side of the tank and the machine gunners started firing at me - I can still see the bullets hitting the water all around." Miraculously, he made it, but he was one of very few from his unit to survive.

Maj. David V. Currie of the South Alberta tank regiment (left-centre with a pistol in hand) supervises the surrender of a group of German soldiers in the little village of St. Lambert-sur-Dives, Normandy. This narrow road was the escape route for the entire German Seventh Army in the retreat from Caen.

"Very few of my C Squadron had landed. My sergeant, I was told, had died, and I learned after the war that we three were the only ones left [alive and unwounded] out of nearly 800 men who had started out." After the war Sole served as a fish and wildlife officer in various places in Alberta, and later farmed in the Evansburg-Drayton Valley area. He retired to Barrhead.

The Calgary Highlanders and the tanks of the South Alberta Regiment were in the thick of the fighting in the two months after D-Day as the Allies attempted to cut off the German retreat from around Caen. As the Allied noose tightened, 19 tanks of the South Albertas, four self-propelled guns and 50 infantry of Canada's Argyll and Sutherland Highlanders moved to block the German retreat at St. Lambert-sur-Dives. For three days the small Canadian force stalled entire German armoured divisions on the narrow road and single bridge leading into the village. When it was over, dozens of tanks and armoured vehicles lay destroyed on the approaches to St. Lambert, 800 enemy troops had been killed or wounded and 2,100 taken prisoner.

As the British and American armies pushed across France towards the River Rhine and Germany, the Canadians were given the less glamorous task of sweeping the Germans from north-west France, Belgium and eventually Holland. In liberated towns and villages they came face to face with the reality of what they were fighting for. James Brady, a Metis soldier from St. Paul, serving with the 50th Battalion of the Royal Canadian Artillery, kept a daily diary throughout the war. On August 27th he wrote: "I talked with a French woman. The SS had whipped her senseless before they left - for no comprehensible reason except a spirit of pure sadism." On September 4th, Brady's unit came across the bodies of civilians shot as suspected members of the resistance. "An RAF bomber crew had been captured by these same SS men. They were hung from trees by their thumbs and shot in the head."

Through the fall of 1944 the Canadians advanced through the battlefields of The Great War, across Flanders, past Ypres, St. Julien and Passchendaele. The ultimate goal was the Belgian port of Antwerp and its approaches through the broad, waterlogged delta where the Scheldt and half a dozen other rivers enter the North Sea. Without control of the port and the patchwork of islands and waterways, the final assault on Germany could not be supplied. The battle for the Scheldt would be one of the most decisive and hard-fought of the war. "It was the worst battleground of the western campaign," war correspondent Ross Munro noted.

During October and November 1944, the Calgary Highlanders and the tanks of the South Alberta's would be in the vanguard of the fighting. In one of their most famous actions of the war, the Highlanders attacked across a narrow causeway which joined the large islands of South Beveland and Walcheren. Over two days of fighting the Calgary regiment suffered heavy losses in attempting to take the heavily-defended causeway, but the assault allowed amphibious landings elsewhere to succeed. A few days later the island was secured and the route to Antwerp was open.

The final Allied assault to push the Germans back across the Rhine, Operation Veritable, began in February, 1945, with the First Canadian Army opening the attack near Nijmegen, Holland. "A great deal of artillery was firing," recalled Frank Holm of the Calgary Highlanders. "We were silent, nervous in anticipation. I believe that after three months of holding positions at the front during the winter, we were genuinely fearful of what was in store for us in this coming offensive. I know I was."

The first major obstacle was a dense forest on the German border known as the Hochwald. Here the tanks of the South Alberta Regiment would encounter the same sort of challenge the Highlanders had faced on the causeway to Walcheren. The goal was a muddy gap through the rolling hills and woodland of the Hochwald, overlooked by heavily fortified German positions. Even light tanks became bogged down in the mud, and so the South Albertas attempted to use a raised railroad embankment that appeared to offer an easier route. "We were now in the open in broad daylight, in sight of the enemy's guns," remembered Trooper David Marshall. "He opened up on us. We could see shells dropping all around, and I never prayed so fervently in all my life. This was the only time in the war that I thought I would not make it." An entire squadron of tanks was destroyed on the embankment. By March 2nd enemy resistance collapsed and the Hochwald was taken, but the South Albertas had lost 61 tanks, their entire strength when the battle had begun.

"It took just over a month for the Canadian Army to clear its sector on the west bank [of the Rhine]," wrote Ross Munro. "This victory at the northern end of the Allied line precipitated the collapse of the entire German front west of the Rhine." The Calgary Highlanders crossed the river on March 29th, and the South Alberta tanks followed

Four Sherman tanks of the South Alberta Regiment's A Troop take a break near the town of Putte in Holland. Towards the end of 1944, the South Alberta's were in the vanguard of the fighting to liberate Holland.

National Archives of Canada PA-132019

Celebrations broke out in communities all over the province at the announcement of the war's end. Above, the streets of downtown Calgary are packed with jubilant crowds.

two days later. There was still fierce resistance in some places, but the war was clearly coming to an end. As British and American forces moved eastwards deeper into Germany, the Canadians were directed north, to liberate the rest of Holland.

The fiercest fighting in these final days came in the ancient city of Groningen, which was full of buildings of historic value. With the war all but won, senior commanders decided not to shell the city and the Calgary Highlanders were sent in to dislodge the SS troops defending it. When the city at last fell, the Highlanders discovered their first task was to protect the German wounded from irate townspeople, enraged after four years of often brutal occupation.

By this time the Loyal Edmonton Regiment and the Calgary Tanks had arrived in Holland to finish the war alongside the other two Alberta units. During April they fought at Voorst, Zutphen and Ede in what Sgt. J.P. Turions of the Loyal Eddies rated as some of the toughest fighting of the war, mopping up stubborn pockets of mostly SS troops who were determined to fight to the last. On April 19th, the high command, anticipating the collapse of German resistance and the end of the war, ordered a halt to all "aggressive action." On May 1st, the *Edmonton Journal* ran its biggest headline of the century: HITLER DEAD. Six days later Germany surrendered, and the war was over.

The victory was bittersweet for the Calgary Highlanders, who had been involved in some of the last fighting of the war (taking their last fatalities at Gruppenbuhren on April 26th). Only 13 men remained from the regiment which had left Calgary in the spring of 1940. The Highlanders had lost a total of 403 killed and 1,354 wounded. One of the 13 originals, Capt. Mark Tennant, said of the moment: "I wanted to get hold of my mother and tell her that I had survived the war. That meant everything to me... None of us knew what we were going back to, we didn't know what we were going to do. But we did know that we had survived." The South Alberta regiment had lost 82 men killed and 339 wounded, a relatively low total considering the fighting it had seen. Regimental historian Donald Graves attributed this to the mental toughness of a tight-knit group of survivors. "The South Albertas never lost its western outlook. Western Canadians tend to be practical, plain-talking people who like to get on with the job."

On August 27th, 1945, gunner James Brady of St. Paul made the final entry in a diary he had kept throughout the war: "Lay in a tulip field and rested for an hour under the stars. What beautiful peace and serenity."

Albertans began returning home from the war, with the first trainloads arriving in June 1945. Some had been away for fully six years, and almost all had been gone for two. Husbands and wives, some of whom had scarcely been married before overseas posting, were reunited. Fathers gazed for the first time on children born after their departure. Older children scanned crowds of soldiers for fathers they scarcely remembered or knew only from photographs. Parents wept in joy for the return of children they feared they would never see again.

Staff Sgt. Dave Shepherd of the Ist Canadian Infantry Brigade had been with the first contingent to leave Calgary in 1939, and was eager to get back to the family hardware business. But he told reporters he had no regrets. "If I had to do it all over again, I would." When the Calgary Highlanders returned home in November they were led along 8th Avenue by their illustrious pipe band. When the last of the Calgary Tanks arrived home on December 2nd, they were met by a cheering crowd of thousands.

There were similar scenes in Edmonton, including a particularly warm welcome for a group of 60 RCAF fliers who returned from captivity in Germany. But the biggest turnout on a rainy Saturday evening in October, was for the arrival of the Loyal Edmonton Regiment. A crowd estimated at 50,000 - half the population of the city - jammed the streets to welcome home the victors of Ortona, with six bands and a floodlit reception in the Market Square (now Sir Winston Churchill Square).

In communities all across the province there were celebrations as their servicemen came home. In November the 17th Light Anti-Aircraft Battery returned to Fort Macleod after six years absence. They had shared a train across the Prairies with the men of Lethbridge's 20th Anti-Tank Battery. Finally, after a long homeward journey over Christmas, the final members of the South Alberta Regiment arrived in Medicine Hat on January 18th, 1946. The city had declared a half-day holiday and crowds of flag-waving children welcomed the men back. The *Medicine Hat News* recorded the numerous political speeches, and also noted that the South Albertas who had already returned home had thoughtfully provided their comrades with "good old Alberta beer."

There was a determination that the end of the wartime economy and the reintegration of 620,000 service personnel into civilian life would be better managed than had been the case after the Great War, and in most instances that was the case. There was a broad public consensus that the veterans of this war must receive better treatment than the many soldiers of 1914-18 who lived and died in poverty and distress. The Veterans' Land Act made farmland available to ex-servicemen (much of it in Alberta), loans were provided to buy homes, and there were programs to assist veterans in completing or augmenting their education. Access to a university education (one month tuition for every month of active service) launched tens of thousands of careers in the professions and business.

Still, the transition to peacetime life - "Civvy Street" as it was popularly known — could be difficult. "Getting used to working again wasn't really hard," Loyal Eddies' veteran J. Bertrand told the *Edmonton Bulletin*. "Everybody was swell to me from the start." He had been seriously wounded in Sicily and had found work as a street railway motorman. The hard part, he said, was "getting used to having a home, a place where you are supposed to stay." Restlessness was common. "I have never been the kind who craved a great deal of excitement, but even I have been restless and found it hard to settle down," reported Harold Gregory, a sergeant with the Seaforth

The children of Hines Creek get caught up in spirit of celebration with their own small parade. For many little ones, war was all they had known.

Provincial Archives of Alberta A-6336

Highlanders. Former air force officer Kenneth Pryor, of Daysland, came up with a solution which suited him. He joined the Edmonton police force and walked more than 30 kms each shift. "That takes care of your restlessness," he said.

In the wake of the world war Alberta's economy would begin a steady climb to prosperity, electricity and telephone service would find its way into every corner of the province, and government services would begin to resemble the support network people would later come to take for granted. But the war worked another remarkable change in Alberta that was all to the good.

The early decades of the century had populated the province's farms and cities with a host of immigrants from beyond the English-speaking world, and until 1939 there had remained a gulf between these newcomers and what was still the established majority. The immigrants had full political and legal rights, and relations between Albertans were, for the most part, cordial. But socially the two groups remained estranged. The war began the final demolition of those barriers as Albertans from varied backgrounds wore the same uniforms and faced the same perils, shoulder to shoulder, regardless of whether they or their parents hailed from Kiev or Birmingham, from Kansas

Provincial Archives of Alberta BL-987/6

or Campania. After 1945, in politics, the arts, and the professions, the unspoken barriers began to disappear. As editor Ted Byfield noted in his foreword to the eighth volume of the original *Alberta In The 20th Century* series, in a peculiar stroke of irony the most destructive war in human history had united Albertans as never before.

That unity would sometimes be sorely tested as the turbulent years ahead strained traditional notions of morality and behaviour. More immediately, in the area south and southwest of the provincial capital, Imperial Oil had spudded no less than 112 dry holes in what seemed to be a fruitless search for oil. But the 113th, a short distance from Leduc, would not be dry. It would, in fact, change the entire course of Alberta history.

Through the winter of 1945-46 Albertans who had served overseas returned to the province in the thousands. Serving so far from home, some had not seen family and friends since the summer of 1940. Cpl. Theodore King gets a warm welcome from his family in Calgary (above). In the capital some 50,000 Albertans were on hand to welcome home the men of the Loyal Edmonton Regiment (left).

The afternoon of February 13, 1947: A crowd gathers around the sump pit of Leduc Number 1 as oil spews from Imperial's new well. Many took jars of "black gold" as souvenirs, but few people would have predicted the dramatic impact the discovery would have on Alberta.

CHAPTER EIGHT

The return of prosperity

THE BABY BOOM AND A NEW AGE OF MATERIALISM
COINCIDE WITH A DRAMATIC DISCOVERY AT LEDUC

The 1950s marked the beginning of a quarter century of sustained economic growth across Canada, the longest such period in the country's history. Canada had prospered before, most notably in the years before the Great War, but now for the first time the vast majority of ordinary citizens could aspire to a level of material wealth undreamed of by previous generations. The population was also growing rapidly, and not simply as a result of the resumption of immigration at the end of the war. An increase in the domestic birth-rate, coupled with advances in medicine and public health that meant almost all children now survived into adulthood, created what would come to be known as the Baby Boom. These dramatic developments would transform Canada, and nowhere more so than Alberta, where the consumer society and population explosion were joined by a third agent of change - oil.

The event that ignited Alberta's development as an economic powerhouse was the much-publicized "coming in" of a new Imperial Oil well on Mike Turta's farm northwest of Leduc. Imperial had given 48-hours notice that something special was expected from this well, which after a series of 112 dry holes was either a display of supreme confidence or just plain foolhardy. By noon on Thursday, February 13th, 1947, some 500 curious people had gathered in Turta's farmyard to see

Driller George Tosh. The faces of Vern Hunter's happy drilling crew were splashed on the front pages of newspapers and magazines across Canada.

which it would be. The dignitaries and journalists in the crowd had been invited, but hundreds of ordinary folk simply turned up to see what all the fuss was about.

The predicted time of the gusher, 1 p.m., came and went, and Imperial treated the restless onlookers to coffee, sandwiches and cake. By 3:30 a good many people were leaving, including Edmonton Mayor Harry Ainlay. It seemed as if Imperial might have yet another dud on its hands. But the confident rig boss, Vernon "Dry Hole" Hunter, kept his crew working, and just before 4 p.m. there was a rumble which many later described a similar to an oncoming freight train. From 5,066 feet below, and 300 million years in the making, Alberta's future came snaking through a three-inch line to the well head - and erupted with a mighty "whoosh!"

Roughneck Johnny Funk had the honour of tossing a burning rag into the volatile mix spewing from the earth. The result, reported the *Daily Oil Bulletin*, was "a roaring column of burning oil and gas, shooting flames some 50 feet into the air and clouds of black smoke hundreds of feet into the sky." As the astonished crowd watched, "The well belched a few times as it cleared itself," Funk recalled years later, and then a perfect smoke ring rose high into the frigid air. Old hands said it was a good omen, and many in the crowd surged forward with bottles and jars to scoop up a souvenir of the miraculous stuff. There was a big party that evening at Edmonton's Hotel

216

Macdonald, and headlines in the newspapers the following day. but it's safe to say that few people understood the full impact Leduc No. 1 would have on Alberta.

Vern Hunter had some inkling. He tested the flow of the well and estimated it might produce a phenomenal thousand barrels-a-day. "I couldn't help but wonder whether the horizon would be dotted with flares before the next year rolled around." He wasn't wrong. Imperial had discovered what was, in essence, a gigantic, multi-level oilfield. Within weeks dozens of rigs were pouring into the province as Shell, British American, California Standard, Gulf, and all the big players arrived on scene. The *Lethbridge Herald* sounded a note of caution: "We would not say that the great oil pool for which Albertans have been searching ever since John Lineham drilled at Waterton Lakes nearly 50 years ago has been found." But the paper did allow that, with luck, within a lifetime the population of Edmonton "might grow to 250.000."

The ownership of mineral rights was suddenly a major issue, and a complicated one. Alberta's history had created a patchwork of ownership, with some farmers owning mineral rights while their neighbours did not. It all depended on whether those rights had been purchased along with the land, or had stayed with the original owners, the Hudson's Bay Company, the Canadian Pacific Railway, and of course the Alberta government - which controlled the mineral rights to more than 90% of the province. Mike Turta, the farmer on whose land Leduc No. 1 had been drilled, didn't own the mineral rights, but after the well came in oil companies were paying hefty bonuses (as much as six figures) for leases to prospect for oil and gas. For those landowners who did own the mineral rights to their property, a strike also meant regular royalty cheques which could turn into a small fortune.

Austrian-born Phillip Schoepp farmed a half-section not far from Leduc No 1. He also didn't own the mineral rights to his land, but like many of his generation was philosophical about not winning the natural resource lottery. "I think I am happier than I would be if I owned the mineral rights," he told reporters. "I have no worries. A lot of money always means a lot of worries."

Mike Turta's father, Anton, farmed two miles west of his son and was of a similar opinion - but he and his family became curious when no one came knocking on his door to ask about a lease. "We thought it was kind of funny," he said later. "People were drilling all around except

Within weeks of the Leduc discovery exploration crews were crawling all over the province. This one has set up a tent in the Brazeau area. Daily life for the crews was reminiscent of conditions experienced by Alberta's pioneer settlers.

Provincial Archives of Alberta P-2134

EXPLORATION
"DOODLEBUG"
REG'D TRADE MARK
TOOLS

There was an explosion of oilfield service companies in the late 1940s, with some arriving from the U.S. but most being home-grown. Seismic supply companies (like this one above) sprouted like dandelions. Princess Elizabeth and Prince Philip visited Calgary during Stampede week in 1951 (opposite page), shortly before she became queen. The city was experiencing a frenetic boom, and 100,000 people turned out to see the "little princess". Calgary's population would grow by 80% over the next decade.

here, so we looked into it." It turned out that when the land had been sold by the CPR in 1908 a clerk had failed to reserve the mineral rights for the company. An employee in the land titles office had later reversed this, but the Supreme Court of Alberta ruled that the original title was valid. So although the son made only a modest profit from the great Leduc strike, royalties from the oil beneath the father's land would eventually be worth an estimated $5 million.

In the decade after Leduc, Alberta experienced a near frenzy of exploration and development of its oil and gas resources, with almost $2 billion being invested in the industry throughout the province. By 1957 almost two-thirds of government revenue came from royalties, leases and rent from Crown land. And it wasn't only Albertans who benefited. In the years after 1945 Canada's exports to war-ravaged Europe boomed, and imports from the United States soared as Canadians bought all manner of manufactured goods. The problem was that Europe bought mostly on credit, and the country was running out of money to pay for American imports. Author James G. MacGregor (*History of Alberta*, Edmonton, Hurtig, 1972) maintained that Alberta oil saved the country from a serious financial crisis. "Not only had oil... put a chicken on every Albertan's table but it had saved every Canadian's bacon," he wrote. "During 1947, just when Canada was running into one of its most serious financial crises, Leduc No. 1 came to its aid." The aid was not, however, always recognized or appreciated beyond the province's borders.

The 50s heralded the arrival in Alberta of a new breed of home-grown oil-patch tycoon, free-spending and confident. Most Albertans took vicarious pride in the business dealings and lavish lifestyles of these men with their Lear jets and homes in California and the Caribbean. They were living the Alberta dream. However, they were not so readily embraced by Alberta's old guard. So unwelcome did the oilmen feel in Calgary's prestigious Ranchmen's Club that they built their own flashy Petroleum Club, described by journalist Frank Dabbs as "an icon of masculine mystique, complete with bronze cowboy sculpture, brass and glass and marble, heavy furniture, drive-in fireplace, and thousand-dollar card games."

What endeared Albertans to this new oil elite was the fact that its members invariably earned their wealth by taking risks and working hard. Typical were the Seaman brothers, from Rouleau, Saskatchewan. All three were engineers, and the eldest, Daryl "Doc" Seaman, was a veteran of wartime service with the RCAF. In 1949 Doc invested his savings in a shot-hole rig (a truck-mounted unit that drilled holes for seismic surveys). Bringing his younger brothers Don and Byron ("BJ") into the business, they gradually expanded and in 1962 created Bow Valley Industries - which would eventually grow into an international corporation with operations from Indonesia to the Middle East and the North Sea.

There were many more. Jack Gallagher, son of an Irish railroad worker, graduated in geology from the University of Manitoba. After working for Shell and Standard Oil, the man they called "Smiling Jack" landed in Calgary in 1948 and eventually joined a new outfit, Dome Petroleum. As the company chairman, Gallagher would turn Dome into an industry powerhouse, and earn himself a substantial personal fortune.

HALIFAX, TRURO & PICTOU MA

219

None among Alberta's new tycoons was more flamboyant than Frank McMahon (after whom the Calgary football stadium is named), who with his brother George built Atlantic Oil and the Westcoast Transmission pipeline company. Frank lived large. He owned race horses (one with Bing Crosby), invested in Broadway shows, and owned a string of homes (including one in Manhattan), but perhaps his most extravagant moment came in 1954 with the wedding of his daughter Marion. He turned Calgary on its ear, flying in 600 guests and renting two floors of the Palliser Hotel. The bride's gown was reportedly designed in Hollywood at a cost of $10,000 (a small fortune in the mid-50s), a Los Angeles florist supplied $25,000 worth of flowers for the church - and when Alberta liquor stores couldn't maintain the flow of champagne, supplies were flown in from Winnipeg and Vancouver.

Politically, Alberta in the 1950s was becoming a very different place to the incredibly turbulent 30s and 40s. As widespread prosperity flowed from the development of oil and gas, the province found itself governed by the right man at the right time. Ernest Manning had been William Aberhart's protégé and deputy, but unlike his mentor had been given time to learn the art of governing. He shared Aberhart's religious faith and decisiveness, but in the 36-year-old Manning these were combined with solid intellect and a gift for practical politics. "I never got any satisfaction from making somebody mad if you could gain your end by more congenial means," he explained in an interview in the 1980s. "I've always thought there was a good deal of truth in the old philosophy that says the greatest victory you could have over any enemy is to make him your friend."

Manning's thoughtful approach produced a government which was radically different in style from Aberhart's. The chaotic (some would say anarchic) Aberhart years were replaced by calm

Inmates of the Fort Saskatchewan prison making automobile licence plates. Vehicle ownership was booming, and the plates had to be replaced each year - creating steady employment for residents of the province's jails.

220

Premier Ernest Manning outside the Alberta Legislature. Only 36 years old, the thoughtful, capable Manning was already a political veteran and a very different leader than his mentor, William Aberhart.

deliberation. As journalist Allan Fotheringham noted, when Ernest Manning was premier Albertans knew someone was in charge.

The new premier was an intensely private and modest person who avoided the limelight, outside of official engagements and his long-running *Back to the Bible Hour* radio show. With his wife Muriel, a classically trained concert pianist (and also a nurse), the couple raised their two sons, Keith and Preston, in an unremarkable two-storey clapboard home in Edmonton's Garneau district. They also spent more than a decade renovating a rundown dairy farm the family bought in 1943, the year Manning became premier. East of Edmonton, the farm - christened *Westerlea* - was a haven away from public life.

Manning's unhurried and understated style has led many Albertans, even during his lifetime, to assume he was austere and rather dull. Dull or not, Social Credit under Manning's leadership provided the province with honest and capable government, and oversaw orderly expansion in a period of unparalleled economic growth during which provincial income quadrupled, and the personal incomes of Albertans tripled to almost $1 billion annually.

There were demands for everything Albertans imagined government ought to provide: schools, hospitals, roads, and support for the elderly, the handicapped and the disadvantaged. And the need was real. What later generations of politicians would call "infrastructure" - utilities, roads, and public buildings - were impoverished after years of economic depression and wartime shortages. In 1958 the Socreds announced an ambitious five-year spending plan that, according to the government," will be the boldest, most aggressive and far-reaching program of its kind ever attempted by any provincial government in Canada." As a result the party swept 61 of 65 seats in the 1959 provincial election. Meeting the promise of the ambitious five-year plan was more difficult, but 29 hospitals, dozens of new schools and nearly six thousand miles of main and secondary highways were built.

There were also the demands of a changing society, and these often proved most troublesome for Socred traditionalists. In 1958, for example, the government moved reluctantly to liberalize Alberta's liquor laws, unchanged since the end of Prohibition in 1923. The sale of alcohol had been permitted only in private clubs and public houses (pubs). In Edmonton and Calgary men and women were not allowed to drink together in public, although some smaller communities permitted this. Now Albertans would be allowed to drink in restaurants, lounges and nightclubs, although individual communities could still ban such decadence. The Manning government drew the line at allowing entertainment or shopping on Sunday.

Albertans in the 1950s were buying homes and appliances as never before, but the one consumer item most emblematic of that thrusting decade is the automobile. From the 100 horsepower, black and basic utility vehicles of the Depression and war years, the automobile morphed into huge, 300 horsepower, chromed and candy-coloured behemoths. These now became much more than conveyances, mere transportation. They were an extrovert statement of personality, exuding confidence and power. An ad for the 1957 Dodge Custom made the point with typical overkill: "It's a dream. Wait 'till you get the full glistening impact of its low, sweeping lines, its jewel-like accents of bright metal, its high-soaring tailfins that dramatize its forward-thrusting look, its wide, gracefully curved expanse of windshield and rear window, its distinctive twin lights that accent the massive bumper grille..."

All of which concerned Alberta's sober and understated premier, Ernest Manning. In a speech at the 1957 annual dinner of the Alberta Automobile Dealers' Association, he questioned the "excessive power" and over-the-top styling of the modern car. "Is public demand the cause of their being produced," he wondered, "or are we so conditioned by modern high-powered methods of publicity and advertising that manufacturers create the demand as such and are then kind enough to meet it?" The audience's reaction is not recorded, but it seems doubtful many Albertans would have agreed with their premier on this issue. During the early 1950s vehicle registrations in the province doubled, and by the end of the decade one in every three Albertans owned a car - far surpassing the national average of one in five.

All these cars needed roads, of course, and the 50s saw the foundation of Alberta's modern road system. The Americans had been building multi-lane roads since the 1920s, and by this time were busy linking them into a national system of interstate highways. The state of Alberta's major roads was summed up in an editorial in the *Calgary Albertan*. "Motoring from Alberta to the Pacific Coast is a chore and a hazard much of the year, except by going through the U.S. The highways from Calgary and Edmonton to Winnipeg are little more than good market roads for most of their distance."

Ottawa was predictably slow to appreciate the need for a Trans-Canada Highway, and although the idea was endorsed in 1949 it would not be officially open until September 1962. Alberta's section opened two years earlier, but not without the usual acrimonious debate over the route should pass through Edmonton or Calgary. Calgary prevailed, and Edmonton would continue to promote its Yellowhead Route along Hwy. 16 for another two decades (until the government of Donald Getty finally twinned what the *Edmonton Sun* labelled "The Highway of Death" after a number of horrific accidents).

Alberta's Mr. Highways throughout this period was Drumheller MLA Gordon Taylor. First

The Universal Sales and Services dealership in Calgary takes delivery of its 1950 models. Automobiles were no longer just about transportation. They were a personal statement.

Provincial Archives of Alberta PA-3727

223

The explosion of automobile ownership drove the creation of new infrastructure and services to support the phenomenon. Edmonton's first A&W drive-in restaurant (above) was one of many new amenities - including motels and shopping centres - that catered to a mobile population. Alberta's great era of road-building culminated with the opening of Highway 2 by Premier Manning (bottom right) in the fall of 1958. Not all developments were so benign. Edmonton's first parking meter was installed on Jasper Avenue (top right) the following year.

Edmonton Archives EA-17-12

appointed in 1951, he was the minister in charge of the province's roads for two decades. A tireless and enthusiastic booster of four-wheeled transport, he would preside over the conversion of much of the province's highway system from gravel to paved "blacktop." In the age of the automobile the importance of highway connections mirrored that of the railways half a century earlier, and the arguments over access were just as ferocious. When Taylor announced the new Highway 2 would miss the town of Wetaskiwin by a full 15 kilometres, Mayor J.E. Pike was furious. "This is not a bypass," he fumed, "this is an abandonment." Wetaskiwin would be the only major centre so seriously bypassed. It would eventually recover, ironically becoming a veritable car dealership mecca.

The four-lane highway between Edmonton and Calgary would not be completed until 1967, but its construction marked the apogee of the age of the car in Alberta - with 20,000 vehicles a day cruising the new route within months of its opening. The old cart track used for more than a century had been transformed. With a 65 mph speed limit - the highest in Canada - travel between Alberta's major cities could now be accomplished in three hours. Taylor's highway would provide yeoman service as Alberta's major thoroughfare for the rest of the century. He also thoughtfully provided a 300-foot right-of-way: enough for his dream of six or even eight lanes one day connecting Edmonton and Calgary. But that would have to wait until a new century.

The forgotten conflict that prevented a world war

CANADA AND THE OTHER DEMOCRACIES PROVED THEIR WILLINGNESS TO FIGHT
AND THE CALGARY-BASED PRINCESS PATS WIN REKNOWN IN DEFENCE OF KAPYONG

In June 1950, the invasion of the Republic of South Korea by troops from the Communist North threatened to turn the Cold War into World War Three. Sponsored by the Soviet Union, Korea was a test of the free world's willingness to oppose Communist aggression with military force. Ottawa originally displayed no such willingness (despite UN backing for the operation), debating what to do for three weeks. It was not until August 7th that Prime Minister Louis St. Laurent, under intense international pressure, announced that Canada would send a brigade to Korea.

By that time the outcome of the war seemed very much in doubt. South Korean and American forces had been pushed into a small area around the port of Pusan, and only a fierce defence allowed the UN to keep a toe-hold in Korea

while fresh troops (including soldiers from Britain, Australia and New Zealand) reinforced those trapped at Pusan.

Alberta and Albertans were at the forefront of the rapidly-assembling Canadian contingent. The Canadian Army Special Force (soon to become the 25th Canadian Infantry Brigade Group) received its training at Wainwright and Calgary, and hundreds of Albertans - many of them veterans of the Second World War - rushed to join up. The Pacific may have seemed a long way off to the government in Ottawa, but it appeared considerably closer from Alberta and British Columbia, where enlistments had doubled even before the announcement of Canada's troop commitment.

The Calgary-based Princess Patricia's Canadian Light Infantry regiment would play a leading role in the fighting. Its commanding officer, Edmontonian Lt.-Col. Jim Stone,

Courtesy of the PPCLI Museum/Museum of the Regiments

The Princess Patricias leave Seattle in 1950. It looked as if the war would be over by the time the regiment reached Korea, but the entry of China into the conflict would prolong the fighting until 1953.

joined the unit as a private at the outbreak of the Second World War and had risen through the ranks. Early in November 1950, as the regiment passed through Edmonton on its way to becoming the first Canadian army unit to leave for Korea, Stone was asked by a *Bulletin* reporter why he had volunteered to go overseas. "I think we're just at the commencement of the biggest war in history," he said. "That's why I joined up." He was not alone in his reasoning. Many feared that defeat in Korea would open the way to full-scale conflict with the Soviet Union and China.

But by the time The Pats sailed from Seattle on November 25, it actually looked as if the war might be over. Led by American General Douglas MacArthur, the American, South Korean and allied forces had pushed back the North Koreans and were on the border with China. The following day six Chinese armies crossed the border and entered the war on the North Korean side. By the time the Pats landed in Pusan on December 18th, much of the north of the country was back under Communist control - and the capital of Seoul would fall for the second time on January 4th, 1951.

The Canadian brigade saw action through a campaign of attacks and counterattacks during the spring of 1951, most famously at Kapyong, a

Four soldiers of the Princess Patricias pose with some pointed messages for home. Were they soldiers fighting a war, or peacekeepers in a "police action"?
Whatever you called it, 516 Canadians would lose their lives in the Korean fighting.

small village northeast of Seoul. There, towards the end of April, the Pats were called upon to cover the withdrawal of UN forces in the face of a large scale attack by the Chinese. Together with American and Australian troops, the Pats occupied high ground overlooking the Kapyong valley and were given the task of slowing the Chinese advance. After 18 hours of fighting the Americans and Australians on the Canadian right were forced to withdraw. Throughout the night of April 24th, and through the next day, the Pats repulsed attack after attack and held their ground.

By the end of June the fighting resulted in a virtual stalemate along the old border between the two Koreas. The war would grind on in this way for another two years, before a ceasefire was concluded on July 27th,

1953. The ceasefire would remain in place until the end of the century and beyond, but the democracies had proved their willingness to fight, if necessary, to block Communist aggression.

Nearly 27,000 Canadian soldiers fought in Korean, and 516 lost their lives there. In stark contrast to the scenes at the end of World War Two, there was no official welcome for returning Canadian troops, and little public interest. Ottawa treated the entire episode with mild embarrassment. "You'd think we were criminals, or something," one chagrined Korean vet told the *Calgary Herald*. The lack of public recognition for those who fought in Korea would continue to be a serious disappointment for the veterans of the conflict. Fifty years on, it would remain Canada's forgotten war.

Calgary's bustling Eighth Avenue in the early 1950s, lined with banks and stores. The automobile would siphon off much business to the suburbs, but the city's downtown business district would eventually rebound.

On December 30, 1952, Lethbridge radio shop owner Roy Fremstad fired up a home-built cathode ray receiver and for about a minute captured the flickering picture of what he thought might have been a boxing match, perhaps from Minneapolis. It was the first recorded television reception in Alberta. A year later Hans Reich and Fraser Keith took off from Lethbridge's Kenyon Field airport in their Stinson airplane with a similar receiver packed into the rear seat. At 11,500 feet they picked up some snatches of music and something that might have been a picture being broadcast from Spokane, Washington, 350 miles away. "Hans and Fraser aren't quite sure whether they saw a soap opera or a blizzard sequence from *Nanook of the North*," snickered a report in the *Lethbridge Herald*. "They didn't hang around too long, however, as ice began forming all over their aircraft and the inside temperature dropped to something less than comfy."

Provincial Archives of Alberta PA-82/1

Jasper Avenue and 101 Street in Edmonton in the 1950s. The crowded downtown was still the beating heart of the city, but the exodus to the suburbs would have a much more serious impact on downtown Edmonton, which unlike Calgary struggled to retain a critical mass of daily commuters.

Provincial Archives of Alberta PA-57/4

In the early 1950s Albertans who were determined to see for themselves this great new development in communications had to be either very inventive or leave the province. What would become the most influential medium of the 20th century had been invented in 1929, commercially available in Britain since 1935 and in the U.S. a decade later. A 1950 survey discovered that 14% of Albertans had seen television while travelling in the U.S., where there were already 108 stations, but in their home province the new wonder remained tantalizingly out of reach - just over the horizon. Unlike radio, television signals did not bounce off the atmosphere to be received many hundreds of miles from their source. In the pre-satellite age, television required a "line of sight" connection, which due to the curvature of the earth rarely extended beyond a hundred miles.

On September 6, 1952 the first CBC television station went on air in Montreal, and two days later Toronto also had its own CBC station. CBC Ottawa television went on air in 1953. That November *Maclean's* magazine had a reporter watch Toronto television for a week to get a feel for this revolutionary new medium. There were 25 hours of Canadian programming, nine British and the rest, 31 hours, were American. After watching the Jackie Gleason and Milton Berle shows, the anonymous author "almost decided to borrow some money and buy a television set." But the rest of the country could only read about all of this. Ottawa was adamant that CBC television would only expand to "the regions" after it had proved itself financially in Ontario and Quebec, which

Albertans take their first look at the new phenomenon of television. The sets were expensive and the broadcasts limited, but it was the beginning of a revolution in home entertainment.

after 18 months of operation seemed as if it might take a while. And when CBC expansion did come, the government decided it would happen first in Vancouver and Winnipeg. Edmonton and Calgary were classified as "secondary" markets, along with Kitchener, Ont., and Chicoutimi, Que.

Ironically, it was this "secondary" status which unleashed television in Alberta. The government decided that in these markets the CBC stations could be privately-owned "affiliates", and that immediately caught the interest of several entrepreneurs. In Calgary H. Gordon Love, majority owner of *CFCN* radio, put together a consortium called Calgary Television and secured a federal TV broadcast licence. In Edmonton Dick Rice's Sunwapta Broadcasting, owner of *CFRN* radio, did the same thing, rapidly followed by *CJLH* in Lethbridge and soon after by *CHCA* in Red Deer. At first it looked as if Calgary would be the first Alberta community with television, but Calgary TV's antenna was damaged while being hoisted into position in September 1954. A month later, on October 17th, *CFRN* became the first Alberta station to begin broadcasting scheduled programming. At 3 p.m. that Sunday afternoon, with the small control room crammed with Dick Rice, his wife Suzy, and a small crowd of invited guests, Don Brinton announced "Ladies and gentlemen, welcome to *CFRN-TV* at the sign of the totem pole, channel three, Edmonton." The "tube" had arrived.

Brinton soon found that television brought with it a level of celebrity radio did not. He was asked for autographs wherever he went. Ed Whalen, the Calgary station's first news and sports director, had a somewhat different experience. Plagued by technical difficulties, *CFCN* was sometimes off the air for a day or two at a time during its first year of broadcasting, which did not sit well with viewers. "At parties, when people asked me what I did for a living, I told them I was a plumber," Whalen recalled in an interview 45 years later. "It was easier than admitting I worked for *CFCN*."

The Calgary Herald thought that perhaps television would restore family life, and people certainly gathered together to share enjoyment of their favourite shows. But were the kids getting enough sleep?

Calgary's Ed Whalen (with glasses) and wrestling patriarch Stu Hart, accosted by Archie "The Stomper" Goldie. Whalen and Hart became the most recognized Calgarians around the world, but neither made money from the international success of Stampede Wrestling.

There were other problems associated with the first live television broadcasts. The presence of Premier Earnest Manning and other VIPs at *CFCN's* first live broadcast made the announcer, Ron Chase, a little nervous, remembered Whalen. "After he'd welcomed the audience to the city's first live television broadcast, he introduced our first locally made show, a 13-week serial on how to train your dog. Rom emphasized that the first lesson was important, the indispensable foundation for all future obedience lessons. In this first program, he said, 'The viewer must teach his dog how to shit - I mean sit.'" This first on-air faux pas caused an enormous fuss, including a meeting of the station's board of directors to discuss the possible firing of Chase. "Common sense prevailed, fortunately," recalled Whalen.

The "least important job" Whalen tackled in those early years was master of ceremonies for the broadcast of Stampede Wrestling, a show produced by Calgary's Hart family. Beginning in 1957, this wrestling extravaganza would by the 1970s become a worldwide phenomenon, distributed in dozens of countries. "While travelling myself, I'd turn on the television in my hotel room and there I'd be on the screen, from Rome to Beijing," said Whalen. He was recognized wherever he went, his face and gravel-throated charms familiar to hundreds of millions of fans, and became arguably Alberta's most famous television product of the 20th century. But neither Whalen nor the wrestling Hart dynasty ever received a cent from this international TV stardom. Their shows were copied and rebroadcast illegally, and no one had the money to track down and sue the video pirates who made millions from this Alberta institution.

The first television sets were expensive, $200 to $400 (a quarter the cost of a car), and usually offered a single channel with about 40 hours a week of black and white programming. Reception, via a roof antenna, was usually snowy and sound reproduction tinny. Compared to radio, which was an established and sophisticated medium with worldwide connections, or the movies, which by now offered lush, widescreen colour productions with stereo sound, early television appeared rather primitive and amateurish. Yet within a handful of years TV would be embraced by Albertans and come to dominate daily life in a way nothing ever had before. Movie attendance dropped by almost half, and restaurants noticed that their evening rush was happening earlier, as people brought meal times forward so as not to miss the prime time TV shows. People started staying

home on Saturday nights to sea what Sid Caesar was up to. Radio drama and variety shows began disappearing in favour of hours of recorded music hosted by "on-air personalities" who rapidly became know as disk jockeys. The same year that television arrived in Alberta, 1954, it became the most lucrative advertising medium in the world.

Not surprisingly, everyone from politicians and the clergy to newspaper editorialists fretted about the impact of this phenomenon. Edmonton Norwood MLA William Tomyn was in not doubt where he stood on the issue. "Only morons, with no sense of moral values, could produce such trash and drivel," he told the Alberta legislative assembly. "Judging by some of the recent productions I sometimes wonder if these individuals need psychiatric care." Calgary pastor Frank Morley thought that television was probably more dangerous than the atom bomb, noting that in one week of TV shows viewers witnessed "91 murders, seven stagecoach hold-ups, three kidnappings, 10 thefts, four burglaries, two case of arson, two jail breaks, a errorist attack which killed 20, two suicides and dozens of assaults."

The *Calgary Herald* thought TV was likely to be a mixed blessing, particularly where the young were concerned. "In the United States is has been found that whereas the automobile shattered family life, the television set is restoring it. Young people stay home evenings instead of gadding around and getting into mischief. Children wander the streets less. But this is not an unadulterated blessing. Children also get less sleep, less than they need. Many of the programs are definitely harmful to their receptive and undiscriminating young minds. People read less. They make their own entertainment less. They are becoming illiterate. It is still not settled whether television is a good or a bad thing, on balance, but the right of people to view it must not be denied."

It was a debate that would continue as television itself continued to grow in influence and diversity, leading the way towards what Edmonton-born media guru Marshall McLuhan called the Global Village. The only certainty was Albertans' seemingly unquenchable appetite for the new medium.

The province's 50th birthday in 1955 was celebrated with parades, picnics, dances and firework displays. Most of Sylvan Lake's population turned out to look at the floats (top) in the town's birthday parade. Merchandising, as it would come to be known, was in its infancy, but items such as this curling sweater (right) proved to be popular mementoes of the birthday celebration.

233

Alberta's baby boomers face an insidious killer

DESPITE ADVANCES IN MEDICINE AND HYGIENE, POLIO RAVAGES THE PROVINCE, UNTIL A VACCINE IS FOUND WHICH ERADICATES THE VIRUS ALMOST OVERNIGHT

Better diet and advances in public hygiene and medicine had by mid-century transformed the health of Albertans. Previously devastating diseases were being controlled and eradicated, the almost miraculous antibiotic drugs were curing infections and aiding recovery from injuries, and people were living longer and healthier lives than ever before.

But there was one disease which appeared almost impervious to medical advances, and indeed seemed almost to thrive with improvements in hygiene. The perverse irony of polio, or "infantile paralysis" as it was commonly known, was that without some exposure in infancy, children failed to develop immunity and stood in greater risk of later infection by more virulent strains. The polio virus had first been

identified in 1908, and throughout the 1930s and 40s research continued to find a cure for the disease which had famously confined U.S. President Franklin D. Roosevelt to a wheelchair. But the number of cases of polio actually began to trend upwards during the post-war Baby Boom, and in 1953 Alberta faced the worst outbreak of polio in the province's history.

On the Kowalski farm near Millet, two of the family's four children became sick. Deanna, 12, got it first and was hospitalized at Wetaskiwin. During a visit to the hospital, her 15-year-old sister, Connie, complained of feeling tired. Within days the two girls were sharing a room in the isolation ward. Deanna's case was relatively mild and she soon recovered, though with a permanent minor disability in one leg.

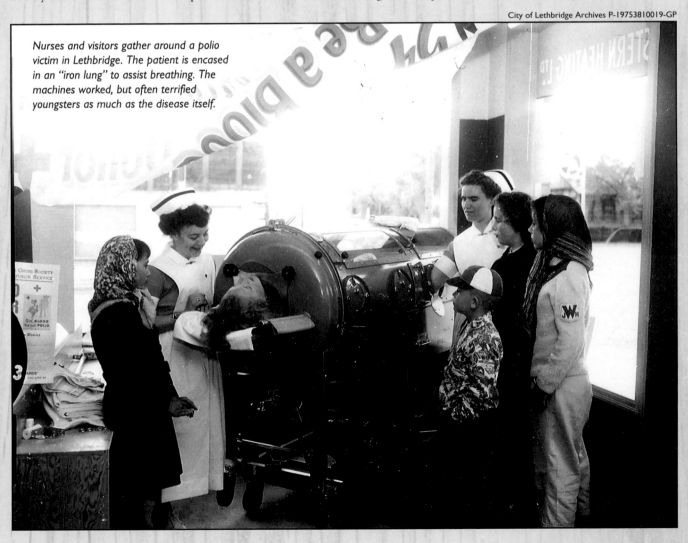

Nurses and visitors gather around a polio victim in Lethbridge. The patient is encased in an "iron lung" to assist breathing. The machines worked, but often terrified youngsters as much as the disease itself.

The vaccine developed by Dr. Jonas Salk, a brilliant professor of bacteriology at the University of Pittsburgh, was available in Alberta by 1955 - only a year after its development. This Calgary schoolgirl is getting her "shot" as part of the province's mass immunization program.

Connie was hit much harder, becoming totally paralyzed. She spent the next 18 months in an iron lung (an artificial breathing machine), and spent the rest of her life as a quadriplegic. She was one of 1,552 cases across the province in 1953, of which 111 were fatal.

Panicked health officials closed swimming pools and movie theatres to children under 16. Many schools were closed and in Calgary churches were asked to suspend Sunday school. When it appeared as if there might not be enough nurses to care for all the victims, retired nurses were urged to return to work. Many did, although polio represented a significant risk for the doctors and nurses treating patients. Donna Graham, a nurse at the isolation hospital attached to Edmonton's Royal Alexandra Hospital, contracted the illness and was totally paralyzed for the rest of her life. Iron lungs were airlifted from Boston by the RCAF, and in an unprecedented move in the days before publicly-funded health care, Alberta agreed to pay almost all the medical bills of those stricken by polio (at a cost of $1 million a year).

The impact of polio was such that in 1954 a vaccine, developed by Dr. Jonas Salk at the University of Pittsburgh, was hurriedly tested on almost half a million American children (including Salk's two sons). When the test proved safe, and 80% successful, Alberta began a mass immunization program. In 1956 there were 81 cases reported, falling to 65 the following year, with just four deaths. After that the threat of polio rapidly receded, although its survivors would carry the scars for decades.

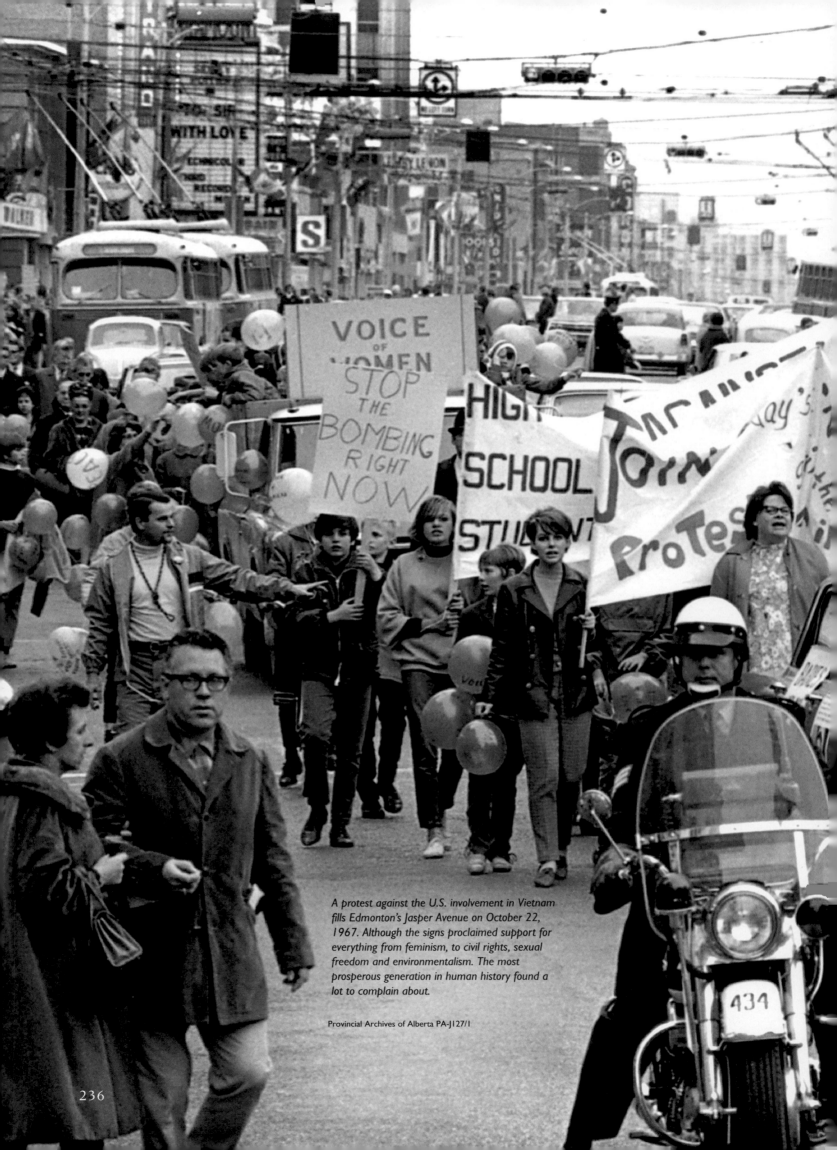

A protest against the U.S. involvement in Vietnam fills Edmonton's Jasper Avenue on October 22, 1967. Although the signs proclaimed support for everything from feminism, to civil rights, sexual freedom and environmentalism. The most prosperous generation in human history found a lot to complain about.

Provincial Archives of Alberta PA-J127/1

CHAPTER NINE

Welcome to the revolution

SOCIAL UPHEAVAL AND POLITICAL UNREST AGAIN SWEEP THE PROVINCE,
AND ALBERTA'S 3RD POLITICAL DYNASTY FALLS TO A NAME FROM THE PAST

In the first half century of its existence Alberta had experienced two world wars, economic boom and bust, droughts which had driven thousands from their homes, and technological change on a scale unprecedented in human history. The province had gone from a sparsely-populated backwater on the edge of empire, to a prosperous, rapidly-urbanizing society plugged in to the "Global Village" so famously predicted by one of its sons. In the shrinking world of the 1960s, most older Albertans probably believed they had seen it all. The generation born into the tumultuous 1920s, who had endured the challenges of the Dirty Thirties, would likely have scoffed at the idea they could be rattled by mere social change. But they were wrong.

The young province had, of course, already witnessed profound social changes: the development of public education, the growing acceptance of women in public life and the workforce, the growth of government and social programs. It is not as if society had stood still in the first half of the 20th century. But what made the 1960s different was the sudden acceleration and breathtaking scope of the changes taking place. It wasn't just one or two traditional beliefs or social mores which were suddenly being questioned. It appeared to be all of them: everything from the traditional relationship with Britain and the symbols of Canada's past, to public morals and deeply-held taboos. Everywhere you looked, it seemed authority and tradition were being challenged, or dismissed as worthless.

To many older Albertans the 60s were the awful decade when "the good old days" came to an end, and their children, for some inexplicable reason, seemed to lose their senses. In the wistful remembrance of those children, middle-aged themselves by the century's end, the 60s are "the good old days," before the responsibilities of earning a living and raising their own families caused the majority to abandon their vaunted idealism and join the rat race. Ironically, most of the ideas on education, social policy and sex which powered the 60s "revolution" were, in fact, the product of the older generation and had been around for years. But it was the Baby Boomers, freed from the economic constraints and military service which had marked the lives of their parents and grandparents, who would become the guinea pigs in this vast social experiment.

On the surface at least, Alberta was far from the cutting edge of the changes taking place. Social Credit still provided shrewd and conventional government under the leadership of Premier Ernest Manning, who although only 56 had already been in power for two almost decades. For Manning the 60s would be a time of continuing electoral success (60 of 63 seats in the 1963 provincial election, and 55 of 65 in 1967), but also of frustration. His Christian world view and his rural values of thrift and self-reliance would put him and his government increasingly out of step with younger Albertans. Manning and the Socreds were backed into a reactionary posture, railing in futile fury against hippies, go-go girls, Sunday commerce and the welfare state. The siege mentality so prevalent during the Aberhart years once again began to manifest itself. "This so-called freedom [of expression] is being made a fetish by a modern cult of non-conformists who think it is intellectually sophisticated to debunk the scriptures, moral values and conventions developed over the years," warned the premier in a 1963 speech to the Socred Women's Auxiliary. Unfortunately, that was precisely what a growing number of young people thought.

It wasn't as if the government didn't try to catch the mood of the times. The government passed the Alberta Human Rights Act, which outlawed discrimination in employment or housing based on gender, race or religion. It established a Department of Youth, headed by a suitably

Mini-skirted cheerleaders at the Social Credit Party's 1968 convention. The Socreds were allegedly out of touch with the changing times, but they certainly tried to get "with it". There was even a resolution from the party's "Young Turks" to legalize marijuana.

youthful Socred MLA, Bob Clark. The department had some success with an Alberta youth corps to rival Ottawa's Company of Young Canadians, but in general touring trailer displays promoting 4-H and Junior Forest Wardens failed to compete with rock and roll and *Playboy* magazine.

The Manning government clashed with Ottawa over taxes designed to limit foreign investment, and over official bilingualism - which the premier concluded was "unrealistic and impracticable." But the biggest fight with the Liberal government of Lester Pearson came over Ottawa's push for a national, universal medical insurance plan along the lines of Saskatchewan's program. There was already a cost-shared federal-provincial hospital insurance plan (inaugurated in 1957), and Alberta was working on a Medical Services Plan which would have made general medical insurance available through a provincial agency or from private insurers (with subsidies available for those with low incomes). But at a 1965 conference Pearson unveiled a national scheme, administered by the provinces, which would cover all doctors' services. Ottawa offered to pay half the annual cost, estimated at $500 million.

Alberta was the only province seriously opposed, and Manning took the unusual step of going on national television to warn that the concept of "free" health care was fundamentally flawed, its costs would be difficult control, and would almost certainly involve "heavy additional taxation." The federal plan, predicted the premier, would set Canada "on the road to a complete welfare state from which there would be no turning back." But even in Alberta the premier's call to resist the lure of "free" health care seemed to fall on deaf ears. Of 60 calls fielded by *CFRN-TV* in Edmonton, where Manning's broadcast originated, 51 were complaints that the premier had pre-empted the popular comedy series, *The Munsters*.

Manning's focus was shifting more to the national scene, and in the wake of the 1967 provincial

election he began to talk about a philosophy of "social conservatism" which he hoped would unite like-minded
Canadians in support of free-enterprise, individual rights
and humanitarian social policies. At the Socred convention
at the end of that year he told the party he was thinking
about retirement, and in September 1968 he made it official. He was, he said, retiring to "a life of ease." Rather he
would work for the "dynamic, constructive revolution"
that he felt Canada needed.

Three months later a leadership convention elected
54-year-old farmer and Manning cabinet minister Harry
Strom as Social Credit leader. Strom had been reluctant
to run, but was widely viewed as decent and capable. It
would not matter. Alberta was about to undergo another
of its periodic political upheavals. The 1967 provincial
vote had seen the election of half a dozen Progressive
Conservatives, including the party's energetic and bright
young leader, Peter Lougheed. A Calgary lawyer and
grandson of Senator James Lougheed, he had rebuilt the
moribund Tory party brick by brick. Charismatic, brainy,
and with an almost photographic memory, Lougheed was
everything the well-meaning but uninspiring Strom was
not. Although few yet predicted it, after three and a half
decades Alberta's third political dynasty was about to
come crashing down.

Of all the many facets of the churning social upheaval
that was the 1960s, none was more explosive, divisive, or
shocking to older Albertans than changing attitudes
towards sex. As the decade opened traditional values
dominated, with sex being a mostly private matter; hope-
fully between consenting, married adults. It wasn't that
older Albertans were naïve or prudish. But to talk about
sex in any detail in mixed company was considered to be
in poor taste, if not downright offensive. Sex as entertainment was virtually unknown in Alberta, but that was
about to change as movie-makers and publishers pushed
the boundaries of what was acceptable.

In 1959 Alberta film censors felt obliged to cut the
word "floozie" from a film called *Shadows* to render it fit
for public consumption. Little more than a decade later
Edmonton's Odeon Theatre would screen *Last Tango in
Paris*, starring Marlon Brando as a dissolute, middle-aged
widower, who works out his mid-life crisis in an explicit,
and often violent, on-screen nude romp with an anonymous young woman. To paraphrase the 60s Bob Dylan
hit, the times they were a-changing. Unfortunately the
Alberta film censor had a knack for fighting over the
wrong movies, which contributed to the growing public
view that it was out of touch with the times. In 1963 it
decided that 70 seconds of footage had to be removed
from the British hit *Tom Jones* before it could be viewed
by Albertans. Based on Henry Fielding's 18th-century
novel of the same name, the film was risqué but harmless
- a relatively accurate reflection of a book which was by
then part of the high school curriculum in Britain.

There was no doubt, however, that chief film censor,

Provincial Archives of Alberta PA-J692/2

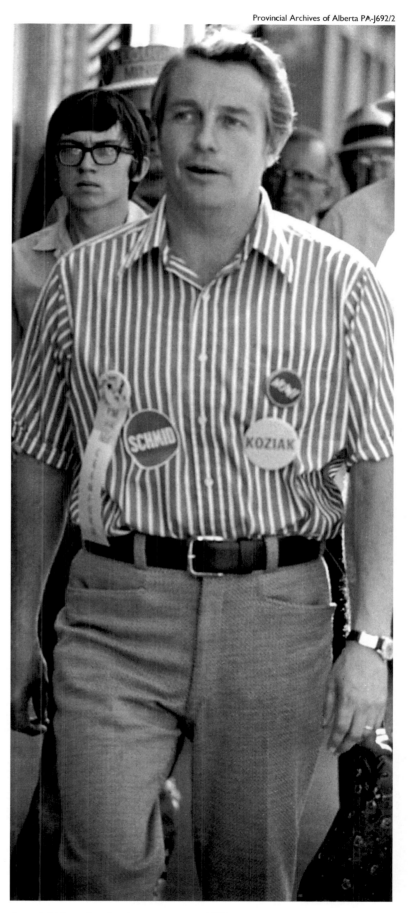

A youthful Peter Lougheed campaigning in 1971. The grandson of Alberta's second senator covered 5,000 miles and literally ran door to door. "This Lougheed fellow... really gets around," marvelled the Red Deer Advocate.

239

Colonel P.J.A. Fleming, was in tune with the views of the government he served. Fleming arranged a private screening of *Tom Jones* for Social Credit MLAs. Edmonton-Norwood representative William Tomyn told the Edmonton Journal he found the film "dangerous" and in "shocking bad taste." Okotoks-High River MLA Ed Benoit suggested "They should take it back to England." Stony Plain representative Cornelia Woods thought it should be burned. Nevertheless, three years later Fleming was out, replaced by Jack Day, a transplanted British public relations officer. Day, it was hoped, would help mitigate the government's image as a creaky political anachronism. But Day's tenure was far from a resounding success. He resigned after being charged with having sex with two under-aged girls (later being acquitted of all charges).

Increasingly explicit movies did not, however, protect Hollywood's revenues from the encroachment of television - which ironically in the 1960s was devoutly smut-free and conformed to a strict moral code abandoned by film producers. Between 1965, when the *Sound of Music* won the Academy Award for Best Picture, and 1969, when the same award went to *Midnight Cowboy*, a bleak story about New York's sordid street life, audiences in movie theatres across Alberta (and North America) had dropped by two-thirds.

The sexual handbook of the 60s was Hugh Hefner's *Playboy* magazine, which had first appeared in 1953 and had rapidly become a fixture of popular culture. Shocking at first, by the mid-60s Hefner's careful public relations placed him on the cover of *Time*, whose editors declared "Hugh Hefner is alive, American, modern, trustworthy, clean, respected, and the country's leading impresario of spectator sex." Edmonton's Rev. Terry Anderson disagreed. At a forum on the "New Morality" at Garneau United Church, he condemned *Playboy* for promoting among young men the notion of disposable sex. The magazine's central message, he said, was "don't get involved with a girl. Use her as an entertainment article and discard her when she begins to get to you." But those who agreed with Rev. Anderson were fighting an uphill battle. There were several dozen people at the Garneau forum, while in 1966 *Playboy's* circulation approached four million. That same year *Gateway*, the University of Alberta's student newspaper, announced a visit to campus by Kelly Burke, a *Playboy* "Playmate of the Month," to sign autographs and model clothing. She was a big hit.

A pipe-smoking older Albertan watches with some interest the Rock Express Festival in Calgary in 1970. The older generation thought they had seen and experienced just about everything. They had not.

As they had four decades earlier, rising hemlines fascinated Alberta's newspapers. This bevy of mini-skirts illustrated a 1969 Calgary Herald feature on the phenomenon.

Christians also got into the swing of things during the 1960s and 70s with their own revival and accompanying demonstrations (like this one by members of Edmonton's Central Pentecostal Tabernacle). Although small compared to earlier revivals, it served to hearten existing churchgoers. But by the end of the 60s the "No Religion" category was the fourth largest reported in the national census.

Provincial Archives of Alberta PA-J598

One of the very last manifestations of the sexual revolution in Alberta was the arrival of gay clubs, which had been in existence in major U.S. cities, and in Toronto and Vancouver, for several years before they made their appearance in the province. Well-known Alberta journalist Paul Jackson was city editor of the *Calgary Albertan* in late 1969 when he received a call inviting the paper to cover a gay costume ball. Until that call, Jackson later recalled, he had "no inkling" that a gay club existed in Calgary. The year-old organization, which met in a large basement hall, claimed 300 members, half under 21. "What type of person comes to the club?" inquired Jackson. "Everyone from a university professor to a sales clerk," replied a member of the club's executive. "We even had a member of the Canadian Senate come down." Jack was suitably impressed. The club, he wrote, was "a quiet oasis in the midst of an alien world of fear, hate, insecurity and often bitter loneliness."

Not everyone agreed. The decriminalization of homosexuality in Britain in 1967 increased pressure for a similar liberalization in Canada. The *Edmonton Journal* argued that eliminating criminal sanctions would amount to "tacit approval of these relations," which were "abnormal and repugnant to the vast majority of Canadians." Worst yet, the *Journal* felt that decriminalizing homosexuality must inevitably lead "to an upswing in the existing tendency among those homosexually inclined to prey on the young." Calgary's Evangelical Ministerial Association agreed, fretting that such a move posed a "great threat to national security." Calgary police chief Ken McIver was quoted as saying "I don't buy the idea that this... is a disease. It's just plain sin."

But the mood of the times and most media coverage was increasing tolerant of gays and lesbians. For the first time in North America sympathetic portraits of homosexuals were turning up in movies and even on television. Federal Justice Minister Pierre Trudeau introduced a huge package of Criminal Code amendments which included one to legalize private homosexual acts between consenting adults. The bill passed in May 1969. It was a seminal victory for Alberta's fledgling gay rights movement, and it emboldened activists to raise their public profile and expand their demands. Two years later the Edmonton-based Gay Alliance Towards Equality was formed, led by Michael Roberts, a South African-born photographer. GATE originally had only

10 members, but it had big ambitions.

Through the 20th century women had been increasingly involved in public life and the workplace, especially in Alberta, where the realities of frontier life often resulted in fewer restrictions - and more demands - on women. So perhaps not surprisingly Alberta was among the first places in the British Empire to allow women to vote, and the first in Canada to elect women MLAs. But faced with the realities of raising families, there was no more than a steady growth in the number of women in public life and in the workplace: Until the 1960s, when changing attitudes and the birth-control pill combined to give young women both the opportunity and the means to begin the final push to liberate themselves from biology and male chauvinism.

It began quietly enough. In September 1961, *Chatelaine* (Alberta's most popular women's magazine) informed its readers they were living in a "time of unsurpassed opportunity." Intelligent women, said the magazine, "are being accepted by men in every capacity." Betraying a critical misunderstanding of emerging feminism, *Chatelaine* advised upwardly-mobile women how to dress and behave - always with the opinions of the male in mind. When meeting with male colleagues, the magazine advised its readers to keep their opinions to themselves "unless you're asked a specific question." And during coffee breaks "she should see to it that every cup is filled and refilled." Edmonton city councillor and Liberal activist Una MacLean Evans (later a citizenship court judge) was no slouch when it came to expressing opinions, but in an interview with the *Red Deer Advocate* she repudiated the growing demands of the feminists: "I don't see the necessity of strident overtures to achieve what, in fact, has already been accomplished."

Of all the manifestations of the 60s' teen revolution, nothing infuriated the older generation more than the popularity of long hair among young men. Out of fashion since the Edwardian era, it now made a vigorous comeback - the hairier the better. This young Calgarian's "Afro" was the height of fashion.

Against this background, marriage and relationships were undergoing an equally volcanic change. Women took to birth control *en masse*, causing a sharp decline in the soaring post-war birth rate and bringing the Baby Boom to an end. In 1966 survey only 1% of Canadian women over 40 said they had lived with a man before marriage. Among women aged 20-29 the figure was 18%. Among women born after 1966, the number would rise to more than 50%. Marriage increasingly became something to be delayed and avoided, or even escaped. In the decade after the introduction of "no-fault" divorce in 1968, the Canadian divorce rate increased sixfold.

"A typical divorce court in Calgary these days resembles a law faculty convocation, as scores of black-robed barristers pore through a record number of divorce petitions," reported the *Calgary Herald*. "This does not mean a rise in the divorce rate, only that a lot of dead marriages are finally being buried," said Edmonton lawyer Gordon S. Wright. In fact, Alberta's divorce rate increased every year throughout the 60s, doubling the national average and becoming by far the highest in the country. In July 1969 the *Edmonton Journal* discovered what it "believed to be the cheapest divorce in Canada - and possibly the world." It had cost just $29.

Most women in Alberta would likely not have agreed with Shulamith Firestone, who wrote in her best-selling book *The Dialectic of Sex* (New York,

Edmonton's Faye Broeksma became a
pioneer among women entering jobs
previously monopolized by men. In
1971 she became the capital's
first female letter carrier.

Bantam books) that "pregnancy is barbaric." But there was certainly a growing consensus that child-bearing constituted a severe restriction on female advancement. Whereas having children had until recently been seen as socially positive, it now became socially responsible to limit the number of your offspring. This change in attitude made a celebrity of Stanford University biologist Dr. Paul Ehrlich, who provided the scientific rationale for this change in attitude. In his 1968 book *The Population Bomb*, Ehrlich predicted that humanity was "breeding itself into oblivion" and within a few years famine, malnutrition and disease would devastate even North America. People would be forced to eat their pets. The answer, said Ehrlich, was to "de-emphasize the reproductive role of sex" and for governments to penalize families through the tax code. He made 25 appearances with Johnny Carson on *The Tonight Show* and his views became widely accepted.

During a lecture series at the University of Lethbridge in 1968, C.F. Bentley (dean of agriculture at the University of Alberta) echoed Ehrlich in predicting famine, half the world's population dying of starvation, and exhausted fuel reserves by the end of the century. Albertans, like other North Americans and Europeans, were getting the message. Maternity wards began to empty. Calgary's birth rate, previously among Canada's highest, dropped 35% between 1962 and 1967. Schools began closing doors, and demographers and city planners began scaling back their growth forecasts.

Against this background it is hardly surprising that "unwanted pregnancies" began to attract attention and debate. Edmonton obstetrician and gynaecologist Dr. Bernard Kredenster was one of many who advocated unrestricted abortion as a solution to the "world wide people crisis." In an interview with *Saint John's Edmonton Report*, he said "We cannot feed, house, clothe and educate those we have." In 1960 abortion was a crime under Canada's criminal code (except where the mother's life was in immediate danger). A decade of protest and of lobbying by the medical profession would result, in August 1969, in a new law which would allow an abortion if a hospital committee agreed continued pregnancy endangered the "health" of the mother. But the debate would continue, to the end of the century and beyond.

Women not only wanted to be liberated from male domination, but also from the tyranny of biology. These women were taking part in a pro-abortion rally in 1970. The astrological symbol for Venus, a looped cross, became the universal icon of the liberation movement.

The end of a century-old Imperial banner

THE DEBATE OVER A NEW CANADIAN FLAG WAS ONE OF THE MOST DIVISIVE EVER,
BUT THE MAPLE LEAF WOULD BECOME OUR MOST POPULAR NATIONAL SYMBOL

On February 15th, 1965, a ceremony was held at the Alberta Legislature in which the Red Ensign - Canada's flag for almost a century - was officially replaced by the Maple Leaf. Premier Ernest Manning called the new flag a symbol "of the national maturity which we have attained," which was doubtless true. The adoption of the Maple Leaf, assured the premier, "in no way lessens our affections for those other symbols associated with our historic heritage and under which Canadians for years have lived and fought and died," which was less accurate.

The Maple Leaf would become Canada's single most unifying symbol, recognized around the world and much-loved at home. But the search for a new flag initiated by the Liberal government of Prime Minister Lester Pearson was part of an agenda to be more distinctly Canadian, and so less overtly British. As both the *Calgary Herald* and *Edmonton Journal* noted, whatever else it might be, getting rid of the Red Ensign (of which the Union Jack was part) was a "massive concession" to Quebec. And it provoked one of the fiercest political and public debates in the country's history.

The government's original design consisted of three red maple leaves on a white background, flanked by two vertical blue bars. A renegade Conservative MP (his party officially opposed a new flag) suggested a single green maple leaf in a white circle centred on two crosses, one red and one blue (representing English and French). Another serious contender was a design from the 1940s, by Edmontonian W. Gordon Harris, which featured a beaver encircled by maple leaves. As the debate raged through the spring and summer of 1964, a committee of 15 MPs was given six weeks to come up with a final design. Their choice was leaked to the *Calgary Albertan* in October, several days before the official announcement. "Surprise!" headlined the newspaper. "Now It's A Single Red Maple Leaf Flag."

Conservative leader John Diefenbaker refused to drop his party's opposition to the flag (despite the defection of his 10 Quebec Conservative MPs), and the Alberta Progressive Conservative Association urged its members to wear black armbands to protest the passing of the Red Ensign. But after the new flag was endorsed by the House of Commons in December, Premier Manning was clear that it would be raised over Alberta's public buildings. His government also announced that the Union Jack would continue to fly over the Legislature Building, because it was the official seat of the lieutenant-governor, the Queen's representative in the province.

The first official raising of the Maple Leaf at the Alberta Legislature, on February 15, 1965. The Red Ensign was gone, but Premier Ernest Manning decreed the Union Jack would continue to fly over the provincial legislature - and it was still there 40 years later.

In 1959 *Time* magazine damned Edmonton with faint praise, calling it "Alberta's first city in almost everything but personality." As the 60s opened, the provincial capital was the fastest growing city in Canada, home to the country's first huge shopping mall - Westmount Shoppers Park - and could boast more cars per capita than any other Canadian centre. But for all that, *Time* cruelly noted that "Edmonton lacks the western dash of Calgary."

The truth was that the two rivals, so different in history and character, were rapidly adopting the same architecture and amenities common to the rest of urban North America. Edmonton and Calgary had, in fact, never been more alike, and outwardly at least would grow even more similar over the next two decades as both experienced large-scale immigration and growth. As a later and more even-handed feature in *Maclean's* would note, during the 60s Edmonton sprouted 45 major buildings downtown, ranging from six to 35 storeys high. "And for visitors to the city who could never contemplate the old Edmonton without wincing and or yawning, the new Edmonton is a surprising, exciting and sometimes bewildering place." Some 70% of the population was under 40, which according to *Maclean's* produced "a lively new exuberance that startled visitors."

For one thing, Edmontonians were the biggest gamblers in the country. By 1963 the Exhibition Association (renamed Edmonton Northlands in 1968) was so flush with cash it revamped the race track grandstand and topped it with the enclosed Sky Paddock lounge. The easing of some of Alberta's archaic liquor regulations were beginning to produce more nightlife than the city had seen since the early years of the century. Music, dancing and drinking were served up by nightclubs like the Capri, the Paddock and Embers. The last was partly owned by Tommy Banks, a Calgary jazz prodigy and leader of the Banknotes, who would become a fixture on the Edmonton music scene. In 1965 he also opened Century II studios, which did much to encourage musical talent from all over the West. Banks' talent, and especially his loyalty to Edmonton, helped the city to develop a music scene that would rival much larger centres and belied its reputation as a cultural backwater.

Public demonstrations were certainly nothing new in Alberta, but organized protests by schoolchildren certainly were. This photo shows a "sit-in" staged by students at a Calgary high school to protest a ban on girls wearing jeans.

Glenbow Archives PA-2864-7005-1A

The era of the Vietnam War marked the beginning of a trend towards strident anti-Americanism, although Albertans would, on the whole, remain much more pro-American than most Canadians. In a demonstration rare for the times, these young Edmontonians express their support for U.S. policy in Southeast Asia.

Edmonton's monied class was both smaller and quieter than Calgary's. It included Francis Winspear, for example, a University of Alberta professor who founded a national accounting company and who would become one of the capital's premier philanthropists. There was also Charles Allard, a surgeon who became a real estate developer almost by accident in the post-war years when he could not find suitable office space for his practice. He built a substantial business empire which later included television and film production.

As the baby boomers began pouring into the housing market in the late 1960s, the entire country faced a housing shortage and rising prices, but nowhere was the shortage so acute as in Canada's fastest growing city (the population soared from 269,000 in 1960 to 410,000 in 1969). The average home price almost doubled during the decade (to $20,000), and the outlying communities of Leduc, Fort Saskatchewan, St. Albert and Spruce Grove began to grow as people looked further afield for affordable housing. The trend would eventually give the Edmonton urban area a more diversified look than Calgary's more unified sprawl. It would also cause the city to undertake its own development of Mill Woods, the largest public land development project in North America - with the province quietly buying nine-square miles of farmland on the southeast corner of Edmonton, which it then sold to the city. In 1968 city council endorsed a study which recommended the annexation of St. Albert, the Namao air base and Strathcona County's rapidly expanding hamlet of Sherwood Park. It would have boosted the city's size from 86 square miles to 292, but it would become the first of several such plans to evaporate in the face of stiff opposition from surrounding municipalities.

It is often said that the flavour of life in Calgary during the 1960s was best captured by a concoction made each July by Mayor Harry Hays (a successful cattle breeder who would become a Liberal cabinet minister and senator). At the annual Hays Stampede Breakfast, he would don a dairymaid's pigtailed wig, parade one of his prized Holsteins before a crowd of 3,000 or so invited guests, and proceed to fill a bath tub with something he called his "syllabub." Legend has it the drink consisted of milk, "alcohol, medicine and lashings of hair restorer." The milk and alcohol were likely real, but only Hays knew the secret recipe. "It was terrible stuff, but hundreds of people actually drank it, "recalled one guest. "Including Prime Minister Lester Pearson, Governor-General Roland Michener, Colonel Harland Sanders and Jack Dempsey."

Hays' annual tradition was a good-natured send-up of the Old West, but reflective of the city Calgary had become. Its cowboy heritage had melded with its newer oil-patch bravado into an

Calgary's McCall Field airport in the 1960s. The city would not get a new international terminal until long after Edmonton had one, but it would be Calgary - Alberta's traditional transportation centre - which would eventually become the airline hub for the province.

Glenbow Archives PA-5093-671

In the 1960s the Bow River (above) was, according to Calgary Mayor Rod Sykes, "a garbage dump with a slaughterhouse on it." But within a few years the river would become the focus of a major clean-up campaign (top) that eventually restored its reputation as a world-class trout stream. For the first time environmental issues grabbed the public consciousness and governments reacted.

unmistakeable civic image in which Calgarians took great pride. Edmonton might be the provincial capital, but Calgary in the 1960s was becoming a business centre of growing wealth and influence. It had a higher proportion of affluent, white-collar workers than any other city in Canada (half of them in some fashion related to the oil business). A university campus was finally under construction, and the new Trans-Canada Highway proved that the city's traditional place as Alberta's transportation hub was still intact. Its insatiable urge for growth fuelled annexations throughout the decade: Forest Lawn in 1961, Montgomery in 1964, and Bowness the year after that.

Calgary's amenities received a significant boost during the tenure of Hay's successor as mayor, former provincial Liberal leader Grant MacEwan. "He played a part in getting Calgary some of its enormous parks - bigger and better than anywhere else in Canada," recalled Roy Farran, a fellow alderman and later a minister in the Lougheed government. He also initiated the city's first major urban renewal plan. But MacEwan's great passion was history (he wrote some 40 books on popular history in his lifetime), and he played an important part in the creation of Heritage Park Historical Village, a collaboration of the Woods Foundation, the Glenbow Foundation and the city. It became one of the continent's largest and most successful "living history" parks, complete with a vintage train, historic buildings and the S.S. Moyie sternwheeler puffing majestically around the Glenmore reservoir.

Calgary's trademark of course was the annual Stampede, but in the early 1960s the new volunteer chairman of the attractions committee didn't think much of the American singers and dancers hired for the event. "When I watched the performers who came up from Chicago, I didn't think they were very good," Peter Lougheed recalled in a 2000 interview. "We thought we'd build our own show, so we went to Chicago, hired Randy Avery, and that's how the Young Canadians began." This spectacular outdoor musical variety show, formed in 1964, became an instant success, with profits going to various youth programs. Offering free training in voice, dance, dramatics and acrobatics, it attracted plenty of talent. Many of its members (including Lougheed's daughter, Andrea) went on to professional careers.

Towards the end of the decade, Calgary's rapidly developing skyline was joined by a building which was destined to become another trademark: the 626-foot Husky Tower, later renamed the Calgary Tower. Completed in 1968, it was the tallest building in the western hemisphere until the

A Social Credit picnic in Edmonton's Laurier Park, 1970. The once formidable organization was suffering dwindling membership rolls, and efforts to rejuvenate the party were fitful at best. Over the next decade or so it would gradually disappear from the scene as a political force.

construction of Toronto's CN Tower eight years later. The problems in building it were formidable. Calgary's core has a very high water table and building on the water-bearing gravel was like building on ball bearings. The solution was to put more of the tower's weight under the ground than above it. The problems associated with the tower's revolving restaurant (most methods used elsewhere had produced a jerky motion that did nothing for diners) were solved by a roughneck and self-taught engineer from Edmonton, Fred Tappenden, designed a system using two washing machine motors (one-half horsepower each) and a cable relay to keep things at a constant speed. It worked, and the tower restaurant would still be rotating smoothly at the century's end.

The man behind the Husky Tower project, vice-president of CPR's Marathon Realty, Rod Sykes, became mayor of Calgary in 1969, and it's doubtful that the city ever had a more outspoken or controversial one. "Calgary was being run by a small, very well-off clique with very low ethical standards," Sykes recalled three decades later. "City hall badly needed a cleaning." The new mayor went to work with gusto, and immediately made enemies. "It was quite a turbulent era. It was not a peaceful, nostalgic love-in," Sykes remembered. "At one point private detectives were hired to get dirt on me so they could shut me up," but after two months they found the mayor's private life so quiet they gave up. "Later two police officers were setting up to plant drugs on my kids - a filthy trick." The plan apparently failed when a young TV reporter, approached to publicize the bust, blew the whistle on the scheme. His name was Ralph Klein, and he would later play his own part in Calgary's future, as well as that of the province.

Many communities in northern Alberta missed out on the post-war economic boom (the Edmonton Journal dubbed the region "Western Canada's Appalachia"). It's clear from this 1967 photo that bustling Barrhead was not among them. But a decade later Alberta's burgeoning prosperity had spread to virtually every corner of the province.

253

Alberta's native people end their long silence

INSPIRED PUBLIC RELATIONS PUT ABORIGINAL ISSUES ON THE NATIONAL AGENDA,
AND THE FOCUS OF THE NEW ACTIVISM IS A YOUNG MAN FROM SUCKER CREEK

In 1960 the Conservative government of Prime Minister John Diefenbaker moved to extend federal voting rights to native Canadians living on reserves. The idea was wholeheartedly endorsed by Canada's only native legislator, Alberta Senator James Gladstone, but was strongly opposed by some native leaders. The concerns ranged from lack of interest in voting in the elections of "a foreign nation" to fears that the franchise would somehow infringe on existing treaty rights. "If I thought for one moment that any of those fears were justified," Gladstone told the Senate, "I would fight this bill to the very end." The legislation eventually passed easily in Ottawa, and similar changes allowing native Albertans to vote in provincial elections were passed in 1965. The granting of voting rights coincided with growing public awareness and concern about the situation of native Canadians, which in some ways mirrored the civil rights movement in the U.S. Most significantly, it coincided with the emergence of a new generation of native leaders who would become adept at using the entire arsenal of modern public relations and political activism to place native concerns on the national agenda.

The most influential of these new leaders was Harold Cardinal, the brilliant product of northern Alberta's Sucker Creek reserve. Educated at the Catholic residential school in Joussard and Edmonton's St. Francis Xavier High School, Cardinal became president of the Canadian Indian Youth Council while studying sociology at St. Patrick's College in Ottawa. He returned to Edmonton in 1968 to take a summer job with the Alberta Native Communications Society, and a rise to prominence which can only be described as meteoric. Within a month of returning to the province he was elected president of the Indian Association of Alberta. He disbanded the IAA's non-native advisory board, and quickly became famous for inaugurating meetings by quietly asking all non-natives to leave the room. Cardinal declared Ottawa's Indian Affairs department a "monstrosity" that had "proven itself incapable a thousand times over." By the end of the year he had become the *de facto* spokesman for Canada's native people, challenging the new federal government of Prime Minister Pierre Trudeau to abolish the Indian Affairs bureaucracy.

In the summer of 1969, the youthful new Minister of Indian Affairs, Jean Chretien, agreed to do just that, within five years. But there was a condition: In exchange for an end to burdensome bureaucracy and continued provision of social services and health care (from the provinces), native people would lose their special status - and in particular would have to begin paying income tax. Cardinal was sceptical the changes Chretien suggested could be accomplished in "200 years," let alone five, and he insisted a "concentration of funds" be turned over the native organizations. In addition, Cardinal warned the public must accept that native people would continue to be "Canadian citizens plus... that we are full citizens but also possess special rights."

The debate dragged on for a full year, before a televised meeting between native leaders - led by Cardinal - and the Trudeau cabinet effectively killed off Chretien's proposal. Cardinal delivered native demands in a 100-page document titled *Citizens Plus* and lectured Trudeau and his minister in front of the cameras until the prime minister admitted the plan had perhaps been "misguided or short-sighted." It was a watershed moment for relations between the federal government and native people. Whether or not they agreed with Cardinal's approach, and some did not, most liked his style. In his short but remarkable career in the public spotlight he had challenged the paternalism and benign neglect which for eight decades had governed relations between native Canadians and the government in Ottawa. The era of quiet stoicism, of suffering in silence, was definitely over. Cardinal had instructed native Canadians in an entirely new arsenal of political, legal, and public relations' weapons, which in the coming years would pay off in major escalations of government funding and a string of court victories. There was also some social progress, but real improvements would continue to be slow and elusive.

In 1971 Cardinal himself became embroiled in a fiscal battle with Chretien, who halted federal funding of the IAA after claims that economic development money had been improperly diverted for other uses. He stood down from the IAA presidency in 1972, but was later elected vice-chief of the Assembly of First Nations. He also became Indigenous Scholar in Residence at the University of Alberta law school, where he pursued a doctorate at the end of the century. Ironically, he also ran unsuccessfully for the federal Liberals, led by Jean Chretien, in the 2000 national election.

After decades of marginalization, in the 1960s aboriginal groups began to demand inclusion in a wider society that had largely passed them by. The Alberta oil patch responded with efforts to include native people in northern development. These Inuit roughnecks were photographed at Edmonton's Petroleum Industry Training Centre in 1968.

The downtown Calgary skyline at night, in a 1970 photograph. The old CPR whistle-stop had been transformed into a shining metropolis, and its citizens were justly proud of the achievement. What they didn't know was that the best was yet to come.

Glenbow Archives NA-2864-4882R

Saudi oil minister Sheik Ahmed Yamani and his wife with Peter and Jeanne Lougheed during a 1978 visit to Alberta. The Mid-East oil crisis made the province a serious energy player, but the sheik was glad to learn that a barrel of synthetic crude from Alberta's oil sands cost 40 times as much to produce as Saudi oil.

Provincial Archives of Alberta PA-J4073

CHAPTER TEN

A second great boom reshapes Alberta

MID-EAST INSTABILITY DRAMATICALLY INCREASES THE VALUE OF OIL, AND PROSPEROUS ALBERTANS DISCOVER THE WONDERS OF 'LIFESTYLE'

In October 1973 events half a world away from Alberta suddenly had a profound impact on the economy of the province. On October 6th, as Israelis celebrated the Jewish holy day of Yom Kippur, Egypt and Syria launched a surprise attack. The fighting would last a mere 20 days, but what became known as the October War dramatically underlined the instability of the world's major oil-producing region. In retaliation for U.S. and Western support of Israel, the Arab states reduced production and raised prices. Saudi Arabia suspended all oil shipments to its largest customer, the U.S.

Until 1973 Alberta's oil had been a valuable resource, but a relatively cheap commodity, its price determined by the availability of vast quantities of easily accessed crude from the oil fields of the Middle East. All of this would now change. The Arab embargo would continue only until March 1974 and never amounted to more than 10% of world demand, but a nervous market had been alerted to the precariousness of supply. There were line-ups for gasoline across North America and Europe, and oil prices rocketed from $3 (US) a barrel to as much as $22. It would temporarily settle in the $12 to $15 range, but it was clear that the era of cheap oil was over - and Alberta was sitting on a commodity that had just quadrupled in value.

A month before the October War, the Canadian government had at long last agreed to the extension of the Alberta-Ontario oil pipeline into Quebec, where Alberta oil had previously been spurned because foreign imports could often be bought at slightly cheaper prices on the open market. This, too, would change. The federal energy minister, Donald Macdonald, imposed an export tax on Alberta oil - beginning at 40 cents a barrel, but rapidly rising to $1.90. The new tax was expected to raise $1 billion for the federal treasury, lower exports and keep Canadian prices below world levels. Albertans, argued Prime Minister Pierre Trudeau, must learn to share their resource wealth. Sharing was not a problem, but the attempt to unilaterally impose federal taxes on a provincial resource triggered a struggle over control of Alberta's energy wealth that would dominate the province's relations with Ottawa for the next dozen years.

Leading Alberta's defence was a new premier, 43-year-old Peter Lougheed, and a new governing party, the Progressive Conservatives. They had replaced the 35-year-old Socred dynasty in the August 1971 election, as the province experienced another of its signature political earthquakes. The PCs had successfully portrayed the Socred government of Premier Harry Strom as tired and out of touch with the changing times. "There was no substantive change in political philosophy," noted Lougheed biographer Allan Hustak (*Peter Lougheed*, Toronto: McClelland and Stewart, 1979). As Lougheed himself later put it: "We weren't asking people to vote Liberal." The PCs were simply conservatives in a hurry, promising youthful enthusiasm and a quantum leap in development. To make this happen would take a lot of money and a lot of government, but Lougheed's timing was perfect. In the early 1970s the belief in government's ability to improve life had never been higher, and now the oil price hike touched off by the October War would fill government coffers and launch the province's second great boom.

Peter Lougheed typified Alberta's penchant for strong leadership, but perhaps no other premier in the 20th century came so strongly to personify the province in the public image - in

Alberta and elsewhere. Grandson of Senator James Lougheed, the young lawyer had studied at Harvard and become vice-president and corporate counsel at Calgary-based Mannix Ltd., at the time Canada's largest construction company. Lougheed was smart, dynamic, and attractive - an increasingly important attribute in the age of television. His vision of "economic diversification" and "province building" captured the public imagination. Alberta would use its non-renewable resource wealth to create a modern, prosperous province which would demand a greater say in national affairs. There would be no return to "have not" status.

After decades of government generally viewed by the Canadian mainstream as rather odd, Albertans were widely viewed as - in the words of *Edmonton Journal* editor Andrew Snaddon - "the funny hick people on the Prairies." But Lougheed's modern and aggressive Alberta cried out for a re-evaluation, and suddenly commanded the serious attention of the national media. "Lougheed has fused big business and big bureaucracy into a tight-knit, and indeed impenetrable, alliance," wrote the *Toronto Star's* Richard Gwyn. As a force to be reckoned with, Gwyn placed the premier on par with C.D. Howe, the legendary federal industry minister. Journalist Christina Newman wrote of the Lougheed government: "The cabinet is like the board of directors of some vast corporation called Alberta Inc. - secretive, self-contained, business-oriented, and run by a president-premier who practices an ideology that might be described as Aggressive Conservatism."

By 1975 Alberta had both the lowest taxes in Canada and an enormous budgetary surplus. The situation allowed the Lougheed government to contemplate what would become its signature legislation and enduring monument: the Heritage Savings Trust Fund. The idea of a "rainy day" fund was first proposed in 1974. Alberta's surplus, warned Lougheed, should be invested "to assure future generations may have an equal opportunity to sustain the same high level of prosperity." The plan was formally announced in the February, 1975 budget, with an initial $1.5 billion endowment. Four years later it would be worth almost $5 billion, and growing by $1.5 billion a year. Ontario Premier William Davis suggested breaking it up and directing Alberta's resource revenues directly to the federal treasury. The fund was also eyed with some suspicion by the federal government, particularly when Alberta began offering low-interest loans to Atlantic Canada. Alberta was by now providing billions to the federal treasury, but in Ottawa there was growing concern over the alleged "fiscal imbalance" created by Alberta's wealth. "At what point do the resources of any one province belong to all Canadians?" Prime Minister Trudeau asked during the 1979 federal election campaign. It was a question which would soon ignite one of the most important political battles in Canadian history, and test the Lougheed government as it had never been tested before.

Allowing students to smoke in school would have been unthinkable before the 1970s - and would become so again - but notions of student empowerment were now at their zenith. These students are taking a smoke break at Edmonton's M.E. Lazerte High School.

For Alberta, the 1970s were a defining moment that transformed the everyday lives of its people, the look of its cities and towns, and the business of its companies and corporations. When people talk about booming Alberta, they generally refer to the decade when growth and development accelerated at a pace which, hitherto, few would have imagined. The Alberta economy was humming along nicely as the decade began, but then it was as if someone hit the fast-forward button. The 1970s were years of superlatives and excess. The province's growth far outstripped that of the other provinces. While unemployment became a fixture of the national economy, Alberta businesses couldn't find enough skilled tradespeople or good help. Inflation was raging everywhere, and double-digit interest rates and wage increases became the norm. In Alberta the cost of everything, from steak to homes, soared along with the boom. The average home in Edmonton cost $22,227 in 1971, and was worth $78,719 eight years later. Homes were even more costly in Calgary, where by 1979 in the Mount Royal-Scarborough district a typical bungalow cost $105,000 - the most expensive housing in Canada.

Part of the reason for high real estate prices was demand. People were pouring into Alberta in ever-increasing numbers. During the decade Calgary grew by an incredible 50% (from 400,000 to 600,000), making it the fastest-growing city in the country. "Every month the city grew by 2,603 people," marvelled one newspaper report. "That's about 650 each week, or 90 each day, or almost four every hour!" Many municipalities were bursting at the seams and gobbling up land from surrounding rural areas. Edmonton and Calgary annexed thousands of acres, while smaller places absorbed land in lesser bites. Medicine Hat, described by Mayor Milt Reinhardt as "probably the wealthiest city per capita in North America," took in 9,100 acres, while Lethbridge swallowed over 14,000 acres to double in size. Drayton Valley optimistically applied for enough land to triple its population to 5,000. Toronto Mayor David Crombie (later a federal Conservative cabinet minister) attended Edmonton's Klondike Days in 1978 and pronounced himself amazed. "In Toronto all you encounter is gloom and doom. Here's it's all eyes forward. Is that ever refreshing!"

It was also, well, nuts. The *Calgary Herald* described the frenetic pace of change engulfing the

As late as 1973 two women had been refused jobs as bus drivers in Edmonton because their feet allegedly couldn't reach the floor pedals. A complaint to the Human Rights Commission was unsuccessful, but by 1977 Calgary Transit employed 26 women drivers, including Marion White (standing) and Lana Boyd.

261

Many Albertans were cool to the 1969 Official Languages Act, but apparently that didn't mean they didn't want their children to learn the French language. By the mid-80s some 115,000 Alberta students studied core French, and 20,000 were enrolled in French immersion programs.

city: "Swinging cranes on every second corner, pounding jackhammers, growling trucks - the whole cacophonous din is evidence that Calgary is reeling into its wildest office-building spree yet. Unless some developers get a bad case of the jitters, the city's employment centre will grow over the next 30 months by 33 buildings and 5.2 million square feet." The cash value of Calgary's city centre building boom was expected to top $1 billion. The province-wide building frenzy had one rather unusual outcome. By 1973, homeowners looking for cement for household projects discovered there was none to be had. Demand had outstripped supply and the province's entire supply of cement had been commandeered by large contractors - and even they were running short.

The economy took off so fast that there was a severe shortage of labour. "You can walk down any street in any town and talk to employers who are looking for workers who aren't available," complained Alberta Manpower Minister Bert Hohol. On a typical weekday in 1974, the *Edmonton Journal* carried up to seven pages of help-wanted ads for positions ranging from labourers to senior executives and engineers. Edmonton's Fibreglass Canada plant was adding 12 people a week, when it could find them. "Everybody I speak to is having trouble," said industrial relations manager R.A. Huth. "It doesn't matter what the industry." Drawn by the job vacancies, migrants created yet another shortage: accommodation. A survey of rental property in Lethbridge in July 1975 couldn't find a single vacant unit. Mid West Property Management reported a waiting list of 500. "It's bloody awful," said Bruce McKillop, of McKillop Agencies. "We don't have one. Not one place for rent."

For most Albertans the inflation of the great boom was seen most obviously in rising food prices. In one week in August 1973 butter jumped seven cents to 79 cents a pound, and the price of ground chuck rose 10 cents to $1.25. By 1978 hamburger would be closing in on $2 a pound. When gasoline prices rose in the summer of 1979, the *Red Deer Advocate* complained, "The $1 gallon of gas, like the $1 pack of cigarettes, is now upon us."

If the 1960s had been all about social revolution, demonstrating and overturning traditions, a decade later as the Baby Boomers settled into careers and began raising families their attention turned to a new concept termed "quality of life." For their parents and grandparents, prosperity had been an end in itself. Life had held its share of enjoyments and entertainments, to be sure, but they were generally modest and of secondary importance. But what, their offspring wondered, was the purpose of prosperity if not to enjoy it? Suddenly bigger homes, recreational opportunities, stylish food and drink, festivals, exotic vacations - what the media now referred to as "lifestyle" - all became vastly important. The boomers spending power soon got the attention of home-builders, retailers, and restaurant owners, and their voting power (the average age of Albertans in 1970 was 24.7 years) got the attention of a government with money to spend.

In Edmonton in 1974 the Lougheed government committed $35 million to begin development of a Capital City Recreation Park along the city's sometimes neglected North Saskatchewan River valley. It was more than the province had spent on all parks over the previous decade. In Calgary the city council froze development of Nose Hill, an area of natural prairie parkland on the city's north side, and the provincial government announced the creation of a 2,800 acre Fish Creek Provincial Park (which would eventually cost $45 million). At the end of the decade plans were announced for parks in Medicine Hat, Lethbridge, Red Deer, Grande Prairie, and Lloydminster that would eventually total $86 million.

In the 1950s and 60s Alberta's Rocky Mountain ski slopes attracted a few thousand intrepid skiers as Jasper's Marmot Basin, Lake Louise, and Norquay and Sunshine in Banff began to develop. By the winter of 1970 a quarter of a million lift tickets were sold at the four hills, but they were still operating at half their capacity. According to historian Bob Sandford, when Hilton Hotels negotiated to buy Canadian Pacific's national chain in the late 1960s, the Banff Springs Hotel, Chateau Lake Louise and Jasper Park Lodge were so run-down that they were excluded from the deal. So when CP spent $11 million to winterize the Banff Springs, it looked like a gamble. With hindsight it was perfectly timed, as Alberta's prosperous middle class discovered skiing and an aggressive marketing campaign began to attract skiers from the U.S., Japan and Europe.

"Before the 70s, skiing was reserved for the elite," recalled Edmonton teacher and lifelong skier Dennis Fitzsimonds. "But in just over a decade it entered the mainstream. Students and working class guys took up the sport. They didn't own European stretch pants, so they skied in insulated work overalls and leather boots. Plastic ski boots were just coming on the scene. Lots of

The phrase "fuddle duddle" entered the Canadian lexicon after it was used as an official euphemism for an obscenity muttered by Pierre Trudeau in the House of Commons. It spawned a host of popular bumper stickers, like these plastered on a Calgarian's car, and even a brand of caramel popcorn.

guys skied with wineskins, which today would not only be illegal but politically incorrect."

A new road and a new chairlift installed in 1970 helped make Marmot Basin more attractive to its core market in Edmonton. Sunshine embarked on a major expansion, which included new lifts, a day lodge and the Sunshine Inn - the first on-mountain ski hotel in the Alberta Rockies. But to get to Sunshine's legendary natural snow skiers still had to endure the long climb from the parking lot, on a one-lane logging road, in an old school bus which chugged and lurched its way up the mountain. By the end of the decade Sunshine would retire the bus and replace it with the world's largest gondola ski lift, with 207 cars capable of whisking 1,800 skiers an hour 1,600 feet up the mountain to the ski area. By the early 1980s the four major resorts closed in on one million lift tickets a season, and had established a reputation as a world-class ski destination. Calgary's 1988 Winter Olympic Games would do much to enhance that reputation and attract more international visitors. Ironically, as Banff and Jasper grew in international popularity, rising prices and a falling Canadian dollar would make it less affordable for many Albertans and regular skiing would once again become a pastime for the well-heeled.

The decade transformed the look of subdivisions throughout the province. Modest, post-war

Feeling and looking good became obsessions during the 1980s, as fitness clubs, aerobics and other forms of physical exercise experienced a boom. Maintaining a healthy-looking tan was difficult in a climate with perhaps six months of winter, and so was born the tanning salon. Rising rates of skin cancer eventually made people think twice about over-doing it.

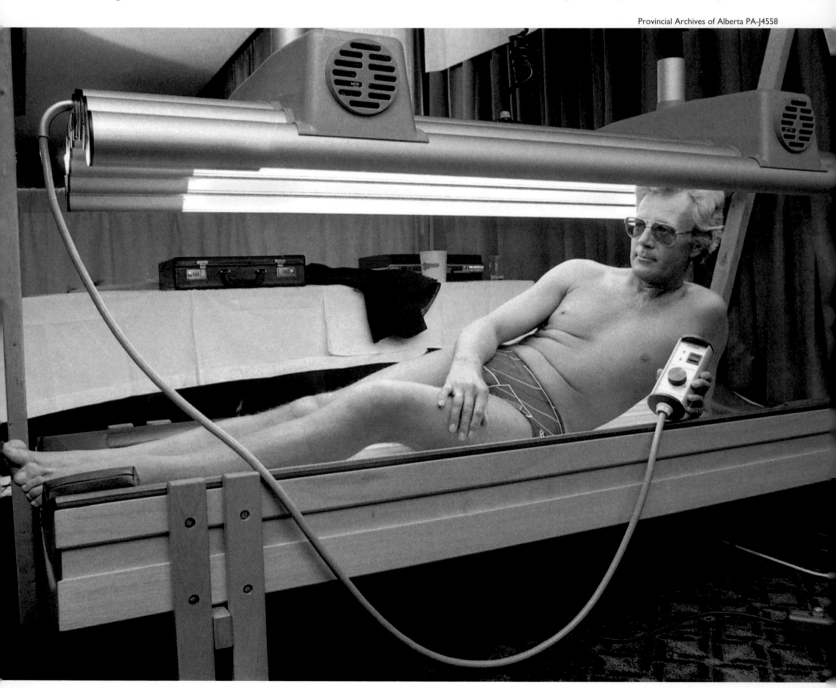

bungalows, typically around 1,200 square feet, were replaced by larger split-level and two-storey homes with attached garages, ensuite bathrooms, main-floor family rooms with fireplaces, and large kitchens with a full range of appliances. Veteran Edmonton realtor Patrick Mooney marvelled at how the standard middle-class family home virtually doubled in size during the 1970s. "As the exuberant economic outlook grew, people became more expansive in their lifestyles, and when it came to houses - as well as many other things - bigger was better. My wife and I were perfect examples of the trend. In 1969 we had a modest house in Sherwood Park. In the mid-70s we moved to a larger house in the new subdivision of Mills Woods, and by 1978 we built a monstrosity, with a fireplace in the master bedroom."

Oddly enough, Albertans were spending less time in their larger homes. Eating out, in particular, was more popular than at any time since the years before the Great War. Edmonton restaurateur Normand Campbell, a waiter at the time, experienced this revolution from a subterranean steakhouse - without windows by order of the Alberta Liquor Control Board - where the wine, the velour furniture and the barely-singed T-bone steaks were all roughly the same colour. It was the flambé era, recalled Campbell in 2001, when Steak Diane or a peppercorn-encrusted New York striploin were the favourites with patrons of Oliver's, The Discovery, or the Edmonton and Calgary renditions of Hy's. Calgary's busiest downtown eateries at the beginning of the 70s were the Greek-run blue-collar joints west of City Hall, crowded each night with cowboys, roughnecks and reporters. In both cities, the white-collar crowd and politicians preferred hotel restaurants, which were doing very well with an upscale version of the steakhouse menu.

All of this began to change as increasingly well-travelled Albertans demanded something a little more sophisticated, a little different. Although restaurants that got too far out in front of Alberta tastes often paid dearly for their adventurism. Prime rib stilled ruled, but Calgary's Inn on Lake Bonavista, La Caille and La Chaumiere, and Edmonton's Bistro Praha, The Creperie and Walden's, began to defy convention and succeed. Walden's was typical of the new trend in restaurant design. "Walking into Walden's is like entering an enchanting rain forest," gushed a *Chatelaine* magazine feature. "Sunshine streams through the ferns and full-sized fiscus trees," and the waiters could be relied upon to inquire "Would you like fresh ground pepper with that?"

Golf began its meteoric rise in popularity during the 1980s, being transformed from a game for older men into a universal pastime. Time at the driving range became essential. Despite the limitations of climate, Alberta would eventually boast more duffers per capita than anywhere else in the world.

Jogging also became popular during this time, as Baby Boomers reaching middle age refused to succumb to expanding waistlines - at least without a fight. This city street scene also underlines the growing informality of Alberta society compared with earlier eras.

While Alberta boomed and racked up record surpluses, the federal government of Liberal Prime Minister Pierre Trudeau struggled with ever-increasing deficits, stubborn unemployment and the threat of Quebec separation. From the Ottawa perspective, Trudeau's vision of Canada as a nation of two founding peoples held together by a strong central government was imperilled by this fiscal imbalance. Entrepreneurial, multi-ethnic, reformist Alberta, as represented by the Lougheed government, saw in its newfound wealth an opportunity to influence the national agenda and secure the economic future of the province. The collision of these very different priorities formed the political backdrop to Alberta's boom, and would eventually bring it to a premature end.

At the federal Conservatives' 1976 leadership convention another Albertan would become a major player in this unfolding drama. Failing to unite behind any of the leading candidates, the party chose instead a 36-year-old MP from Alberta, Joe Clark. In his home province, Clark's surprise victory was welcomed as yet another sign that power and influence were moving westward, but it would, in fact, become a serious complication in Alberta's relationship with Ottawa.

Not that it needed much more complicating. In an interview years after, Lougheed recalled that Alberta's relationship with Ottawa always seemed to come down to a desire to "control" the province. "They see us as being able, physically, to be independent and that means we would have influence with other provinces. When I look back on the Heritage fund... we just thought we should be participating in the Canadian mosaic. But actually... lending money to Nova Scotia and Newfoundland just drove the federal bureaucrats wild. It shook the foundations of their position. We probably, in hindsight, shouldn't have done that... [but] we thought we were expressing our patriotism."

Whether having both parents work was a choice or a necessity, the late 1970s saw the first expressions of the view that childcare ought to be available as a social benefit, and subsidized by the taxpayer. This demonstration took place in Edmonton in 1979.

Provincial Archives of Alberta PA-J4587/1

High River's Joe Clark was the surprise victor at the 1976 federal Conservative leadership convention. The 36-year-old Albertan vaulted ahead of Brian Mulroney and Claude Wagner to take the prize.

Lougheed warned Albertans to prepare for a federal grab at Alberta's resource revenue, but with the national economy stalling, and Trudeau's seeming inability to halt Quebec separatism, the Liberals went down to defeat in a federal election in May 1979. Basking in the glow of victory at the arena in Spruce Grove, west of Edmonton, the new prime minister, Joe Clark, vowed his new minority government would be a "partnership" with Canadians. With an Albertan ensconced at 24 Sussex Drive, it seemed to many as if Alberta's time had come. "It was fully expected," wrote journalist Allan Fotheringham, "that the decision-making bodies and all those non-elected boards in Ottawa would suddenly flower with these energetic and tough-minded Alberta men who had been denied their say for so long. There was talk of an Alberta figure heading the *CBC* and another getting a major position in the CNR. Once young Joe found the levers of power in Ottawa, it was expected (a natural expectation) that all those havens of patronage filled with fatted Liberals would be cleansed with lean-jawed Tories, a good percentage of them from Alberta."

With the impending departure from politics of Alberta's nemesis it was widely assumed that relations with Ottawa would improve, and on some fronts that was indeed the case, but an energy agreement between Alberta and the federal government remained elusive. "With Conservative governments in a majority of provinces we thought a speedy agreement could be reached on a new energy policy," Clark's finance minister, Newfoundland MP John Crosbie, recalled in his memoirs. "But as negotiations with Alberta dragged on our political position was undermined by the public perception in Ontario that we were caving in to Alberta. Premier Davis waged a deliberate campaign to discredit our federal energy policy in order to protect the popularity of his own provincial party in Ontario. Rather than prepare his people for the higher oil and natural gas prices that had to come, Davis told Ontarians that any increase in oil prices would be disastrous."

In Montreal on Thanksgiving Day 1979, Clark, Crosbie and federal Energy Minister Ray Hnatyshyn met with Lougheed and several Alberta ministers. "The meeting was a disaster," remembers Crosbie. "There was no sense that we were all members of the same political party seeking a solution to a common problem." Lougheed, says Crosbie, was "far more formidable than Bill Davis, in appearance, intellect and pugnacity," and he was in no mood to make a major compromise for the sake of Conservative unity. "There were no pleasantries and no collegiality," says Crosbie. "Lougheed laid down the Alberta position and told us to take it or leave it. We left it."

The Clark government introduced a budget on December 13, and was defeated on a confidence vote two days later. Clark's Conservatives were at first confident they would be returned with a majority, but in the federal vote of February 18, 1980, it was the Liberals and Alberta's old nemesis, Pierre Trudeau, who were returned to power with a majority. Towards the end of the election campaign Trudeau had given a speech in Halifax which contained hints of a massive federal intervention in the oil patch. "I read the Halifax speech and I said 'Wow, we're in for it,'" Lougheed recalled later.

Prime Minister Joe Clark and Premier Peter Lougheed met at 24 Sussex Drive, the PM's Ottawa residence, in November 1979 to discuss a deal on oil pricing. The fact the two Albertans had been close (Clark had worked on Lougheed's early campaigns) did not make their relationship noticeably easier.

Canadian Press CP-3959028

Joe Clark: The prime minister from High River

IT WAS A LONG WAY FROM ORGANIZING THE UNIVERSITY OF ALBERTA'S FIRST STUDENT DEMO, BUT FOR CANADA'S ONLY ALBERTA-BORN PM, POLITICS WERE DEFINITELY IN THE BLOOD

The only Alberta-born prime minister of Canada, Joe Clark grew up in the rangeland town of High River, 40 kilometres south of Calgary, surrounded by the competing influences of newspapering and politics.

The eldest son of Charles A. Clark, publisher of the *High River Times* weekly newspaper, and Grace Welch, a lumber merchant's daughter, Joe was born on June 5, 1939 into a family with a political history (his grandfather's brother had been a member of the Ontario legislature and an MP) and a host of more current political connections (including another Conservative prime minister, family friend Arthur Meighen). Yet it was assumed that Joe would follow his father and grandfather into the family business. Indeed, in 1955 the Golden Jubilee issue of the *Times* noted with some pride: "It is encouraging evidence of family continuity that young Joe Clark has been contributing to the paper in special assignments during the past year."

Clark's interest in journalism was genuine. After graduating from High School in 1957, he spent the summer as a sports reporter at the *Calgary Herald*, and during his university years he worked for first the *Edmonton Journal* and later the *Albertan*. He is also remembered as one of the most aggressive editors in the history of the University of Alberta's student newspaper, the *Gateway*. The radical young Clark used his editorial perch to lecture his fellow students on their lack of interest in politics and their general "narrowness and selfishness."

He also helped organize the university's first recorded student demonstration, when in March 1960 several hundred students marched on the Legislature to demand more student housing. According to biographer David L. Humphreys (*Joe Clark — A Portrait*, Montreal, Depeau and Greenberg, 1978), the demo and Clark's rabble-rousing editorials earned him a stern three-hour lecture from Dr. Walter Johns, the university's president. "He said I was trying to destroy freedom of the press," recalled Dr. Johns. "I said he was trying to destroy the university."

Clark's first real political involvement came while at university in 1958, when he worked on Alan Lazerte's bid for the provincial Conservative leadership, and during the 1959 provincial election as a driver and speech writer for Conservative leader W.J.C. Kirby. But these were not good times for Alberta Tories (the party won one seat in the 1959 election) and Clark turned for a time to the youth wing of the federal party. After an unsuccessful attempt at law (at

Dalhousie and UBC), Clark returned to the U of A as a graduate student to study political science. At the same time he began working for a friend of his father's, Peter Lougheed, who had won the provincial Tory leadership in 1965. Over the next two years the young Clark was a key organizer as Lougheed rebuilt the party and the two men became friends.

As the 1967 provincial election loomed, Lougheed talked Clark out of running in Okotoks-High River, a seat he might well have won. Instead Clark ran, quite literally, in Calgary South. Clark had helped develop the Tories' new strategy (borrowed from the NDP) of blitzing constituencies door-to-door, with advance teams identifying homes which might offer potential support. Lougheed himself took to running door-to-door, providing the media with a new and startling photo-op. Humphreys says Clark enthusiastically adopted the leader's fast-paced style, with unfortunate results. "The mind was willing but the flesh was weak. With three days to go, Clark's knees began to puff and he was forced to stop campaigning."

Clark lost the election by a mere 462 votes, while Lougheed and five others went on to become the "Original Six" MLAs who would form the core of the revitalized Progressive Conservative Party of Alberta — and in 1971 the heart of Lougheed's first government. Clark was left on the outside looking in.

In the October 1972 federal election, after a year of campaigning, Clark was elected to the House of Commons as the member for Rocky Mountain, an enormous and sprawling Alberta constituency stretching from the U.S. border to the Peace River country. Around the same time, the rookie MP hired as a research assistant Maureen McTeer, a serious-minded young law student from Eastern Ontario whose Conservative political roots and student involvement mirrored his own. The 34-year-old MP married his 21-year-old researcher in June 1973. McTeer planned to finish law school and decided to keep using her own name. "I thought it would be nice to practise in my own name and have a McTeer on a law firm door somewhere, something my parents could be proud of," McTeer explained to biographer Humphreys. In keeping with the times, but in the eyes of more traditional Tories it would be one more reason to doubt the conservatism of the man from High River.

When Clark decided to contest the 1976 PC leadership contest to replace Robert Stanfield, he was far from being the unknown and untried challenger of his media

Joe Clark with his parents, Grace and Charles. When the national media questioned his son's ability, Charles Clark wondered "if they even know Joe?" Ironically, in later years (when the former prime minister returned to the leadership of the federal Progressive Conservatives) his son would get much better press outside Alberta than within it.

image. He had been involved in Conservative politics for two decades, knew everyone worth knowing in the party and was a veteran political campaigner. But he was seen as a long shot for the leadership, an up and coming young MP running to raise his profile. Outspoken Alberta MP Jack Horner was thought by many to have a better chance than Clark, but when the first ballot votes were counted at the Ottawa Civic Centre on a snowy Sunday afternoon in February, even Clark and his supporters were stunned to find he was in third place behind front runners Claude Wagner and Brian Mulroney. On the second ballot he edged Mulroney for second place, and when the final votes were counted Clark (who was the second choice for many delegates) found himself the winner - just 65 votes ahead of Wagner.

The *Toronto Star* welcomed the new Tory leader with the headline "Joe Who?" It was a nickname which stuck,

and which bothered Clark's father. "They just haven't done their homework," the elder Clark complained of the eastern media. "They don't know anything about him. I question if they even know Joe." Despite the continuing media barbs, numerous mistakes and miscues in opposition, and a lack of public enthusiasm for Clark personally, the Conservatives were elected as a minority government on May 22, 1979. On June 4, one day short of his 40th birthday, Joe Clark was sworn in as Canada's sixteenth and youngest prime minister.

For Charles Clark, the election was vindication. "If my son is such a stumbling, bumbling dummy, how in the world could he get to this position?" While for Grace Clark it was all a little bewildering. "I woke up this morning thinking I'd had one of my outrageous dreams... I can't quite say that word - prime minister!"

On March 3, 1979, a propane explosion damaged a pipeline which ran under the southwest quadrant of Edmonton, filling sewers and basements in the Mill Woods district with gas and turning homes into potential bombs. It prompted the evacuation of 20,000 people - the largest such operation in Canadian history. One person was severely burned in the original explosion, but the gas dissipated over the following 24 hours without further damage or injury.

The Edmonton Sun

The raid on Alberta's prosperity was, of course, conducted in the name of the national interest. "The government of Canada and its ministers are elected to seek the good of the whole of the country," Trudeau explained. "So sometimes that means saying no to one region and yes to another in order to redistribute equality of opportunity." In his 1985 autobiography, veteran Trudeau cabinet minister and future prime minister Jean Chretien explained this thinking more bluntly. "Some Westerners, in their time of success, had forgotten the concept of sharing on which Canada had been built. They argued that their resources belonged to them and were not to be shared with the less fortunate parts of the country. Alberta accumulated an enormous trust fund for its citizens and howled when Ottawa tried to get some of the wealth for the rest of the nation."

By the late '70s this serious and divisive charge had become widely accepted as fact in the media and by many people in Central and Eastern Canada. To Albertans it just didn't ring true. The Alberta government claimed that between 1973 and 1979 the provinces contribution to lower Canadian energy prices had already amounted to $15 billion. Figures compiled by economist Robert Mansell at the University of Calgary later put the figure much higher. Rather than the greedy brat of confederation, unwilling to share, Alberta had in fact been by far the most significant contributor to the running of the country. Between 1961 and 1992 Alberta's net contribution to the federal treasury totalled $139 billion, the largest per capita transfer of wealth ever recorded in a democratic nation.

In the House of Commons on October 28, 1980, federal Finance Minister Allan MacEachen introduced a budget which relied heavily on a new National Energy Program to generate revenue. In effect, the federal government had unilaterally decided how Alberta's oil and gas would be developed and who would get what portion of the profits. Alberta's response to the program was rapid and decisive. On October 30, 48 hours after the NEP had been unveiled in Ottawa, Peter Lougheed went on television to inform Albertans that "the Ottawa government has, without negotiation, without agreement, simply walked into our home and occupied the living room." The

Canadian Press CP-2213474

15%
LESS
ALBERTA'SCRUDE

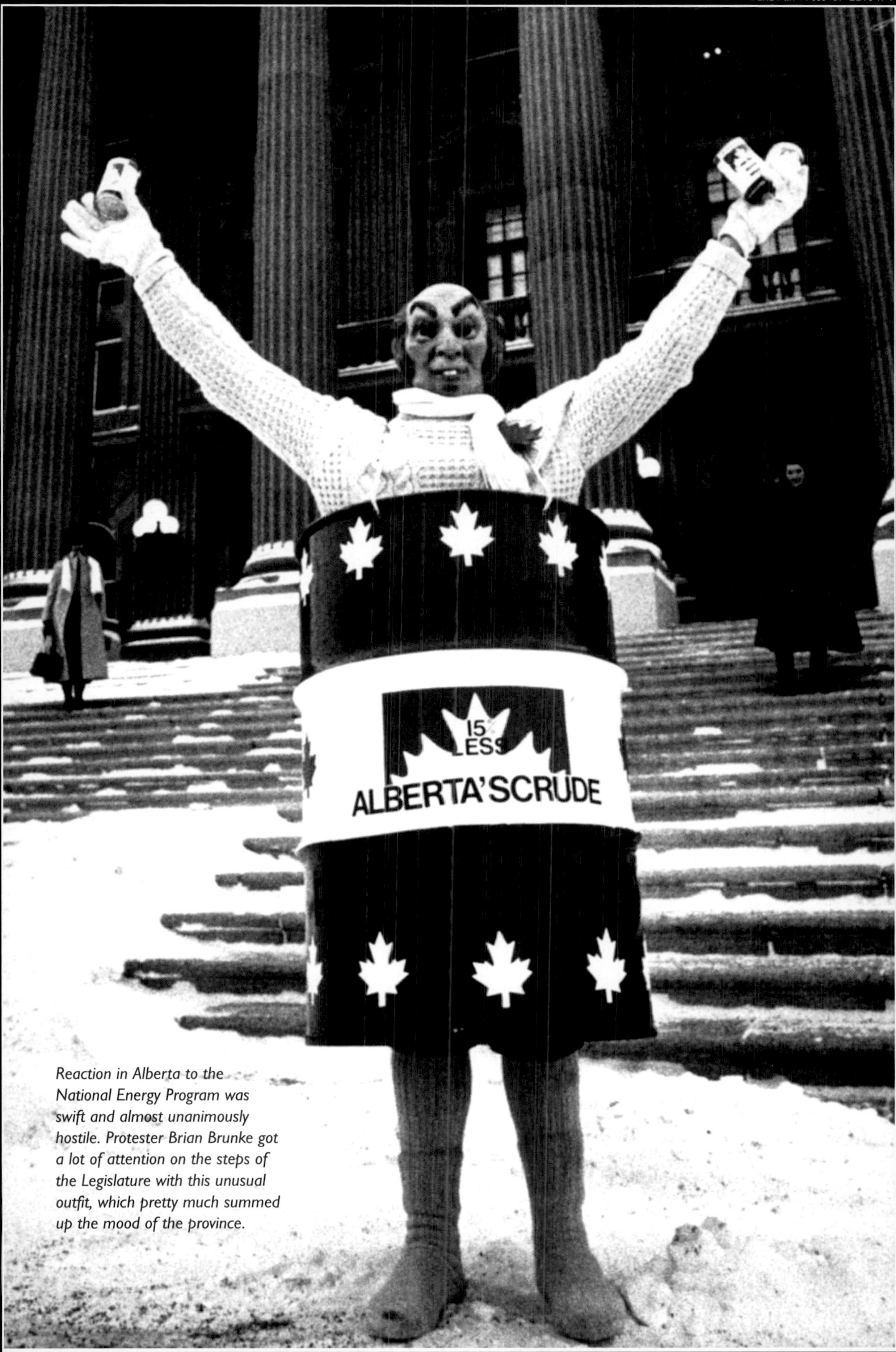

Reaction in Alberta to the National Energy Program was swift and almost unanimously hostile. Protester Brian Brunke got a lot of attention on the steps of the Legislature with this unusual outfit, which pretty much summed up the mood of the province.

A sign of the times in Swan Hills, in the wake of the National Energy Program and a slowdown of the economy. After a decade of spectacular growth, suddenly Alberta ground almost to a halt.

federal budget and energy measures were more than just another round in the simmering energy conflict between Ottawa and Alberta, explained Lougheed. "They are an outright attempt to take over the resources of this province, owned by each of you as Albertans."

Lougheed warned that the province faced a political crisis which directly threatened the constitutional rights of ordinary Albertans: "What we're facing here is a situation where more and more decision-making, more and more control, will be in the hands of the decision makers in Ottawa, and your provincial government will become less and less able to influence your future and to provide for job security and opportunity." After decades as a have-not province, Alberta would not be coerced into giving up its hard-won prosperity, vowed the premier, and it would not be bullied into selling its resources at less than a fair price. Alberta would fight back.

Lougheed announced that over the next nine months the province would reduce its oil output by 15% (beginning March 1st). Shipments of oil to the rest of Canada would be cut by 180,000 barrels a day (in 60,000 barrel increments), and $16 billion in oilsands and heavy oil development would be re-evaluated and possibly shelved. The province would also launch a legal challenge to the new export tax on natural gas. Lougheed promised production would be restored in the event of a fuel shortage. Knowing the move would be controversial, the government launched a major public relations effort to inform Albertans and bolster support for the tough stance. "We kept up a steady series of television communications," recalled Lougheed. "We constantly used the phrase that [the NEP] was the worst public policy decision in Canadian history. We got quite a bit of media support." In Alberta, public support was behind Lougheed. In one of several public meetings in support of the government, 200 hundred people attended a hastily organized rally in Brooks. An opinion poll taken for the *Calgary Herald* and *Edmonton Journal* in the week after Lougheed's television address found two-thirds' support for the provincial government's response to the NEP and almost 75% support for the premier personally. An *Edmonton Sun* poll two weeks later found 80% supported the provincial government or thought the response should have been "much stronger."

The impact of the NEP was disastrous. Customs brokers at the Coutts border crossing between Alberta and Montana reported that in the month of November they had been swamped by the departure of 28 drilling rigs loaded on more than 700 trucks, and the exodus was increasing every week. A survey of drilling companies by the *Calgary Herald* found that another 200 rigs were likely to head for Texas, Oklahoma, Wyoming and other U.S. destinations by the end of February 1981.

With them would go 12,000 jobs and $2 billion in economic activity. Oil industry analysts feared drilling activity for 1981 could drop by 40%, or more. Rob Hunt, general manager for Montgomery Drilling, told the *Herald* that with each departing rig, 23 to 25 Canadians would lose their jobs. In addition, each rig spent in the region of $1 million a year in local communities for food, fuel and other supplies. What upset him most, reported Hunt, was the attitude of the locals. "They really believe that if things turn around [in Alberta] tomorrow, all of the rigs moving to the U.S. would be moving back." It cost an average of $300,000 to dismantle a rig and move it south, he explained. "These rigs are not coming back. When the decision is made to go, that move is pretty well permanent."

The oil war dragged on for almost a year. Then, on September 1st, 1981, as the third round of Alberta cutbacks came into effect, Lougheed and Trudeau signed a five-year energy pricing agreement and the two leaders celebrated with a champagne toast for the assembled media cameras. After months of bitter disagreement and acrimony the photo-op was meant to signal a fresh beginning and a victory for Canadian federalism, but Lougheed would later come to regret it as bad public relations. Two decades later he insisted that the 1981 energy agreement had been a good one for Alberta, in the circumstances, but it was not a public relations triumph. "We oversold in the television announcement of how well we had done. And I also shook hands with Mr. Trudeau and clinked champagne glasses — which was a dumb thing to do. Courteous westerner," he chuckled.

The provincial government was criticized by some Albertans, particularly from within the oil patch, for compromising with Trudeau, but from Lougheed's point of view a compromise had been inevitable. "They have to back away, as they did, significantly, and we have to live with some other things. It was a compromise. Here was our major industry in turmoil, so we figured we had to make a deal." A decade after the NEP, Marc Lalonde explained Ottawa's reasoning. "The major factor behind the NEP wasn't Canadianization or getting more from the industry, or even self-sufficiency," the former federal energy minister admitted. "The determinant factor was the fiscal imbalance between the provinces [Alberta] and the federal government, in which provincial revenues would go up with the price of oil while Ottawa's share of the larger and larger pie got smaller and smaller."

At the beginning of 1982 it seemed as if life might continue as before, despite the NEP and a

The famous photograph of Premier Peter Lougheed and Prime Minister Pierre Trudeau toasting their energy agreement of September 1981. Lougheed always defended the deal, but years later admitted he wished he'd never posed for the photograph.

Canadian Press CP-376985

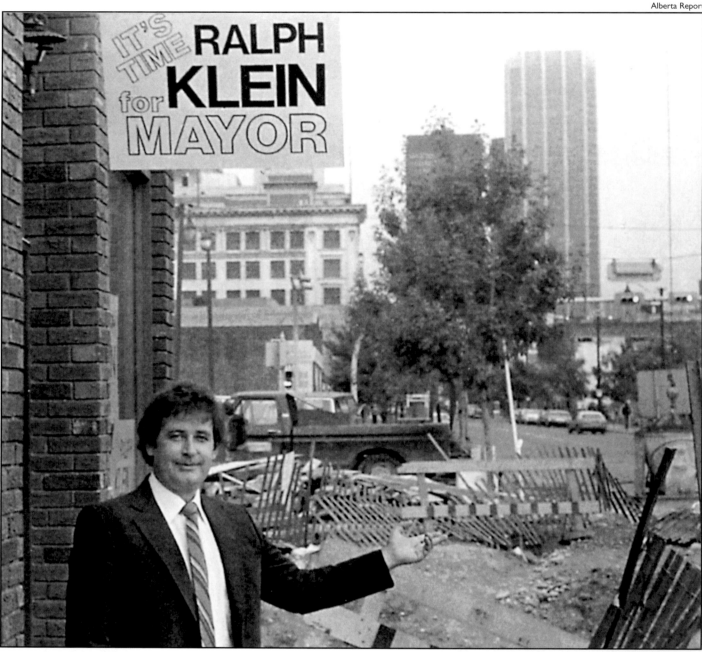

A rising political star. Ralph Klein outside his campaign office during his successful 1980 attempt to become Calgary's mayor. The charismatic former television reporter surprised a lot of people, but it was just the beginning of a stellar political career that would eventually carry him to the premiership of the province.

growing international recession. At the beginning of the year unemployment still hovered around 4%, but it would rise quickly - to 12% by year's end. In addition to the carnage in the oil patch, a quarter of all construction jobs and 30% of jobs in the forest industry simply evaporated as the building boom ground to a halt. By the fall of 1983 there were almost 70,000 Albertans looking for work. Not surprisingly the influx of workers stopped, and then reversed. Alberta's population declined for the first time since the Depression and Calgary's shrunk for the first time in 100 years. The impact of the sudden end of the boom hit everyone, from CEOs to secretaries, from engineers to labourers. Edmonton's homeless shelters were suddenly half empty, prompting the Journal to ask "Where have all the transients gone?"

Alberta's housing market began to deflate at frightening speed. After peaking at $106,000, the average house price in Calgary plunged to $87,000 in little more than a year. If you could sell. Upscale homes dropped in price by as much as 40%, and thousands of Albertans simply walked away from homes which were by now worth less than the mortgages on them. When the devastation was tallied, Alberta's 500,000 homeowners had collectively lost a staggering $5 billion in equity. The *Toronto Star* noted that "until a couple of years ago [Calgary] was certain it was to become Houston North." The paper quoted an oil executive who now speculated that "maybe we're destined to become another Winnipeg." The boom was over.

The opening ceremonies of the 1978
Commonwealth Games in Edmonton. Canada came
first with 45 gold medals. It was the first of a series
of spectacular sports events in the province which
would culminate in Calgary's hosting of the 1988
Winter Olympic Games.

The Edmonton Sun

277

The Calgary Stampeders' 1971 Grey Cup victory was the beginning of two decades of sporting triumphs for Albertans. The crowd which welcomed the cup in the Calgary Corral (top left) was fully appreciative of the city's first CFL championship in 23 years. In 1975 it was the turn of the Edmonton Eskimos, who beat Montreal in Calgary in the first Grey Cup game to be held in Alberta. Jasper Avenue was packed with well-wishers (bottom left) when the boys brought the cup home. In 1979 some were doubtful a skinny 17-year-old Wayne Gretzky could make it as a pro hockey player, but when he signed with the World Hockey Association's Edmonton Oilers, at centre-ice in the Northlands Coliseum (above), it was the beginning of a golden era of hockey in the capital city. Albertan Bill Hunter (below) was the driving force behind the creation of the WHA, which would shortly become a route into the NHL for both Edmonton and Calgary.

A strike at Edmonton's Gainers' meat packing plant in the summer of 1986 brought back memories of the province's turbulent labour history. In this evocative photograph, a police officer climbs on the front of a damaged bus carrying non-union workers. The strike would be settled in December, but the city's once-flourishing meat-packing industry was clearly on life-support.

CHAPTER ELEVEN

Recession tests Alberta's mettle

EDMONTON AND CALGARY DEVELOP ALONG DIFFERENT LINES,
AND FOR SOME THE LACKUSTRE 1980S BECOMES A LOST DECADE

For some Albertans the recession of 1981-82 was the first blow in what many would come to think of as a lost decade. After 40 years of nearly uninterrupted economic growth and increasing prosperity, unemployment hit double digits. businesses large and small collapsed, the booming construction industry ground almost to a standstill, and the real estate market deflated like a punctured balloon. For those Albertans born after the Great Depression, and they were the majority, it was a stunning reversal of fortunes they had never before experienced and had never expected to see. The government of Premier Peter Lougheed tried to put a brave face on the situation, but as Preston Manning, then a management consultant and soon to launch his own political movement, told *Alberta Report* magazine: "Don't be fooled. You can rationalize it any way you want... but it won't change the fact that 175,000 or so people out on the street need jobs."

Alberta's economy continued to shrink at an alarming rate, courtesy of oil prices that dipped below $15 (US) a barrel. By the middle of the decade 62,000 Albertans were receiving welfare - numbers not seen in over four decades. The oil patch, the engine of the economy, bore the brunt of the slowdown. Some 150 drilling rigs sat idle through the 1986 drilling season. "We're not making any money now," said Fred Fleming, president of Regent Drilling. "We're surviving. We're in an emergency state. We're prostituting ourselves to the oil companies." Some drilling companies weren't even able to do that. Guthrie McLaren Drilling of Nisku was one of many companies that went into receivership, laying off its entire workforce of 225. "It's like a morgue around here," reported Bill Briscoe, who was winding up the company on behalf of the receiver.

Grande Prairie's Ed Skrepnek had spent two decades building his oil-well servicing business, like so many home-grown success stories beginning small and building a substantial company through the booming 1970s. Now most of his fleet of trucks were idle or sold. "In 28 years [in the oil patch] I've seen it come and go, but never like this. There's no place to run and no place to hide. I've cleaned out my savings account like everyone else, and I'm just hanging on." His words were echoed by Lloydminster's Lyle Abraham, co-owner of Slurry Cementers. "This is the worst it's been since I was a teenager and broke into the business. If we could shut down for a year, I'd do it, but people have to feed their children."

The double-recession of the early 80s was a severe test for Albertans, but 1987 oil prices had started to recover and the oil patch began the long haul back to prosperity. It also helped that Alberta in the 1980s was not the same province it had been half a century earlier. With a population now approaching three million and an economy more diversified than ever before, it had attained what many economists called the "critical mass" necessary to weather a recession, even one centred on its most important industry. In particular what differed most were the size and wealth of the province's two major cities. Edmonton and Calgary were closing in on a million people each and were home to almost 70% of Albertans. They had become the two most dynamic cities in the country. The traditional fierce competition remained, but what marked this era was the increasing divergence in the character and economies of the two cities.

Despite the depredations of the National Energy Program and the end of the energy boom, in

1985 Calgary was still home to the head offices of 57 of the top 500 Canadian companies. Edmonton was home to 14. Calgary had always had better road and rail connections, and since the construction of its new international airport in the late 1970s it had added more and better air links to its list of advantages. By the summer of 1987 almost every economic indicator showed Calgary's revival and Edmonton's continuing malaise. The capital was home to 40% of the province's unemployed. "It's clear," Edmonton deputy mayor Jan Reimer told the *Edmonton Journal*, "that the three levels of government haven't been able to develop any action plan to deal with unemployment here in our city."

In fact, government was the source of much of the unemployment in a city where 10% of the workforce (some 35,000 people) toiled in the public sector. Traditionally a source of steady employment in tough times, governments were at long last reacting to mounting levels of debt. Thousands of civil servants lost their jobs as the provincial government grappled with a $3.3 billion deficit (per capita, Canada's highest). Most of the cuts came in Edmonton. These job losses came on the heels of the post-NEP contraction of Edmonton's once-thriving oil patch service sector. As late as 1986 the industry lost an estimated 25,000 Edmonton-based jobs in that year alone. By the end of 1987 there were 26,800 people on welfare in Edmonton, compared to 19,000 in Calgary.

In Calgary the better news just kept on coming. Energy companies hired additional management and professional staff in anticipation of the busiest drilling schedule in years, and the city began to feel the impact of $1.3 billion in spending related to the upcoming 1988 Winter Olympics. Calgary's rebounding confidence was summed up in an official song - chosen from among 921 entries in the "Song for Calgary" contest. The bouncy winner, *Neighbours Of The World*, was actually penned by two middle-aged songwriters from Victoria, B.C. (urban planner Tom Loney and radio host Barry Bowman) and produced by Edmonton's Tommy Banks, but the lyrics caught the mood of the city.

> *This is the time*
> *Here is the place to be*
> *Stay and set your spirits free*
> *Come now, now, now, now*
> *Let everyone know*
> *Let everyone come to see our dreams turn into reality*
> *A place for us to share*
> *Chorus:*
> *For we are neighbours of the world*
> *A shining city we call Calgary*
> *For we are neighbours of the world*
> *A place for you, a place for me*

The diverging characters of Calgary and Edmonton during the second half of the 1980s can perhaps best be seen in their changing politics. Conservative Calgary had become Canada's most politically homogenous city, and true to form voted overwhelmingly for the governing Tories in the 1986 and '89 provincial elections. Edmonton had never quite forgotten its old Liberal traditions, but the city had been supportive of the Tories during the Lougheed years, and with the party now led by Donald Getty, an Edmontonian and popular former Eskimos' quarterback, it was widely assumed that the trend would continue.

Even Premier Lougheed became concerned with the state of Alberta education, and the government reintroduced provincial exams and expanded parental choice and control. Nevertheless, some parents - and the occasional teacher - simply fled the public system. In the early 1980s Diane Cummings (below) left her teaching job to set up an unlicensed school for eight children in her Calgary apartment. Her Banbury Crossroads Independent School operated for three years.

Despite the growing differences between Alberta's two major cities, the one thing most Albertans seemed to share was a love of shopping. The 1980s saw a retail boom in which malls proliferated and districts such as Edmonton's Old Strathcona and Calgary's Kensington filled up with specialty stores. The debate over which major city had the better shopping seemed to be decided with the opening of West Edmonton Mall, the world's largest shopping centre, with 800 stores, restaurants, bars and amusements covering 119 acres.

West Edmonton Mall

It did not. The lingering economic malaise had eroded support for the government and encouraged political dissent. The result in the 1986 provincial vote was the election of 13 opposition members from Edmonton (11 New Democrats and four Liberals). No less than six Getty cabinet ministers went down to defeat in the capital. The post-election headline in the *Edmonton Sun* summed up the city's new image: "Redmonton!" It was a label which would define the city's politics for the next decade as an island of left wing opposition in a province which remained staunchly Conservative.

Despite the sharp differences in economic fortunes and voting preferences, Alberta's big cities still shared some interesting similarities — shopping, for example. Despite the difficult economic climate of the 1980s, Calgarians and Edmontonians continued to be the country's most avid consumers, alternately leading all Canadian cities in retail sales. By the late '80s the province had a mind-boggling 435 shopping malls, with the majority located in the two major cities. Some of the new malls, like Calgary's South Centre, were enormous temples to consumerism, but the thriving retail scene meant that even older, smaller shopping centres and strip malls could afford face-lifts and renovations totalling $1.5 billion.

In the opinions of some, this meant too many stores. "We're over-malled and over-stored for the population of both Edmonton and Calgary," complained Jack Robinson, Alberta general manager for the Retail Merchants Association of Canada. "I honestly can't figure it out," said Sally Hall, the Edmonton-based president of the Consumers Association of Canada. "The economy nosedived, yet retail space is expanding at an incredible rate. Edmontonians and Calgarians are shopping crazy. Go figure."

Being Edmonton and Calgary of course, the question of which city had the better shopping amenities was a matter of civic pride. The issue was settled decisively in Edmonton's favour with the expansion of West Edmonton Mall into the world's largest shopping centre. Even *Calgary Herald*

The search for the perfect lifestyle continued, with ever more ostentatious accessories. The hot tub migrated to Alberta from California. Originally designed for a mellow climate, it caught on as something Albertans could enjoy throughout the province's frigid winters - with additional insulation, of course.

The summer of 1986 saw flooding in much of north-central Alberta, brought on by heavy rains. More than 100,000 acres of farmland along the North Saskatchewan and Pembina rivers were submerged, but nowhere was more affected than Edmonton's river flats. The North Saskatchewan rose 12 metres above normal, inundating neighbourhoods of Rossdale, Riverdale and Cloverdale. Almost 1,000 people were forced from their homes, including this couple, who rescued as much as they could transport in their fishing boat.

The Edmonton Sun

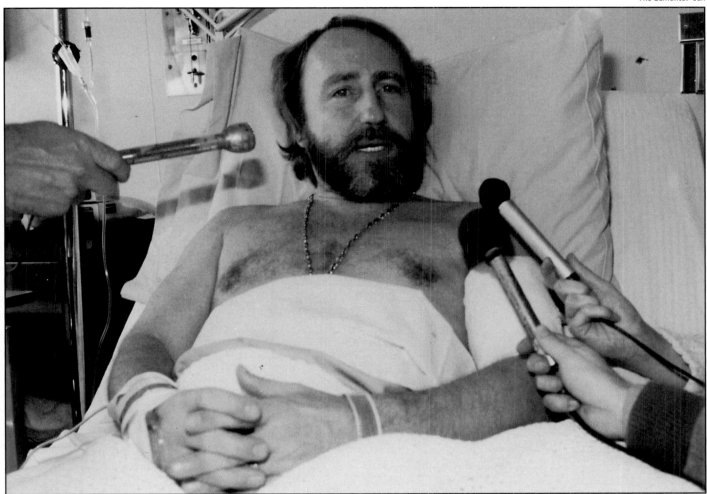

columnist Don Martin was impressed, noting that "while the locals are blasé about their *Guinness Book of World Records* entry (it's the world's largest parking lot), many of its 7.8 million annual visitors inevitably gasp at this grandiose shrine to consumerism that outdraws Banff for tourist spending."

Begun in 1981 by Triple Five Corporation, owned by Edmonton's Ghermezian family, the suburban shopping centre had grown through several phases into a monster with 800 stores, cinemas, an indoor water park, skating rink, amusement complex, bars and restaurants, covering 119 acres and employing 16,000 people. Most Edmontonians took pride in the fact their city was now famous for something other than Wayne Gretzky and the Oilers, but the growth of the mall - which by 1988 accounted for one third of all retail sales in the city - was dogged by controversy. If the enormous project had been planned, it was a plan known only to the secretive Ghermezians.

But even local residents, who had been fearful of the huge development, soon came to realize that the huge mall had a positive effect on property values and encouraged the city to spend money on the area. "The west end is the fastest growing residential area in the city," an enthusiastic Geoff King, director of planning for the Edmonton Transportation Department, told the *Edmonton Journal*. In 1985-87 more than half the residential development in the city went up within four kilometres of the mall. It attracted almost nine million tourists, never mind local shoppers, who injected an estimated $1.6 billion into the Edmonton economy. The city scrambled to make $40 million worth of road improvements to ease the traffic crush around the new attraction.

Not everyone liked malls, particularly during the summer, and smaller, more traditional shopping districts also thrived - generally without the assistance of large developers or civic planners. Burgeoning inner-city "villages," like Edmonton's Old Strathcona and Calgary's Kensington and 17th Avenue districts, attracted individualists, merchants as well as customers, looking for an alternative to the big-box, national chain shopping experience. It was all part of a burgeoning new concern for "quality of life."

Ironically, many people argued that the quality of life in Alberta's big cities seemed actually to improve in the years after the boom. The frenetic pace of life moderated and the huge number of recent arrivals put down roots, raised families and got involved in their communities. The raw,

Flamboyant Edmonton Oilers' owner Peter Pocklington recovers in hospital in April 1982 after being taken hostage in his home. He was wounded as police attempted to rescue him from disgruntled Yugoslav immigrant Mirko Petrovic, who demanded $1 million. Petrovic served five years in prison before being deported. Pocklington later ran for the leadership of the federal Progressive Conservative Party, unsuccessfully.

The twisted wreckage of a VIA Rail passenger train that hit a westbound freight train near Hinton on February 8, 1986. Twenty three people were killed in the accident, and dozens more injured. The authorities used water bombers to douse the burning passenger cars, which caught fire after being covered in a flammable mixture of fuel oil, sulphur and ethylene dichloride from the freight train.

unfinished quality which had been so prevalent in Calgary and Edmonton during the 1970s faded in the 80s as people stopped thinking of themselves as temporary residents. Newcomers and native Calgarians and Edmontonians finally began to meld, and to take pride in the cities they were building. As *Edmonton Sun* columnist Graham Hicks put it: "In an odd way the end of the boom actually created a better, more liveable environment. People are more involved and more concerned with community. We have time to smell the roses."

Of course this set off another argument between the two cities, over which had the better quality of life and public amenities. In fact both were in a good position to respond to the new and growing public desire for "lifestyle" which blossomed in the post-boom years.

At first Calgary appeared to have the edge. With its amenities and profile boosted by the 1988 Winter Olympics, the city had developed an enviable reputation as a tourist destination and was drawing in large numbers of American, Japanese and European visitors. The big attractions, of course, were the nearby Rocky Mountains; world famous Banff National Park, and the Kananaskis Country provincial playground. But the Bow River had developed an enviable reputation as one of the best and most accessible trout rivers in the world, and the Winter Games produced a legacy of superb sports venues, including Canada Olympic Park with its bobsled run and ski jumps.

Edmonton had its lush North Saskatchewan River valley, more urban parkland than any other city in North America, and was no slouch when it came to outdoor amenities. But it was in cultural and community events that the capital city now began to shine. The Citadel Theatre acted as a performing arts incubator, helping to encourage around two dozen professional theatre companies - which in turn spawned the hugely successful Fringe theatre festival. By the end of the 1980s the week-long Fringe was selling 250,000 tickets and attracting a similar number of people who just wanted to take in the atmosphere and free street activities. The Jazz City festival enjoyed similar success (drawing 110,000 fans in 1988), as did the city's Folk Music Festival.

Within a few years Edmonton was hosting a string of popular arts festivals that kept the city hopping through the summer. The city's Heritage Days, held over the August long weekend, had grown into one of the largest multi-cultural celebrations in the country, regularly attracting 350,000 visitors and bringing traffic to a standstill. Edmonton also experimented with winter festivals, and when the weather co-operated they enjoyed considerable success - but the inescapable reality of the Prairie winter meant they would never achieve the popularity of the summer events.

The lighting of the Olympic flame in Calgary on February 13, 1988. The games pumped an estimated $1.3 billion into the Calgary economy and raised the city's profile immeasurably. Always full of confidence, Calgary welcomed the world with typical Alberta verve.

Balloons fill the air during the opening ceremonies for the 1988 Olympic Winter Games at Calgary's McMahon Stadium. The largest city to host a winter games, Calgary raised the bar with an event that was an enormous success. Those who had worried that a large city would produce an impersonal event were pleasantly surprised. Calgarians, predictably, turned it into a gigantic, citywide party.

The Edmonton Sun

Alberta attracted some prominent visitors during the
1980s. The Prince and Princess of Wales, newlyweds
and probably the two most famous people in the
world at the time, visited the province in the summer
of 1983. Dressed suitably in Klondike attire, the royal
couple paid a visit to Fort Edmonton Park (right).
Princess Diana chats with Premier Peter Lougheed
(above) at the opening ceremonies of Universiade
(the world university games) on July 1. In 1987 it was
the turn of the Queen's second son, Prince Andrew,
and his new wife, Duchess of York Sarah Ferguson, to
visit the province. Fergie, as she was known, hefts a
backpack in preparation for a wilderness trek (far
right, this page). The accompanying British press went
wild when Premier Don Getty presented the couple
with matching fur coats, which was considered
seriously politically incorrect in Britain. But certainly
the most popular visit of the decade was that of Pope
John Paul II to Edmonton in September 1984. A
crowd of 300,000 people lined the route from
Canadian Forces Base Namao to St. Joseph's Basilica
in the city centre. An outdoor mass at Namao
(opposite page) as part of the Pope's "pilgrimage of
hope" drew another 200,000 people. The pontiff also
took time to hike in Elk Island National Park, and said
it reminded him of his boyhood home in Poland. He
was particularly touched by the crowds who lined the
roadside to see him. "It was wonderful," he said.
"Especially the groups of singers and dancers who
met me on the road."

Edmonton was the first city in North America with a population of under one million to build a rapid transit system - the city's LRT, which opened in time for the 1978 Commonwealth Games. The capital originally spent some $350 million building a single, 12-km line (4.7 km underground) from the city centre to Clareview in the northeast. Edmonton's controversial system was later extended to the banks of the North Saskatchewan, with the crew (above) celebrating the successful completion of the tunnelling on December 9, 1987. It eventually crossed the river to the University of Alberta, and in the province's centennial year discussions were underway to take an above-ground line into the city's southern suburbs.

The sluggish economy of the late 1980s did not entirely dampen developers' enthusiasm for Alberta's major cities. If you believed the economy would eventually improve and the cities continue their impressive growth, and many developers obviously did, it made sense to buy property and land while it was cheap, and build while costs were low and tradesmen plentiful. The result was a building boom at a time when the economy was supposed to be in recovery! Calgary saw the construction of the new Eaton's Centre, the beginning of Bankers Hall (which would eventually boast twin 47-storey office towers), and the Canterra Tower, Cascade Tower and Amoco Tower office complexes. In Edmonton there was a new downtown Eaton's Centre, the two-stage Manulife development and a new $200 million federal building, the rose-coloured Canada Place, overlooking the North Saskatchewan. In 1988 alone, commercial building in Edmonton totalled $842 million, and in Calgary $539 million.

The construction boom of the late '80s would dominate the downtown skylines of both Edmonton and Calgary for the remainder of the century. It also allowed visiting easterners to exhume a standing joke from the 1970s: that these might be "nice cities - when they're finished." But despite the superficial similarities between Calgary and Edmonton's new downtown office buildings, the two city centres had, in fact, developed along quite different lines. The biggest difference could be found in the number of people working downtown. In Calgary upwards of 85,000 commuters flooded towards the city centre each morning, and the number was growing. In Edmonton the number of people working downtown was estimated to be 65,000 and falling, thanks to provincial layoffs.

The flow of workers in and out of Calgary's core each day made its rapid transit "C-Train" system an instant hit, and by the late '80s encouraged its extension to the southern, northern and eastern suburbs. Edmonton's decision to run its LRT underneath the city centre (never a serious option in Calgary) made it less intrusive but much more expensive. After each city had spent a decade and hundreds of millions of dollars on rapid transit, Calgary had the outline of a functioning, citywide network, while Edmonton had one line running between downtown and the northeast that was

Calgary's C-Train system opened in 1981 (left), with a single line starting at Anderson Road and ending at 8th Street S.W. The above-ground system was eventually developed into a 40-km, three-line system with 34 stations. Despite the inevitable public controversy over expansion through established neighbourhoods, the C-Train quickly became a hit with commuters - with an average of 187,000 people using it each week day, compared to the 42,000 commuters using Edmonton's LRT.

only heavily used when the Oilers or Eskimos had a home game. A dozen years after the opening of Edmonton's LRT, a city survey found that most residents had never used it and many visitors didn't even know it existed.

Edmonton's civic leaders had taken a rather haughty approach to the building of freeways, which in the words of one city planner could only be "detrimental to the concept of a liveable city." Many Edmontonians believed that Calgary had made a terrible error in going into considerable debt to build a network of modern freeways criss-crossing the city. But by the late 80s it was beginning to look as if Calgary had the best of both worlds: good roadways and a user-friendly rapid transit system.

Edmonton's supposed preference for public transit was contradicted by declining use and the fact it had one parking stall for every two people working downtown (50% more than Calgary's larger city centre). The city itself was the second-largest owner of downtown parking lots, yet city councillors continued to fret that people were avoiding the heart of the city because there was not enough parking. Despite the public's seeming indifference to taking the bus or train, in 1986 Edmonton decided to spend $125 million to extend the LRT southwards, across the North Saskatchewan to the University of Alberta. As late as 1989 city planners were confidently predicting that by the end of the 90s the system would reach Southgate Mall (centrally located in the city's southern suburbs) and would also complete a "circle route" through the downtown.

Neither would happen. The idea of expensive LRT extensions remained controversial, despite considerable media support. "We are forced to ask ourselves, what exactly, is the usefulness of a partial or limited LRT system?" wondered a 1989 editorial in the *Edmonton Sun*. "Extending the LRT may be expensive, and many balk at the idea, but in the long run can it be more costly to the city than the maintenance of a white elephant?"

Edmonton's economic revival received a blow with the release in 1990 of Statistics Canada study that showed traffic at the city's international airport had fallen to two million passengers annually - 324,000 less than in 1980! By contrast, traffic at Calgary International had grown during

The most remarkable hockey dynasty of all time, Viking's Sutter brothers: (clockwise from top left) Ron, Rich, Brent, Darryl, Brian and Duane. At least one Sutter brother was active in the NHL between 1976 and 2001, and for a stretch of five years in the mid-80s all six played in the league at the same time. Between them they played 5,000 games and racked up nearly 2,000 points. One memorable night in 1983, there were four brothers playing in a game between the New York Islanders and Philadelphia Flyers. Three of the brothers, Darryl, Duane and Brian, went on to become coaches in the NHL.

the decade by half a million passengers, to a total of 4.5 million. As a result, fares were higher for Edmonton travellers (as much as $100 a ticket) and connections fewer.

Edmonton had been losing its international flights for years as major airlines followed a world-wide trend towards consolidating long-haul services in regional "hubs" which could draw passengers from a wide area. With its larger share of business travellers and tourist traffic, Calgary naturally developed as an airline hub for the Prairies. Passengers from across the region, bound for the U.S., Europe and Asia, increasingly found themselves having to make connections in Calgary. But while that was an inconvenience for many, for Edmontonians the thought of having to connect through Calgary was intolerable - a throwback to the bad old days when the city had been forsaken by the CPR.

Part of the problem was that Edmonton's Municipal Airport (known as the Muni) had seen passenger numbers grow during the 1980s to almost a million passengers a year. But splitting air service made Edmonton the most expensive Canadian city for airlines, while the 30 km distance between the two airports made connections almost impossible. The issue went to a plebiscite in the municipal elections of October 1992, and 108,000 people voted to keep two airports while 84,500 voted to consolidate flights at the International. The vote was largely moot, due to the announcement that same year that Canadian Airlines, the Muni's largest tenant, was to be absorbed by Air Canada, the major tenant at the International. Air Canada could save $12 million a year by consolidating operations at the International, which sealed the Muni's fate. "Plebiscite or no plebiscite," said an editorial in the *Edmonton Journal*, "the Muni is probably headed for a long, cold winter." After yet more acrimonious debate it would be closed to most commercial traffic, but the debate would linger on into a new century.

Calgary, meanwhile, announced major improvements to its bustling, 15-year-old air terminal, which was having difficulty coping with increased traffic. "We intend to keep our long-haul

The Lougheed government's goal to diversify the Alberta economy led to public ownership of Pacific Western Airlines, with the headquarters and 1,200 jobs moved from Vancouver to Calgary. The company was eventually sold to Edmonton's Wardair, but airline consolidation later in the century saw Alberta's airline merged first into Canadian Pacific and later into Air Canada. Calgary then spawned another upstart air carrier, WestJet, which at the end of the province's first century had grown to become Canada's second largest airline.

flights and hub status," said Calgary Airport manager Richard Paquette. "It's as simple as that." As it had done a century earlier with the CPR, Calgary could once again trumpet its transportation supremacy. It was also winning the battle for jobs. For half a century Edmonton had more employment than Calgary; around 50,000 more jobs than the southern city. But by 1990 Edmonton's lead in employment had been trimmed to a mere 5,000 jobs (375,000 to Calgary's 370,000). Public sector cutbacks had taken their toll on the capital city, which had the highest proportion of public sector employees of any city in western Canada. Seven of the 10 largest employers in Edmonton were in the public sector, including the provincial and federal governments, the University of Alberta, school boards, and hospitals.

But the numbers were a little misleading. Calgary's private sector downsizing had, in fact, been more severe, particularly in the energy industry. Before the NEP there had been 150,000 workers in Calgary's oil patch, but by the end of the 1980s that number had been cut in half. "We've been lucky in that the economy as a whole kept expanding, if slowly at times," Calgary management consultant Ron Caputo told the *Edmonton Journal*. A lot of those who were laid off were able to find employment elsewhere or joined the growing army of the self-employed.

In the summer of 1991 Edmonton's historic Hotel Macdonald, now owned by Canadian Pacific Hotels, reopened to much public fanfare after a $20 million renovation; its marble, hardwood and plaster restored to their original Edwardian splendour. The reopening of the mothballed landmark was greeted by Edmontonians as a harbinger of better times. "After eight years the old girl is back," wrote *Edmonton Sun* columnist Donna Marie Artuso. There were other positive signs, too. In 1992 the Ford Motor Company of Canada picked Edmonton rather than Calgary for a huge new regional parts distribution centre. It seemed to be the beginning of a trend. Proctor and Gamble, the food and household products multi-national, chose the Alberta capital for its western Canadian distribution centre, and Allied Van Lines, one of Canada's largest moving companies, relocated its head office from Scarborough, Ontario.

All that good news led to Edmonton being picked by the *Globe and Mail's Report On Business* magazine as one of the five best places in Canada to do business - ahead of business-friendly Calgary. Or perhaps it was the result of a ferocious lobbying effort? "Yes, we lobbied awfully hard for this," Doug Clement, a vice-president at Economic Development Edmonton (EDE) admitted to *Alberta Report*. "Let's face it, the folks in central Canada think the country ends at Lake Superior. We had to show them that Edmonton is a great place to live and work. We even flew to Toronto

On May 19, 1984, the Edmonton Oilers defeated the New York Islanders to win Alberta's first Stanley Cup. It was the first of five NHL championships to be won by the Edmonton team between 1984 and 1990, with superstar Wayne Gretzky leading the team to victory in the first four.

and met with the magazine's editorial board."

The diverging economies of the two cities was nicely summed up in the *Financial Post's* annual rankings of Canada's top 500 companies. Edmonton was home to a dozen of these, with substantial revenues of $5.5 billion and assets of $10.2 billion. But the capital's numbers were dwarfed by Calgary's. No less than 67 of the 82 Alberta-based companies on the *Post's* list were to be found in the southern city, with revenues of $51.2 billion and assets of almost $80 billion! It was no contest.

Calgary's growing reputation as a business centre had by now caught the attention of the national media. Calgary became emblematic of the "New West" and it seemed that whenever a newspaper, television program or magazine wanted the typical western view on everything from food to fashion to entertainment they went to Calgary. *Canadian Living* fashion editor Rhonda Rovan gave a typical explanation for why her magazine chose Calgary rather than Edmonton as the Alberta representative in a 1992 "Fashion Across The Nation" feature. "Calgary, with its cowboy mythology, is just more colourful." Besides, she added, "we already had Winnipeg and doing two 'parka cities' would have been redundant." Ouch.

CBC radio host Arthur Black thought there was more to it than that. He thought Calgary's upbeat image was related to the 1988 Winter Olympic Games. "The city underwent a consciousness raising as a result of that. It used to be Cowtown, but since the Olympics the world got a different impression of Calgary. It was such an enthusiastic games." An article in the *Globe and Mail*, headlined "Cowtown Finally Gets some Respect," went on at length about the city's "vigour, maturity and civic pride."

Edmonton's estrangement from the ruling Conservative dynasty continued in the June 1993 provincial election. While the rest of the province voted overwhelmingly for a new Tory government under the new leadership of former Calgary mayor Ralph Klein, Edmonton didn't elect a single Conservative MLA. The city opted, not surprisingly, for a provincial Liberal party now led by its most popular mayor ever, Laurence Decore. Alberta New Democrat leader Ray Martin also kept his Edmonton seat, and noted that the election had offered Albertans a choice between "Massive Cuts Klein and Brutal Cuts Decore." But with no government representation and the majority of provincial public service employees, it would be the provincial capital which would bear the brunt of the new job losses. "Is this what we can look forward to with a former mayor of Cowtown running the province?" wondered the *Edmonton Sun's* Graham Hicks.

It was a view Calgarians had little time for. "Edmonton seeks a handy scapegoat for its many problems," columnist Don Braid wrote in the *Calgary Herald*, "and we are elected, largely because of one fact: Premier Klein is a Calgarian. Too many Edmontonians read conspiracy into this accident of geography." Braid, who had worked for 16 years for Edmonton's two daily newspapers, pointed to the fact that the private sector in Calgary was still laying off as many employees as the provincial government was shedding in Edmonton, with hardly a whimper of protest in Cowtown. "Most Edmontonians are far too tough and proud to blame Calgary for their problems, but Edmonton politicians, eager to avoid responsibility, have turned Calgary-bashing into an art."

"It's hard to go anywhere or talk to anyone in this city without the conversation turning to complaints," noted the *Sun's* Hicks, who promised to dedicate himself to improving Edmonton's' self-image. "First of all," he suggested, "we have to stop comparing everything to Calgary all the time." Edmonton lawyer John McDougall, a scion of the city's venerable McDougall and Secord clan, founded the Spirit of Edmonton Association, which was also dedicated to repairing the capital's bruised morale. But it was hard to do. Even Edmonton booster McDougall had to admit that Calgarians had the right attitude.

Local hero Lanny McDonald hoists the Stanley Cup after the Calgary Flames 1989 victory over the Montreal Canadiens. If anything could have topped the 1988 Winter Olympic Games, this was surely it. Captain Lanny and his team also had the added bonus of replacing the Edmonton Oilers as the province's top NHL team - at least temporarily.

"There's a different mindset in Calgary these days," he told the *Sun.* "It comes down to the entrepreneurial spirit in Calgary. They have businessmen. We have bureaucrats." McDougall insisted he was optimistic about the future, but didn't sound like it. "The [civic] leadership is trying," he said. "We'll either see a change in five years, or Edmonton will be a much smaller town." It was a prognosis that might have shocked McDougall's great-grandfather, John A. McDougall, who in 1905 had used his storefront for that memorable opening salvo in the Battle of Alberta.

One of the many injured from eastside businesses destroyed
by the deadly twister. Twenty seven people were killed and
150 injured as the tornado struck virtually without warning.

Out of the foothills comes a killer storm

A 400 KMPH TORNADO CUTS A SWATH THROUGH HOMES AND BUSINESSES,
AND AN HOUR LATER 27 ARE DEAD, HUNDREDS INJURED, AND 1,000 HOMELESS

The 1987 August long weekend promised Edmontonians some much needed relief from a week of unusually hot, muggy weather that had seen temperatures regularly top 30 degrees. The Environment Canada forecast for Friday, July 31 called for a high near 26, "afternoon clouds with scattered thundershowers," and much cooler weather by Saturday.

Some people complained that, as usual, the heat wave was destined to end with the work week, before they could take advantage of it. But most residents of the capital region had been unsettled by a series of thunderous evening storms and "severe weather" watches. They were looking forward to the end of what many would later remember as a period of "ominous" and "oppressive" weather.

Unfortunately, the worst was yet to come.

Shortly before lunch on Friday, staff at Environment Canada's Atmospheric Environment Service office in southeast Edmonton had noticed a storm building up over the foothills southwest of Rocky Mountain House. They charted

its path as it moved northwards at speeds of up to 70 kilometres an hour, and began issuing severe weather advisories warning of high winds, heavy rain and the possibility of hail.

Just before 3 p.m. Leduc pharmacist Thomas Taylor was feeding his two Labrador retrievers behind his home on an acreage outside the town. He watched, fascinated, as a small funnel cloud snaked out of black skies and briefly swirled across nearby farmland. Then, suddenly, everything changed. Instead of quickly withering back into the sky, the funnel cloud touched down and began to expand. "It went from a dormant state to a full-blown tornado and it didn't take a second," Taylor told *Alberta Report* magazine. "It was like turning on a switch." The pharmacist called the Edmonton weather office and spoke to meteorologist Garry Atchison, head of Environment Canada's severe weather team. After getting Taylor to carefully describe what he'd seen, Atchison was in no doubt that it was a full-blown tornado. His office issued an alert to city media at 3:17 p.m.

The storm ploughed on northeast of Leduc, and then

A firefighter checks beneath an overturned car for signs of life. There would eventually be 60,000 insurance claims as a result of the storm, totalling $330 million.

Ken Bond, a resident of the Evergreen mobile home park, finds time to care for a frightened kitten. More than 100 pets were found amid the wreckage of homes, and taken to the SPCA's Edmonton shelter.

skirted the small community of Beaumont. The funnel was, by now, ten times the size of the one Taylor had seen near Leduc and was ripping trees and power poles out of the ground. Southeast of Beaumont it destroyed a barn and a farmhouse. It sucked cows into the air, slamming them back to earth and killing them instantly.

If this had been a typical Alberta tornado, it would have burned itself out in the countryside and dissipated as suddenly as it had appeared - but this tornado was far from typical. It veered north, picking up speed and power, and clipped the eastern side of south Edmonton's Mill Woods residential district. It destroyed several homes, tossed cars into the air and churned on its way, following 34th Street northwards to the Sherwood Park Freeway, where it swept vehicles off the highway and registered its first fatality.

By now the twister had grown to cover several city blocks and reared 300 metres into the air. As it moved into the industrial area which separates Edmonton from Sherwood Park and Strathcona Country, its churning winds reached speeds estimated at more than 400 kmh and witnesses described the sound as resembling a monstrous freight train. With little or no warning, workers took cover as best they could, but few buildings were able to withstand the destructive power of the twister. It was all over in less than 15 minutes, leaving a sprawl of twisted wreckage several kilometres long, seven dead and 150 injured.

The twister continued moving northeast and appeared to be heading for the cluster of oil refineries at Baseline Road

and 17th Street in Strathcona County. It tossed several giant oil storage tanks around like beach balls and derailed a dozen CN railway freight cars - before lifting from the ground and turning directly northwards, away from the Esso, Gulf and Petro-Canada refineries.

It touched down again in the North Saskatchewan River valley, just north of the Highway 16 bridge. The river was bloated with an estimated 20 inches of runoff, and one witness described it as "more like the Atlantic than the North Saskatchewan" as the twister veered from one side of the valley to the other before emerging into the Clareview residential district. It destroyed half a dozen homes, damaged dozens more, before again veering away from the residential area and heading northeast out of the city.

By now the twister had killed a dozen people and injured many more, but it had miraculously avoided most residential areas. If it had ended here, Edmonton might have considered itself battered but lucky. But it did not. The tornado reserved its most terrible destruction for last, as it bore down on the 700 homes of the sprawling Evergreen Mobile Home Park.

With no basements to hide in, the Evergreen residents who were home that afternoon had little protection from a 400 kmh vortex filled with lethal debris. Within moments 100 of the park's mobile homes were obliterated, with 100 more damaged beyond repair. For Ken Bond it was his worst nightmare come true. He survived unscathed but his first thoughts were for his daughter, Wendy Chrisp, who had been babysitting five of his grandchildren in a nearby trailer.

"I ran over to see how she was, and her trailer was gone. Just gone," Bond told *Alberta Report*. Over the next few minutes the frantic Bond was able to find three of his grandchildren wandering amid the destruction. He also found his shocked and injured daughter and drove her to hospital. Bond's four-year-old grandson, Troy, was rushed to hospital with his left arm almost severed by flying debris. He was close to death, but staff at Edmonton's Charles Camsell hospital was able to save his life and his arm.

The youngest of Bond's five grandchildren, three-month-old Tyler, was found later that night, covered by debris on an access road 300 metres from his mother's trailer. He had suffered a fractured skull and a severed spine which left him a paraplegic, but he, too, would survive.

The final toll of destruction was 27 dead (15 at Evergreen), several hundred injured, almost 1,000 left homeless and $330 million in damage. Edmonton Mayor Laurence Decore toured the devastation at Evergreen, talking to volunteers, emergency workers and survivors. As he left the site a crowd of reporters asked the visibly shaken, soaking wet mayor for a comment. He turned towards the cameras and tried, but with tears streaming down his ashen face he remained speechless. It was beyond words.

No one lost more that afternoon than Arlean Reimer. Her husband Marvin and her three children - Dianne, Dawn, and Darcy - were all killed in the destruction of their trailer at Evergreen. "I try not to think about it too much," she told the *Edmonton Sun's* Kerry Diotte in an interview for the 10th anniversary of the tornado. "I just try to make it through the birthdays. It's tough around those times. Sometimes I can't do anything then."

The tornado, which also killed the family's dog and cat, left her with nothing beyond a few stuffed animals and a few photographs. She told Diotte she had been back to Evergreen just once, for a memorial service commemorating the first anniversary of the day remembered by Edmontonians as Black Friday. "Going there that day almost killed me."

Offers of assistance poured in from across North America and around the world, but it was mostly Edmontonians themselves who donated food, clothing and furniture for the survivors. An army of municipal, utility, railway and disaster relief workers from across the province worked round the clock to repair utilities, clear roads and clean away the mountains of debris.

The emotional scars took longer to heal. The certainty of Edmontonians that tornadoes weren't a threat in Alberta had been destroyed. Despite a new Emergency Public Warning System (which broadcasts warnings on television and radio) and Environment Canada's adoption of advanced Doppler radar technology (which is better able to track tornadoes), it was years before most Edmontonians could sit through a severe thunder storm without looking at the sky and wondering if it might happen again.

Red Deer musician Jim Morrison in the wreckage of his van near the Sherwood Park Freeway. He lost two guitars, but he survived unscathed.

It was just one cow. An Albertan demonstrates the widespread support for a beef industry devastated after the discovery of a case of BSE, mad cow disease, in the spring of 2003.

The Edmonton Sun

CHAPTER TWELVE

'Alberta Advantage' kicks in

CREATING A PROVINCE LIKE NO OTHER, DEBT FREE AND PROSPEROUS,
YET DESPITE HUGE CHANGES THE SPIRIT OF THE FRONTIER LIVES ON

On its 90th birthday, Alberta was a very different province than at its birth. Eight out of ten Albertans now lived in cities and towns. To the railways that had opened the province to settlement had been added highways, air services and instantaneous communication that made Alberta's original remoteness a long-forgotten memory. The rest of the world was now no more than a plane ticket or computer keyboard away. Immigrants still arrived by the thousands each year, except now the majority came from Asia rather than Europe, and your neighbour, doctor or plumber was as likely to have been born in Hong Kong as Medicine Hat. Increasingly prosperous and urbane, Alberta had weathered the uneven economy of the previous decade and a half, and was once more firing on all cylinders. Doubts and uncertainties seemed to evaporate, and Albertans once again looked to the future with confidence and optimism.

In November 1995, CP Rail announced it was moving its head office from Montreal to Calgary. It was an event of enormous symbolic importance to a city which traced so much of its early development and success to the arrival of the Canadian Pacific more than a century before. The former CP whistle-stop had finally become the railway's headquarters. CP's president and CEO, David O'Brien, said it was "strictly a business decision," but there was no denying the symbolism. CP Rail was the 93rd company to locate its head office in Calgary, now surpassed in corporate headquarters only by Toronto (118) and far ahead of any other western city. Calgary had become Canada's second city of business.

Calgary's mayor, Al Duerr, declared himself "pleased and encouraged" by the news. From the phlegmatic Duerr this was the equivalent of a traditional Calgary "Yahoo!" Others were not so restrained. The *Calgary Herald* suggested the city was "no longer Alberta's second city, but truly western Canada's capital."

Another newspaper article (this one in *Financial Post*) listed the reasons why Calgary was "hot": The "Alberta Advantage" of low taxes, including no provincial sales tax, business costs lower than most other major Canadian centres, high worker productivity, a well-educated workforce (almost half of Albertans had a post-secondary degree or diploma), great urban amenities and a short drive to the Rockies. A few weeks later another glowing *Post* story declared, "Calgary is now the nation's hot spot for investors looking to park capital." In fact, the buzz about Calgary and Alberta was becoming international in scope. "We're getting calls from investors all over the world who have read about the Klein government policies and the opportunities here," explained Larry Mason, Calgary manager for commercial real estate company Colliers, Macaulay and Nicolls.

Edmontonians felt they had just as much to offer as Calgary - with the obvious exception of the short drive to the mountains. In fact, real estate prices and business taxes in Edmonton were now substantially lower than in Calgary. Surely it was just a matter of time before Calgary's dramatic growth spread north? Edmonton's new mayor, the ebullient Bill Smith, certainly thought so, famously declaring the capital to be "the best city in the best province in the best country in the world." Another former Edmonton Eskimo turned politician, former tire store owner Smith had not been endorsed by the business community (which in Edmonton tended to be the kiss of death anyway), but he was a complete change from his predecessor, Jan Reimer, who had a cool relationship with the business community - but who could quote sections of the Municipal Government Act by heart.

"Booster Bill," as he was christened by the *Edmonton Sun*, was elected in 1995 on a pro-business, pro-development platform to "Keep Edmonton Working." When a reporter tackled Smith on his lack of specific policies, the mayor pointed out that he was but one vote on city council. "But I can represent this city," declared Smith. "I can be an effective voice for Edmonton in promoting the city and changing people's perceptions. I can sell Edmonton." And he did. Even those who had doubted Smith's political credentials came to appreciate his formidable work ethic and his infectious enthusiasm. "He's here, he's there, he's everywhere," noted an editorial in the *Edmonton Sun*. "The mayor never stops promoting the city, locally, nationally, and internationally. He's a one-man advertising campaign."

The capital's economy and self-confidence received a major boost from the federal government in 1996 with the creation of a military "super base" at Canadian Forces Base Edmonton, on the northeast edge of the city. In a bid to save money Ottawa consolidated a number of army establishments from across the West, relocating almost 3,500 troops from B.C., Manitoba, and Calgary. In total, 10,000 servicemen and women and their families moved to Edmonton and surrounding communities, boosting the local economy to the tune of half a billion dollars. More than half of the new compliment of troops at CFB Edmonton was from Calgary. The entire First Canadian Mechanized Brigade, including Calgary's beloved Lord Strathcona's Horse regiment (raised in the area in 1899 to fight in the Boer War), moved north.

There was much bitterness in Calgary over this. As had been the case nine decades before (when Edmonton was named provincial capital and site of the University of Alberta), political skulduggery was identified as the culprit. At the time the decision was made to create the Edmonton "super base" the city had four Liberal MPs (the only ones in Alberta), including future deputy prime minister Anne McLellan. "I suppose there has to be an advantage in electing Liberal MPs," noted Calgary Reform MP (and future federal Conservative leader) Stephen Harper. "Is it a

A memorial service in Edmonton in April 2002, for four members of the famed Princess Patricia's Canadian Light Infantry, killed in a friendly fire incident in Afghanistan. The loss prompted a national outpouring of grief, but nowhere more profound than in Alberta.

payoff? Of course it is." Edmonton had once more successfully used its political clout to scoop a government prize to balance against Calgary's continued predominance as a transportation and business centre. Some things never changed.

There was some trepidation among the troops and families who moved to Edmonton, but it didn't last long. To say that the city opened its arms to the incoming military was an understatement. Led by a beaming Mayor Smith the city embraced the newcomers in an astonishing display of warmth and affection. There were endless official welcomes and parties organized by community groups. "I was worried about the move, but this is astonishing," one military wife told the *Edmonton Journal*. It seemed to be a match made in Heaven, and was the beginning of a relationship which would quickly deepen as troops from Edmonton saw much dangerous service overseas in the Balkans, Somalia and Afghanistan. As an editorial in the *Edmonton Sun* noted: "These are no longer anonymous soldiers from somewhere else, serving in places we know little about. They are ours."

By the time Bill Smith won his second election in 1998 (in a romp, with 50.6% of the vote), Edmonton's economy had turned the corner and the city was beginning to feel much better about itself. People were even beginning to use the boom word again, if more quietly than 20 years earlier. Unemployment was down, investment was up and even real estate prices were finally recovering from a decade and more of depression. Even Premier Klein was finally able to say "I like

Edmonton Mayor Bill Smith greets soldiers transferred to Edmonton in 1996 as part of a consolidation of western army establishments. Some army families were concerned about the move, but the sign promised a welcome, and that was exactly what the capital provided.

307

Albertans played a central role in national politics during these years. Former prime minister Joe Clark, who led the federal Conservatives for a second time at the end of the 20th century, and Reform Party leader Preston Manning, at a policy conference in 1999 aimed at uniting Canada's fractured conservatives. The right would eventually unite, under yet another Albertan: Calgary's Stephen Harper.

Edmonton." At an Edmonton Chamber of Commerce event in 1999 the former Calgary mayor conceded that, after living most of the time in Edmonton during the previous decade, the city had grown on him. "I think this is a dynamic city with a great future," he admitted. "I want to see Edmonton do well," said the premier. The *Sun* celebrated the statement the following morning with a banner headline: "He Likes Us!"

Most of all, the competition between Alberta's two major cities seemed to translate into productivity and prosperity. At the end of the 20th century what was becoming known as the "Calgary-Edmonton corridor" had a standard of living which outranked all Organization for Economic Co-operation and Development member countries - with the exception of tiny Luxembourg. The output of the region's economy rose to $40,000 (US) per resident, 40% higher than the Canadian average and even 10% higher than American metropolitan areas. Employment growth ranked ahead of Boston, Chicago, San Francisco, New York and all Canadian cities. At the turn of the century, a glowing report from the TD Financial Group, charting the corridor's economic growth, noted that it had been successful in piling up American-style wealth while retaining a Canadian-style quality of life. "If there is [an economic] tiger in Canada, it's spending a fair amount of time patrolling up and down Highway 2," said the bank.

Early in 2004 the government of Premier Ralph Klein announced that its major centennial gift to Alberta would be the final retirement of the provincial debt - which a decade before had stood at a staggering $24 billion. In addition to being the only Canadian province without a provincial sales tax, Alberta would celebrate its 100th birthday by becoming the only province - and one of only a handful of jurisdictions in the world - without any accumulated government debt. The Klein government's centennial Throne Speech, delivered by new Lieutenant-Governor Norman Kwong on March 2nd, 2005, noted that "Alberta now enters its second century with a strong economy, no debt, nation-leading rates of growth and employment, a high standard of living, and an enviable quality of life."

It confirmed what many commentators had begun saying, that Alberta's economy was once again rapidly outpacing the rest of the country. "There are the other provinces, and then there is Alberta," noted Don Martin, a former *Calgary Herald* columnist now based in Ottawa for the *National Post*. "Alberta is becoming a super province."

In the fall of 2004 oil had broken the "psychological barrier" of $50(US) a barrel. "It's great to be in Alberta," said the province's exuberant finance minister, Pat Black. The Toronto *Globe and Mail* immediately dispatched a team of journalists to look for signs of Albertans revelling in this new petro-wealth. " 'Help Wanted' signs hang in windows left and right," the *Globe* reported breathlessly, "a flush waiter boasts of a 50% tip and Mercedes-Benzes fly out of showrooms where there is little regard for six-figure price tags, And, it seems, oil money is stuffed in every pocket." Premier Ralph Klein noted that "no one was sending reporters when oil was selling for $12-a-barrel, and we had the country's biggest [per capita] government deficit."

In truth, Albertans approached their province's third great boom with more caution than had been in evidence in the 1970s or the early years of the 20th century. Times were good, with record activity in the oil patch and the economy bubbling along, but Albertans were less cocky than a generation earlier. In a series of articles for the *National Post*, Don Martin dubbed the new attitude "Uneasy Street," which seemed entirely appropriate. "Albertans will not be fooled again into believing their energy-driven boom is immune to an overnight bust," he wrote.

Former premier Peter Lougheed offered another note of caution. The 76-year-old elder statesman of Alberta politics had avoided public statements through the turbulent 1990s, but in the new century he was prepared to offer some sage advice to Ralph Klein: "Keep your head down. Make sure you're not doing anything that's too flamboyant. It's a very delicate judgement to make sure that, with the best of intentions, you don't get into expenditures that embarrass the people in other less advantaged parts of Canada."

Not everyone was in agreement. "I don't happen to be a federalist," said Alberta Environment Minister Lorne Taylor. "I'm an Albertan first. If Canada works for us, then fine. If it doesn't, we'll look at other arrangements along the lines of the European Union. If they come after more money from us, and last year we contributed something like $3,000 for every man, woman and child to the rest of the country, Albertans are going to push their government to look at different arrangements." Outspoken Calgary Conservative MP Jason Kenney was also reluctant to apologize for Alberta's wealth. "It's a good thing to have a province like Alberta setting the standard," he told the *National Post* in 2002. "It's either

Premier Ralph Klein sporting a native headdress in the Alberta Legislature as he tables a First Nations Sacred Ceremonial Objects Repatriation Act in the spring of 2000. The populist Klein, a one-time Liberal, rescued the Progressive Conservative dynasty, straightened the province's finances, and was unfailingly colourful in the process.

The Edmonton Sun

The incomparable Kurt Browning. The man from Caroline revolutionized men's figure skating (being the first to land a quad jump) and helped make the sport enormously popular. One of several champions who called Edmonton's Royal Glenora Club home, Browning also won a fourth world championship to go with the three gold medals he's holding in this 1991 photo. Caroline renamed the town arena in honour of its famous son.

everybody's equally mediocre or you create pools of excellence which encourage other jurisdictions to stay competitive."

Regardless of whether Albertans were cocky or cautious, there was clearly more stability to Alberta's economy at the century's end. Energy was still king, but Lougheed's goal of economic diversification was finally becoming a reality. Alberta's prosperity was no longer a mile wide and an inch deep. The young and the restless from across Canada were still drawn to the oil patch and booming construction, but there were now opportunities in every field from high finance to medicine and scientific research. Doctors and nurses arriving from other parts of Canada could expect to immediately increase their earnings by 20%, well-funded university research chairs were established to attract the best and the brightest, and the province's rapidly-expanding hi-tech sector began to compete with Ontario for capital investment.

One thing that had not changed was the stubborn streak of political independence and unconventionality which had first manifested itself with the election of the United Farmers' government eight decades earlier. When a new Liberal government, led by Prime Minister Paul Martin, called a federal-provincial summit conference to solve a health-care funding crisis, Premier Klein said he wasn't inclined to take part in a "Gong Show" (a reference to a television game show in which the elimination of contestants was accompanied by the banging of a large gong). "Thankfully, we are not reliant on Ottawa to fund Alberta's health care system," he noted. "We intend to do our own thing." The premier sat through one day of the week-long Ottawa summit, and then left.

Alberta was not immune, however, to the rapidly escalating costs associated with socialized medicine. And in common with other Canadians, in survey after survey Albertans identified health care as their number one concern and by far the most important of the myriad social programs now funded by government. Consequently, in 2004 the Klein government spent a staggering $7 billion on health care for the province's three million inhabitants - roughly equal to all the government revenues generated by oil and natural gas. The province promised to scour the world for answers to the medicare funding dilemma, and also drew the ire of the federal Liberal government with suggestions it would consider private delivery of health services if that promised greater efficiency or cost savings. But as an *Edmonton Sun* editorial noted, "We've had a decade of promises of health-care reform, and so far not much of anything has been done beyond shovelling more money at the problem." Albertans also noted with interest that other provinces, most notably Quebec, were quietly allowing the privatization of some health care services without any hostile response from Ottawa.

As Alberta approached its centennial the Klein government also found itself as the lone

The Edmonton Sun

defender of the traditional definition of marriage. The social revolution that had begun in the 1960s had served to undermine many of the institutions and traditions that had once dominated Canadian life - and none more so than the family, which had already been subjected to no end of official persecution through the tax code and re-definition by government and the courts. But the determination of the Martin government to open marriage to gay and lesbian couples finally prompted widespread public concern. The only government willing to oppose the move, however, was Alberta's. Premier Klein was blunt in his reasoning. "My reading of the situation is that the majority of Albertans are opposed." He was equally direct when asked to explain his personal views on the subject. "I'm against it [same-sex marriage] because I feel it's morally wrong. I believe in the traditional form of marriage."

It was not clear if Alberta could go it alone in opposing the official redefinition of marriage (a federal responsibility), but Premier Klein insisted his government would "pursue all legal and political avenues" to resist its implementation in the province. When puzzled reporters asked Klein if he was afraid of being out of step with other governments, and of perhaps being labelled a "dinosaur," he was unfazed. "Well, we've done a lot of things that were different," he replied. He meant his own government, but his words echoed those of his predecessors through eighty years of opposition to centrally-mandated change and the political status quo. There could be no doubt that Alberta at the end of its first century was a very different place than in the early years of provincehood, but clearly some things had not changed.

Perhaps the most famous Albertan of the 20th century was actually from Brantford, Ontario, but Wayne Gretzky will always be remembered as an Edmonton Oiler. He rewrote the NHL record book and won four Stanley Cups as an Albertan, and in at the end of the century he returned to the provincial capital to see his number retired and Capilano Drive renamed in his honour. Thousands of people braved an early snowstorm to gather in Winston Churchill Square on October 1, 1999, where Mayor Bill Smith presented Number 99 with a framed copy of the new street sign. "I was an Oiler again," said an emotional Gretzky.

311

Newfoundland's third largest community

SAILING ON A SEA OF BITUMEN, FORT MCMURRAY IS A CHILD OF THE ENERGY BOOM,
BUT THE MAYOR WORRIES THAT 'THE WORD AFFORDABLE IS A MYSTERY TO US ALL'

At the end of Alberta's first century perhaps no community personified Canada's most dynamic and rapidly-growing province as completely as Fort McMurray. The product of the 1970s' boom, and a victim of the 1980s' bust, Fort Mac took off again in the mid-1990s on another wild ride, courtesy of proposed oilsands and northern gas developments which by 2004 totalled a staggering $55 billion. Between 1996 and 2001 the town grew by almost 18% to 41,466 residents, and was expected to reach 80,000 by 2010.

"It's unreal, it's grown quite a lot and it's getting bigger and bigger," Newfoundlander Melvin Picket told the *Globe and Mail* newspaper. "It's all fast-paced up here, you're always going, going, going." Picket was among many Newfoundlanders to settle in Fort Mac. The town's supercharged economy drew people from all over the world, but it seemed to hold a particular attraction for Newfoundlanders. One third of the town's population hailed from The Rock. Picket moved to the town in 1977 to work as a heavy-equipment operator at Suncor Energy, and in the following years helped many family members relocate to

what many Newfoundlanders joked was their third largest community (after St. John's and Gander).

Many of the newcomers gathered at the McMurray Newfoundlanders Club, including new arrival Walter Andrews, who moved to the town early in 2002. "The money is good and there's so much of it you don't have to worry about it," he explained. "It's a lot steadier, a lot more secure than it is back home, that's for sure."

The rapid growth of Fort McMurray was not, however, without its attendant problems. Most serious was the lack of housing, affordable or otherwise. During the summer nearby campgrounds were full of newcomers who were unable to find apartments or homes. The average price for a home in the town topped $300,000 in Alberta's centennial year, and one-bedroom apartments were renting for $1,000 a month. "The word affordable is a mystery to us all," said former mayor Doug Faulkner, another Newfoundlander who moved to the city in 1980 with $26 in his pocket. "What is affordable in Fort McMurray? The prices are so high." The former clergyman advised immigrants to stay away unless they had a job and a place to stay. "Yes there are jobs here, but they are jobs for skilled labour, jobs for tradesmen, jobs for engineers."

Fort McMurray's retail stores and restaurants regularly paid $3 to $4 an hour above Alberta's minimum wage of $5.90, and still had trouble finding staff and keeping them. Advertisements for service-sector jobs would receive little or no response, and those who did respond were often looking for temporary employment until something better opened up in the oil patch. The boom-time economy was of concern to Mayor Faulkner, who, having lived through one bust, was acutely aware that his city's economy lived or died with the price of oil. "I don't want to be responsible for young couples losing everything. That's my biggest nightmare," he worried.

Oilsands' output was predicted to triple to at least 2.8 million barrels daily by 2015, and perhaps as much as 4.1 million barrels if oil prices stayed high. With crude oil hovering around $55 (U.S.)-a-barrel, and a growing awareness of the strategic value of a secure and seemingly limitless source of energy trapped within Alberta's oilsands, there seemed little danger to Fort McMurray's growing prosperity. It had become a microcosm of the surging vitality of Canada's most dynamic province.

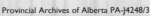

Provincial Archives of Alberta PA-J4248/3

The mammoth Syncrude plant near Fort McMurray. Alberta's oilsands contain perhaps a third of the world's recoverable oil reserves - some 300 billion barrels. Enough oil to satisfy global demand for a century.

A giant bucket wheel excavator bites into
Alberta's oilsands. Enormously expensive to
develop, but rising energy prices at the
century's end meant that billions more
dollars would be invested in the oilsands.

The closing of the U.S. border to Canadian beef after a case of mad cow disease was discovered at Wanham, Alberta, prompted literally hundreds of barbecues and other demonstrations of support for the province's beleaguered beef industry. Here a group of riders leads a convoy of cattle trucks to draw public attention to the industry's plight.

The Edmonton Sun

314

In sharp contrast to the booming oil patch and soaring urban economy, the final years of the 20th century were a time of trial for much of rural Alberta. Drought, grasshoppers, and a new disease that attacked the thriving cattle industry, presented the greatest threat to the rural economy in four decades, and generated great concern over the future of the family farm.

Much of the prairies were severely parched at least some of the time during the last quarter of the century. Drought was something Alberta farmers had faced before but unlike the 1920s and 30s - when it was the southern grasslands that suffered most - this time parts of northern and eastern Alberta bore the brunt of the drought. Water levels declined precipitously at some of north eastern Alberta's prized recreational lakes, turning beaches into mud holes and leaving boat docks high, dry and useless. In east-central Alberta lakes and sloughs, some of which had been a part of the landscape as long as people could remember, gradually dried out - and in some cases disappeared altogether.

John Tackaberry was a government agriculturalist in the Vermillion area in the late 1970s when he

Glum faces at an Alberta cattle auction. Stock prices began falling within minutes of the news of a case of mad cow disease.

began noting the changes. "At that time we used to hunt a lot of ducks," he recalled in a 2002 interview. "You'd walk in there with sloughs all over the place. You needed chest waders. Five years later you needed hip waders. Five years after that, gum boots. Pretty soon the duck patterns changed."

Farmers in southern Alberta were used to lack of moisture, but even here there was concern when crested wheat grass, the drought-resistant forage used in combination with alfalfa since the 1930s, failed to turn green by the end of April. For the first time in many years, billowing clouds of topsoil were a common sight, although farming practices like minimum till reduced the damage and prevented a return to the devastation of earlier times. With fears of global warming common fare in the media, even city residents took note of unseasonably warm winter weather. Bizarre events like the winter prairie fires around Fort MacLeod in December 1997 made headlines. Hundreds of hectares of parched grassland burned, destroying buildings and fences and killing hundreds of cattle. By the end of the century it was rare indeed to see a farmer burning stubble in the fields.

With a growing awareness of environmental concerns, water quality was also an issue. A 2001 study by the Pembina Institute found that between 1961 and 1999, cattle numbers, and wheat, barley and canola production, had all increased by at least 100%. Much of the increased production was the result of a massive increase in the use of fertilizers, herbicides and pesticides. A five-year federal-provincial study in the mid-1990s found that farming practices were indeed contributing to the degradation of water quality, as farmers struggling to make a living pushed their land close to its limits. And nor was the impact restricted to rural Alberta. Calgary taxpayers were forced to spend $76 million upgrading the city's Glenmore Water Treatment Plant. The upgrade was precipitated, at least in part, by an increase in nutrients from agricultural run-off. "What folks have realized," said John Tackaberry, "is that environmental issues and economics are a lot closer tied than they thought."

On a bright Tuesday morning in May 2003, the weekly cattle auction at Olds got underway

316

A rabid Edmonton Eskimo fan at Edmonton's Commonwealth Stadium. The Eskimos and the Calgary Stampeders continued to be the heart and soul of the Canadian Football League. At the end of the century the Battle of Alberta was alive and well in both football and hockey.

with more than 1,000 head for sale. Shortly after bidding opened word began to spread that a single cow in northern Alberta had been identified as suffering from bovine spongiform encephalopathy, better known as BSE or mad cow disease. Within minutes the auction ground to a halt as nervous buyers withdrew their offers. By the end of the week 13 farms had been quarantined, the U.S. had closed its border to Canadian beef, stock prices of multinational fast-food companies had fallen, and the live cattle futures market had collapsed. It was the beginning of a two-year nightmare for Canada's cattle industry.

BSE, a brain-wasting disease which can be transmitted to humans, had first been recognized in Britain in the mid-1980s and within a few years had devastated that country's cattle industry. It is thought to have been spread through the practice of feeding ruminant protein to cattle. A case had been identified near Red Deer in 1993, but that animal had been imported from Britain and the rapid destruction of the farm's entire herd had ended the matter. The second case involved a seven-year-old, Canadian-born cow on a farm at Wanham in north western Alberta. Although it was a single case, it confirmed the presence of the disease in Canadian cattle and brought to an end the country's BSE-free status. As a cattle producer free of the taint of BSE, Alberta during the 1990s had experienced a booming market for beef exports. Drought and escalating feed prices had taken some of the steam out of the industry by the turn of the century, but many ranchers had remained optimistic.

Among them was Myron Pearman of Rimbey, who together with his brother had almost doubled the size of his herd in the months before the Wanham animal was diagnosed with BSE. "It was just such a shock," Pearman told *Maclean's* magazine. "You can adjust for weather and bugs, but this is a blindside you have no control over." But he wasn't about to lose faith. "I came home tonight and we ate hamburgers. Tomorrow I'm heading to town, maybe to buy some cows. I have no fear of that."

In the old ranching town of Cochrane automobile dealer Corry Baum came up with an innovative way to help the farmers who made up a significant percentage of his clientele. For two weeks at the beginning of 2005 he accepted cattle as a trade-in on new vehicles. For example, up to 10 head of cattle against the price of a new diesel truck, and up to five on the gasoline model. "These [farmers] have been sitting on the cattle for close to two years," explained Baum. "We're just doing something to try and help them out." Other customers were given boxed steak and ground beef.

In Europe and Japan the discovery of BSE had been accompanied by public panic and a drop in beef consumption that had devastated local producers. In Alberta consumption of beef actually increased during the BSE scare. There were hundreds of barbecues in support of the ranchers, and in parking lots all across the province you could find beef being sold by the truckload. It was a remarkable show of solidarity from a population which was by now 80% urban, and only remotely acquainted with the day-to-day realities of Alberta's oldest industry. Or perhaps it was yet another indication that the surest way of getting stubbornly independent Albertans to do anything was to tell them it went against conventional wisdom.

In 1905 there were around 180,000 residents of the new province named for Queen Victoria's fourth daughter - Princess Louise Caroline Alberta. One hundred years later there were more than three million, and they were among the most prosperous and productive people in North America. From its humble beginnings as a distant frontier of empire, the least populous and least prosperous of the prairie provinces, Alberta was now the world's ninth largest oil producer and third largest natural gas producer, each year exporting energy worth a staggering $40 billion.

The province had become the United States' number one source of oil and refined products (followed by Saudi Arabia), and its major supplier of natural gas (accounting for 15% of the U.S. total). Government revenues from these non-renewable resources topped $9 billion in the province's 99th year. That included $1 billion just from drilling leases on Crown land. Mike Turta, the farmer on whose land Leduc No.1 had been drilled, would no doubt have been impressed.

Rising oil prices, which topped $56 (U.S.)-a-barrel in early 2005, provided the government with surplus cash to cover the remainder of the province's accumulated debt ($3.7 billion) and allowed

Preston Manning encouraged his followers to "Think Big' and accept the transformation of the Reform Party into the Canadian Alliance. They did, but in 2000 also concluded that the premier's son was not the man to lead the new party, opting instead for former Alberta treasurer Stockwell Day.

Alberta to enter its second century effectively debt free. But perhaps even more remarkable was that two thirds of government revenue now came from elsewhere within the province's rapidly diversifying economy. Oil and gas remained the icing on the Alberta cake, and the province's 51 million acres of agricultural land still generated almost $9 billion a year in farm revenue, but tourism was now a $5 billion industry, forestry $4 billion and telecommunications $5.8 billion. By some estimates Alberta's information technology industry (computers and software) - which had hardly existed 20 years earlier - was expected to become a $30 billion industry by 2010.

Yet there was little doubt that the key to prosperity in Alberta's second century would continue to be oil and gas. "We're very much poised to become a significant global player," Roger Thomas, president of Calgary-based energy company Nexen, told the *Edmonton Journal*. "When we talk billions of barrels my eyes start to spin a little bit. But that's the size of the resource base we have. It's just huge, and the opportunity is very significant."

Perhaps the most tantalizing prospect was the development of a pipeline to carry oilsands' output to the Pacific for export to the emerging China market, forecast to be the world's major economy in the 21st century. One proposal suggested a pipeline from Fort McMurray directly to Kitimat or Prince Rupert on the B.C. coast. But there was also strong support for a southern route to Edmonton, via what was becoming known as the "Heartland" district northeast of the capital - where dozens of facilities could turn the oilsands' bitumen into refined products, petrochemicals and plastics. Much would depend on the final choice. Alberta's new energy minister, Greg Melchin, seemed to have no doubt as to the right decision for the province. "As Albertans we are charged with being stewards of our hydrocarbon resources. We really do have a responsibility to see how we can maximize value and opportunities."

Lieutenant-Governor Lois Hole, Alberta's "Queen of Hugs," presents an award to a woman in uniform. The outgoing and much-loved St. Albert market gardener passed away shortly before the province entered its centennial year. She was succeeded by Calgarian Norman Kwong, a popular former CFL star and retired businessman whose task it would be to escort the Queen during her visit to the province in May 2005.

319

Young Albertans on the farm in the 1930s. In good times and bad, most Albertans never lost their faith in the future, and the accomplishments of the century belong to them. "We've come a long way in Alberta's first 100 years," noted Premier Ralph Klein in 2005. "It's certainly a journey worth celebrating."

In the spring of 2005, Melchin's predecessor, Murray Smith, went to Washington D.C. as the province's new representative in the American capital. It was a controversial decision, since a decade before Smith had been the minister who had closed Alberta's foreign trade offices as a blatant waste of money. Now retired from politics, Smith had become convinced of the value of promoting the province's oil and gas as a strategic North American resource. "Here is our big chance as Albertans," he told the *Edmonton Journal*. "We are on edge of the next province-building opportunity." Smith pointed out that Alberta was the only jurisdiction where energy reserves were growing and production increasing, and summed up what his message to the Americans would be. "These commodities are located right next to the largest consuming market in the world. This beautiful supply and demand balance usually exists only in text books."

At the beginning of Alberta's second century, the focus of many politicians and commentators was on absorbing the lessons of the past and formulating a plan for the future. The vast majority of Alberta's three million people, or their forebears, came to the province seeking an opportunity to prosper and find better opportunities for themselves and their children. At times, particularly in the 1930s, many Albertans struggled to achieve those goals, but by any reasonable yardstick you would have to say the vast majority succeeded - and in the process created a vibrant and dynamic society that stands as a living monument to their perseverance and sacrifice through a century of often turbulent history. That sentiment was echoed by Premier Ralph Klein in a centennial television address in February 2005. "We've come a long way in Alberta's first 100 years," he noted. "It's certainly a journey worth celebrating - especially the hard work and determination of all Albertans who have achieved such great things for themselves, their families and this province."

In the booming years immediately before the Great War, a pamphlet from the Calgary Board of Trade trumpeted the astonishing growth and unlimited potential of a young province "larger than Austria-Hungary, and over double the area of Great Britain and Ireland." The language of the pamphlet now appears dated, but the enthusiasm of the times shines through. "Alberta is another name for achievement. In the early days of the railroad it was a No Man's Land. It was said by many to be incapable of producing crops... now it is admitted to be one of the most productive provinces of the Dominion of Canada. Its wealth lies in its splendid climate, its soil, and in its resources of mine and forest; little wonder that its history is a story of achievement - a phenomenal record of material progress." The author of those words, living in a province not yet 10-years-old, could not have foreseen the astonishing progress of the next nine decades,

Yet Alberta's prosperity was not simply due to happy accidents of geology and geography, although they had surely helped. It was also the result of countless battles fought on behalf of Albertans by a succession of leaders and governments: Frederick Haultain's arguments in 1905 that Alberta and Saskatchewan should have powers equal to the original provinces; John Brownlee's fight for control over Crown lands and natural resources; William Aberhart's spirited defence of provincial rights; Ernest Manning's efforts to prevent federal intrusion into gas pipelines and healthcare; Peter Lougheed's decade-long struggle to protect energy revenues, and his determination to achieve a constitutional amending formula based on equality of the provinces; and Ralph Klein's victory over debt and deficit and his preservation of Alberta's fiscal independence. Underlying all of this, of course, was an accurate reflection of the wish of a majority of the province's people to control their own destiny.

In his first speech in the Legislature in March, 2005, Dr. Ted Morton, the new Conservative MLA for Foothills-Rocky View constituency, recalled this history and Alberta's turbulent road to prosperity. "What a way to turn 100! And when the history books are written, they will show again that Alberta's enviable status was not by accident, but on purpose." Morton, a California-born academic who had taught political science at the University of Calgary for a quarter century, was in some ways reminiscent of Henry Wise Wood, the American-born Albertan who had been the intellectual force behind the Social Credit movement. As Albertans looked for a renewed vision to guide the province into its second century, he offered these words of advice to the Legislature: "A society that forgets its past has no future. The path to our present can serve as our guide to that future."

Photo and Archival Sources

The publisher gratefully acknowledges the particular assistance of the News Research Department of the Edmonton Sun and Editor in Chief Graham Dalziel. The publisher also wishes to acknowledge the generous assistance of the other sources of archive material and photographs contained in this volume: The Calgary Sun, Edmonton Journal, Calgary Herald, the Provincial Archives of Alberta, the Glenbow Museum and Archives, the City of Edmonton Archives, the National Archives of Canada, the City of Lethbridge Archives, Medicine Hat Museum and Archives, Red Deer and District Archives, and the Canadian Press.

Index

324

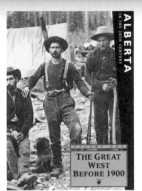

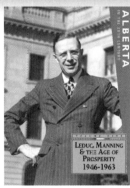

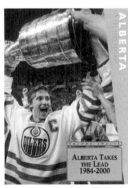